Destiny
at Your
Fingertips

Destiny
at Your
Fingertips

Discover the

Inner Purpose

of Your Life and

What It Takes to Live It

Ronelle Coburn

Llewellyn Publications
Woodbury, Minnesota

First Edition
First Printing, 2008

Cover design by Gavin Dayton Duffy
Interior book design by Joanna Willis
Interior fingerprint images and symbols by Richard Unger

Llewellyn is a registered trademark of Llewellyn Worldwide, Ltd.

Library of Congress Cataloging-in-Publication Data
Coburn, Ronelle, 1967–
  Destiny at your fingertips : discover the inner purpose of your life and what it takes to live it / Ronelle Coburn.
      p. cm.
  Includes bibliographical references.
  ISBN 978-0-7387-1324-3
  1. Fingerprints. 2. Self-actualization (Psychology) I. Title.
  BF1891.F5C63 2008
  133.6—dc22
                                                              2008013974

Llewellyn Publications
A Division of Llewellyn Worldwide, Ltd.
2143 Wooddale Drive, Dept. 978-0-7387-1324-3
Woodbury, MN 55125-2989, U.S.A.
www.llewellyn.com

 Printed in the United States of America on recycled paper

CONTENTS

ACKNOWLEDGMENTS

Unending gratitude to:

Alana and Richard Unger, my mentors, colleagues, friends, and spiritual parents who have seen who I could be from the start, who have held my feet to the fire with phenomenal patience and encouragement, and who continue to do so.

My Eight of Diamonds for chaining me to the table at the café, for alternately spurring me on and distracting me, and for offering a camping and fishing trip reward for finishing, as well as threatening severe disappointment if I didn't finish.

Suzanne Hawley, best friend extraordinaire who listened to uncountable moments of rant, exuberance, frustration, and excitement for all the years this book has taken to get here.

Chris Zydel, dear friend who provided me a safe, loving sanctuary during the turbulent life changes happening at the time the book was coming into being.

My students, colleagues, and friends who read various pieces of the manuscript: Joyce Sarahan, Darlene Katsanes, Sandra Edwards, and Elizabeth Walkup. And to Stacy Davenport for letting me pick her brain!

Friendly and supportive cafés and their owners, like Tanya and Sanri at the Hudson Bay Cafe in Oakland, California, who allow writers to take up time and space for too little pay, and support us in getting our work done—without losing our minds in the lonely madness inherent in the writing process.

Carrie Obry of Llewellyn Worldwide, who guided me with skill and grace through the publishing process.

PART I

HEEDING THE CALL

1   Life:
Not What I Expected

If you don't know where you are going, every road seems like the wrong one.

SUSAN PAGE, *The Shortest Distance Between You and*
a Published Book

Poor little old human beings—they're jerked into this world without having any idea where they came from or what it is they are supposed to do, or how long they have to do it in. Or where they are gonna wind up after that. But bless their hearts, most of them wake up every morning and keep on trying to make some sense out of it. Why, you can't help but love them, can you? I just wonder why more of them aren't as crazy as betsy bugs.

FANNIE FLAGG, *Welcome to the World, Baby Girl*

When Push Comes to Shove

Awaking anxiously, I lifted my head off the pillow to find that I'd woken before the alarm. I sprang out of bed to get ready to go to the first day at my new job. Excited and nervous, I drove across town, where I would meet new people and hopefully really enjoy what I would get to do.

I had just left a highly functioning nonprofit grant-making foundation with wonderful people, high ideals, and fantastic pay and benefits—but after four years I realized that although the mission we were all working for was important, I didn't want to get an advanced degree in energy policy studies in order to make a lifelong career commitment to go deeper into the work of saving the environment. Although my values were well met and I was contributing to the betterment of the world by doing what I was skilled at, I wasn't waking up feeling like I was making a contribution only I could make. It felt like others with similar values and skills could fill my shoes just fine. Day by day, the actual work I was doing felt less and less personally meaningful. Even though it was hard to leave people I cared about and a supportive working environment most people envied me for, I took this new position, which promised to be more in alignment with my master's degree in writing and my love of literature. I took a cut in pay, vacation time, retirement benefits, and health care benefits, all in the search for work that would put a bounce back in my step. Little did I know that the cosmic bouncer was about to give me the boot.

I arrived at the parking lot and walked across the street. I was in my nicest clothes and hoped that no one would notice I was sweating a little in anticipation. Up the elevator I went, and then down the drab linoleum-tiled hall to the appointed door. Taking a deep breath, I entered to find the three other people with whom I would share a cramped room, originally meant as office space for just two university professors, and they greeted me pleasantly. Then, I looked at my new desk to find . . . nothing. No computer, no pens, no paperclips, no paper, no phone, not even a chair, just a desk. I realized vaguely that I'd made a terrible mistake! But it was too late to rewind the film of the last few weeks. I made the decision to make the best of it and hoped things would get better once I got myself set up. Mistake number two.

After six months, I was still struggling to make the job work, between visits to the bathroom to panic, cry, and breathe deeply, then returning to my desk to answer to the three uncoordinated heads of the organization amongst a thoroughly disheartened staff working too many hours for too little pay. The business was disorganized and its leaders had no desire to be otherwise. After seven months, I didn't even want to get out of bed in the morning. At my review, I was told that I was not getting the promised raise because the executive director, who was out of the office seven days out of ten and who wouldn't tell me what he wanted, needed someone who could "read his mind"—and, no surprise, I was not succeeding at this. The next day I gave one month's notice via e-mail. I had $1,000 in the bank and $28,000 in student loan debt.

I have always prided myself on my survival skills, my toughness, and my ability to get by. I've been the super-responsible girl who has worked full-time since the age of fifteen. But this time, I was unable to will myself to go out and get just another job. I wondered if I was going crazy. I didn't know how I was going to pay my rent. How could I raise some money? I looked around to see if I had anything to sell. After putting myself through all those years of school, the only thing I had was . . . *books*. Gulp. All my lovely books, many of them my dearest friends. I packed up three-quarters of them and went to Moe's, a bookstore near UC Berkeley, where the buyer sorted through them, one by one. It felt like he was sorting through my underwear drawer. I held my breath until all my books passed through his appraising hands. He scratched for a minute on a piece of paper, calculating I suppose, and then looked up to say, "Would you like cash or a credit slip?" I hadn't sold books before, so I stood there not understanding the question. "If you want cash, it's $150. A credit slip is $300." Before I knew it, a voice squeaked softly, "I'll take the credit slip, please." I'm not sure who had spoken, but since I was the only one standing there, it must have been me.

About this time, through all of the ups and downs, I realized something. What I'd been doing all along was studying *people*. In my spare time, I read psychology books and studied personality systems like the Myers-Briggs Typology Inventory, the Enneagram, and the MMPI, and I observed people—what makes them tick, how they get along, and why they rub each other the wrong way. I was two classes shy of a psychology degree as an undergrad, but, at the time, I decided that two majors was enough (literary studies and creative writing) and that I'd rather go to school in communist Hungary for a term instead.

What struck me most during my career crisis was the way my interests overlapped. Isn't literature really the earliest form of psychology? When you read good fiction, it's all about the characters, their motivations, and what they are driven to do. Thrilling stories have us on the edge of our seats, wondering whether the characters we sympathize with will choose to do something different . . . or stay stuck. Real people's lives are no different. We are all protagonists in our own stories and come face to face with ourselves at some point in our lives. So I decided to check out psychology graduate schools. I attended their open houses and contemplated borrowing more money to pay the tuition, but every time I visited a school, things felt wrong, and it was all I could do to sit through the panels and presentations. My bewildering sense of being in the wrong place was so strong that I snuck out of every open house before it was over and headed for the bookstore.

After one such open house, feeling lost, I headed to Moe's with my giant credit slip like a kid with a free ticket to the candy store. I went up the familiar concrete stairs to the wall of used psychology books on the third floor and proceeded to poke among them. A random book caught my eye. I reached up to pull it off the shelf and another hefty book came down with it and whacked flat onto the floor. I picked it up to find that it was *The Benham Book of Palmistry: A Practical Treatise on the Laws of Scientific Hand Reading*, published in 1900. Hmmm. Palmistry? Scientific? Yeah, right! Out of sheer curiosity, I opened the book up, even though palmistry was just a bunch of gobbledy gook as far as I was concerned. The thing was, though, I was surprised at what I read. The hand and the brain are connected, and the hand is a representation of the brain. William Benham was a skeptic who ended up devoting decades of his life to studying hands during a time when there was almost no research on the matter. I thought it might be interesting entertainment to browse this book and see how crazy it was! I had a lot of store credit, so why not take it home?

As soon as I sat down with the book, I was hooked. It was *fascinating*, even with its tortuous, florid Victorian language and biases. Before I knew it, I was looking at my own hands, my friends' hands, and even strangers' hands at any gathering I attended. I liked how this practice wasn't about making predictions but about determining one's personality, aptitudes, emotional preferences, and the way a person thinks. It fit in with what I understood about myself, the people I knew, and the psychology I'd been studying. It was a rewarding challenge, like when I studied foreign languages, working with the basic letters of an alphabet, then words, and then stringing the words into sentences and saying them aloud. When I talked about people's hands, they started opening up to me to talk about things they'd never told anyone. I had "seen" them in their hands.

At this point, one friend, and then another acquaintance, asked me if I had heard of a man named Richard Unger and his hand analysis institute. Intrigued, I made a phone call, talked with Richard Unger, and the rest is history. I borrowed money and enthusiastically signed up to study modern hand analysis at the International Institute of Hand Analysis. Even with the popular misconceptions about reading hands, the ridicule I might face in making it a profession, and the fact that I had no idea how to start my own business or much less make it pay my rent, I knew right away that this was what I wanted to do. Hands were for me. That was 1998, and here I am now, loving my work and doing something that was the last thing in the world I expected to be doing. I read the hands of thousands of people, from exotic dancers to corporate heads to spiritual seekers, I am privy to their inner life experience, and my work takes me around the world. If anyone would have told me this is what I would do with my life, I would have said they were crazy.

Ten Years Later and Counting

In my career as a Life Purpose Analyst, people work with me when they're searching for a life rich with purpose and fulfillment. They are seeking their core selves, longing to understand and use their unique talents, and looking for their place in the world. In short, they are seeking the meaning of their own lives and questioning how the lives they have fit into the larger scheme of things. They are intrigued by the idea that their Life Purpose, their *destiny* ("the inner purpose of a life that can be discovered and realized," according to the *Encarta Dictionary*), is mapped out in their own unique fingerprints and that it is entirely up to them whether they choose to live it or not.

When they trustingly show me their fingerprints, I enter the world of their lives as they are living them right now and, at the same time, step into the lives they yearn to live at the deepest levels of their identity. The immediate questions, life crises, and confusions that compel people to visit me are the ones we all have at one time or another:

- What job do I take?

- Why am I dissatisfied at work?

- Is this relationship right for me?

- Why can't I seem to have a satisfying relationship?

- Am I using all of my talents? Living up to my full potential?

- Who am I supposed to be?

- What am I supposed to do?

- What's wrong with me? (I have a good job, a good relationship, and a house, but something's missing. There must be more. Is this *it*?)

- I have the urge to do *x*, but is it what I should really do?

- I feel stuck and don't know what to do!

My experience, gained from seeing thousands of people and their fingerprints, is that there is nothing more constantly dissatisfying and painful than living a life that feels devoid of meaning, disconnected from yourself, with no sense of personal purpose. It seems that a lucky few know early in life what they want to *be* and *do* and manage to stick to it, and a mystical vision or a serendipitous occurrence pulls a few others into alignment with themselves—but most of us feel somewhat lost and bewildered, sensing an untapped potential for a personally meaningful contribution to the world that seems just around the corner but just beyond the veil of conscious awareness. Some inherent part of each of us knows life can feel better when lived with a sense of internal purpose that guides our external direction. In short, everyone wishes to live in accordance with his or her individual Life Purpose, to wake up in the morning and say, "I've got someone to *be* and things to go *do*!"

Sounds great, doesn't it? I am asked repeatedly, "How do I figure out what my Life Purpose is so I can live it?" And this has been the sticking point . . . a lack of an objective, reliable way to determine Life Purpose. Many extremely valuable subjective systems exist to help you assess and understand various aspects of yourself from the inside out; they ask a question and you answer the best you can from your inner sense of yourself. These systems rely on your personal opinions or feelings about things rather than on external facts or evidence. What these systems primarily measure is your personality psychology and/or what you are "good" at doing, although it doesn't necessarily follow that you get a strong sense of meaning from doing it. I'm very orderly, but that doesn't mean I get a larger sense of fulfillment by creating filing systems all day long.

Many popular books are on the shelves now on how to find your Life Purpose, but the majority are all from a subjective standpoint as well, and after pondering their questions you may get lucky and hit upon your purpose, but most likely you'll come out with a better definition of your values, your principles, or your goals. Life Purpose is something bigger than your values, it pre-exists and goes beyond them. It is transpersonal—transcending or going beyond your changeable personal beliefs and personality characteristics.

Life Purpose Fingerprint Analysis is an "outside-in," or objective, tool for looking at the purpose of your life. The language of your fingerprints operates *objectively*, "free of any bias or prejudice caused by personal feelings" (*Encarta World English Dictionary*, 1st ed.). Any person trained to decode fingerprints in this manner will get the same results, just as any person trained to translate Greek will translate the same basic meaning from the same Greek phrase. All that may differ are the vocabulary words used to describe the translated information. This is where the "art" of fingerprint analysis comes in—just as some people are more poetic in their ability to translate from one language to another.

It is now possible for you to know objectively and definitively what your Life Purpose is from your own fingerprints. You don't have to guess or intuit it. You don't have to take any tests. This book is here to help you decode the first aspect of it directly from your own fingerprints and then learn what it's about so you can start working with it consciously right away. Immediately, you can be more empowered about the decisions you make for yourself because you will be clearer about what your inner self desires and what makes you feel most alive. Your increasing awareness of the role you play in shaping your own life will help you create the inherent meaning and satisfaction you yearn for because you will begin to understand the underlying structure of your own life story. You can choose to engage in soul-feeding activities and steer clear of self-defeating actions.

Perhaps most importantly, this book will invite you to see yourself and your life in a startling new way—with an increased lack of judgment that fosters self-acceptance. Looking at yourself is most often like viewing a photograph held right against your nose—you can make out some general shapes and colors, but you cannot see the details too well . . . they're too blurry, you're too close, it's hard to get a clear perspective. When you know and begin to understand your Life Purpose, you acquire a different vantage point; you can step back a bit and gain a broader view of yourself and your life circumstances. You can begin to discern the underlying structures governing your life and choose to direct your energy toward working with your trouble spots and steering yourself into your arenas of fulfillment. You will likely be aware of and recognize some parts of yourself, while others you may not be well acquainted with and even resist befriending. Overall, the more willing you are to know and integrate all parts of yourself, the more you will come to accept yourself with compassion and become comfortable in your own skin.

You can approach this book in two different ways:

1. Start with the background information in the first few chapters for a full context before identifying your own fingerprints and Life Purpose; or

2. Begin by identifying your fingerprints and reading about your Life Purpose, then return to the background information for a fuller context in which to understand and consider your life.

This book is for anyone who wants to become truly acquainted with themselves, the workings of their inner and outer lives, and their unique place in the world. I sincerely hope this information helps you to better understand and accept yourself and the people around you and inspires you to choose to get aligned with your Life Purpose. As you will discover, *it is up to you to step up to your highest potential*. I feel much more passionate about life and live with a deep sense of meaning and freedom now that I am consciously embodying my life's purpose, and I know you can feel this way too.

A Special Note to My Favorite Folks: The Skeptics!

If you are skeptical, as many are, about the possibility that you can actually know your own personal reason for being from your fingerprints, congratulations! You are someone who wants to think for yourself! To you I say, "Don't believe anything anyone tells you, including me!" Check it out for yourself, gain your own experience, and then go from there. But don't just dismiss it out of hand without your own investigation . . . that would mean you're so skeptical that you aren't rational, which is what you most wish to be as a skeptic—rational and questioning rather than closed-minded and judgmental. Rational people do their own investigation to see if something has validity for themselves and others. I've come across quite a few people who say, "I don't know anything about what you do, but I don't believe in it and I know it doesn't work." What kind of sense does this make? How can you know *nothing* about something yet pass judgment on it based on no experience whatsoever? How *logical* is this piece of thinking? I don't "believe" in fingerprints either, any more than I believe or don't believe in aspirin. (Do you refuse to take an aspirin when you have a headache or fever just because its mechanism of efficacy is still not completely understood?) I certainly didn't expect to be looking at fingerprints as my full-time profession, but like aspirin, they work consistently with everyone, their analysis is teachable and repeatable, and their interpretation is empirically validated by over thirty-five years of research, observation, and use with over 150,000 people.

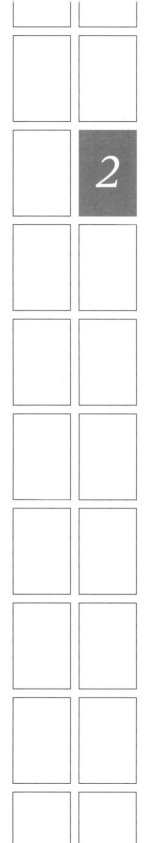

2 Fingerprints, Free Will, and Destiny

At the dawn of the new millennium we need to understand that DNA prints and fingerprints are ultimately just reflections of something far deeper—the Soul Print.

MARC GAFNI, *Soul Prints*

You Have a Destiny and You Can Know It

For millennia, humans have been searching for the meaning of life and have wondered about their destiny. And although the meaning of life as a whole remains a mystery, the particular meaning of your life—your Life Purpose—doesn't have to be a secret.

Just as all living and natural things develop according to the pattern of what they are, you also have a blueprint for your life's unfolding in accordance with who you are. An acorn grows into an oak tree, a caterpillar becomes a butterfly. What is different about humans is the capacity to *choose* what we do—whether it is in accordance with our true being or not.

You have a Life Purpose—a particular state of consciousness or sense of being you yearn to live in during every moment of your life—which generates your ultimate sense of fulfillment. Your singular Life Purpose is available to you as soon as you are ready to choose to inhabit it. There are only two things in question:

- Will you choose to *know* it?

- Will you choose to *live* it?

If you are longing to know the inner purpose of your life so you can choose to live it, this book is expressly for you. It is finally possible for you to know your Life Purpose because it is eloquently written in the language of your unique fingerprints. You've been carrying the answer to the question of the meaning of life—*your life*—around with you since five months before you were born, when your fingerprints were formed. All you need to do is translate the meaning of your fingerprints, the meaning of your life, into English, and this book will teach you how to do it. Knowing who you want to *be* and, as an outgrowth of this, what you yearn to *do* is the most valuable thing you can ever possess—the missing key to becoming fully integrated with your authentic self.

Most people are familiar with the fact that your fingerprints identify you as physically unique, yet this was discovered relatively recently in the late 1800s. Criminal investigative work and our understanding of each person's individuality have been revolutionized by the study of the patterns carved into our skin at the tips of our fingers. These patterns are called dermatoglyphs (literally "skin carvings") and law enforcement agents utilize the microscopic patterns (called pattern minutiae) forming the individual ridges of the fingerprints to physically identify people.

When you stop for a moment and ponder the fact that we each have a built-in system of individual physical identification, a personal tagging system, it is a wonder to behold. In the 1880s an entire world was discovered in the fingerprints, and the power of this information has changed the way people think about themselves as individuals. Now that we are familiar with these facts, they seem natural. *Of course* our fingerprints show who we are physically, and *of course* the image of a fingerprint has come to represent the idea of individuality. The marks your fingertips leave behind are your personal physical signature.

And given that fingerprints say so much about who we are physically, and are seen as a reflection of our DNA, it's been suspected that our fingerprints may tell us more about ourselves as a natural matter of course. All phenomena have identifiable patterns or structures—from bird calls to heartbeats to molecules—unique signatures that indicate something about their essential nature. Much study and research is conducted to identify these patterns and what they tell us about ourselves and everything in the world around us.

I regularly come across quotes that make an implicit connection between fingerprints and the core of who we are (our inner patterns, uniqueness, signatures, or marks), which extends beyond the physical. There is a collective "hunch" emerging about fingerprints that sees them as the next missing link to be unraveled between science and consciousness, between body and soul or psyche. And guess what? The collective hunch is right, and this link has already been decoded.

Fingerprints

Your fingerprints were completely formed five months before your birth, and they stay the same over your lifetime. The Navajo people have a saying: "The Great Spirit breathes in the breath of life, and the tracks of that breath become our fingerprints." There are many theories about why we have fingerprints and our own particular arrangement of fingerprint types, and much is understood about how the fingerprints actually form, but there is no definitive scientific answer as to why we possess them. Is it genetics, the intrauterine environment, physical evolution, the Divine, or karma? If our fingerprints are solely determined by genetics, then it would seem reasonable to presume that all members of a family would be likely to have the same overall fingerprint patterns, but research shows that often this is not the case. Even within my own small family group, there are two of us with completely different fingerprint types and overall patterns (of all ten prints together) than the rest of the family. So there must be something more than genetics at play.

It seems that fingerprints are a unique expression of each individual person, both on a physical-identification level and beyond, an expression of each person's central, pre-ferred state of being. And why shouldn't this be so? Doesn't everything about a person's physical form tell us something about the person? It is well known in the biological sciences that the hand and the brain are very intimately connected. As our ancestors developed and came up off all fours, the hands became free to manipulate the environ-ment. As our ancestors tried to pick up rocks, the brain had to map it, and brain capac-ity literally increased. Then the brain told the hand to bang the rock, and then the brain mapped the movement, and so on. As the human hand developed, the brain developed and vice versa. (For a fascinating exploration of and meditation on the inseparable rela-tionship between the hands and the brain, career, and being human, see Frank Wilson's book *The Hand*.)

Our hands are a direct expression of brain activity, and one of the primary ways we interact with the world is by using our hands. Notice how most people gesticulate with their hands while talking to emphasize and enhance what they are trying to say. Given how much of the bandwidth of the brain is dedicated to the hands, it seems possible that looking at someone's fingerprints and hands can tell us much about a person's inner work-ings. When we study hands we find that this is so. Your fingerprints and hands are like a user's manual for understanding yourself and your life. We may not yet have a definitive answer for why we have fingerprints, but given that we have them, they can be studied. The deeper layers of their meaning are being discovered over time.

A New Model of Consciousness Is Discovered

In 1979, after studying more than 12,000 pairs of hands and spending countless hours researching fingerprints in medical libraries, Richard Unger, founder of the International Institute of Hand Analysis, developed this system of fingerprint analysis. Today, more than 150,000 people have had their fingerprints analyzed and hundreds have been trained to analyze fingerprints for Life Purpose.

The fingerprints represent a previously unknown map of human consciousness that is separate from the already-recognized understanding of personality worked with in traditional psychology. We call this part of human existence your *soul psychology*. For an expanded discussion, see *LifePrints* by Richard Unger.

It is important to understand that there are three inextricably interwoven building blocks of your overall soul psychology. Taken together, they are called your *Life Agenda*. These components build on each other to create your specific formula for a fulfilling life. Here is a brief look at each one and how they work together:

Life Agenda = Life School + Life Lesson + Life Purpose

Life School: Your Life School is like the water you swim in. It's the general flavor of all of your experiences, the particular lens through which you experience all the circumstances of your life.

Life Lesson: Your Life Lesson is the weakest part of your swimming stroke (that left leg that is hard to kick well with) that needs much practice, patience, and expansion of your awareness. It's your least evolved skill on a spiritual and practical level. It's that part of yourself that you wish you didn't have and that you try to avoid, because there's so much uncomfortable work to be done to become aware of it and learn it.

Life Purpose: Your Life Purpose is the swimming stroke you want to be able to do. It's the "I am" you are meant to be. It's your most evolved skill on a soul level waiting to be activated, and the place where you have a deeply personal sense that life has meaning.

The aspects of your Life Agenda build on one another and are the pieces of your personal, spiritual, and practical training program. They work in concert with one another. When you work on any part of your Life Agenda, it activates the other parts as well. To use the swimming analogy: if you want to *be* the person who can *do* the breast stroke (Life Purpose), then you must be willing to work on the scissor kick, which you happen to be lousy at and would rather not have to learn (Life Lesson), and to try and swim at all you must be willing to get into and learn about the water (Life School).

This book introduces you to your Life Purpose and what you must do to live it. Understanding your Life Purpose allows you the freedom to begin consciously choosing your most fulfilled life.

What Is Life Purpose?

Let's stop and take a closer look at what "Life Purpose" means. As the phrase has entered mainstream usage, its meaning has gotten fuzzy and has been defined in many different ways, but fingerprints consistently indicate that Life Purpose is something very specific. For starters, let's take a look at what it *isn't* to try and understand what it *is*.

What You Want to Achieve (Your Goals)

Some believe that Life Purpose is a goal to be achieved. Winning the gold medal at the Olympics, making a certain amount of money, owning a house, and having children are worthwhile goals many people aspire to. Others feel that Life Purpose is some kind of challenge to overcome. Losing weight, quitting smoking, drugs, or other habits, and overcoming resistance to exercising are surely life-enhancing activities. But the unasked question is *what's next?* Once the gold medal is achieved, the house is bought, the fortune is made, love is found, weight is shed, the cigarettes are extinguished, and exercise has become a happy routine (or not), what then? Does the person who achieves any of these things no longer have a purpose in life? Is that all there is? Is life over at that point?

In the 2002 Olympics, Sarah Hughes won the women's figure-skating gold medal at the age of sixteen. Up to that point, her entire life goal and dream was to win the Olympic medal in her extremely competitive sport. In a stunning, breath-holding competition of beautiful performances, she narrowly beat out the two top favored contenders.

Imagine yourself in this situation. You've worked most of your life toward the possibility of this moment. It must be absolutely thrilling to be an Olympic champion and to achieve it at least four years earlier than expected. You're being interviewed by the media and you're invited to travel and appear all over the United States, and everyone wants your autograph. This busy, noisy, intense schedule goes on for a year or two, you tour to constant acclaim with skating shows like *Champions on Ice*, and then one day you wake up and wonder, *What am I going to do with the rest of my life?*

Would you think that you no longer had a Life Purpose now that your all-consuming goal and dream was fulfilled? It sure might feel like it for a while, but hopefully not. Sarah Hughes has a larger, more enduring Life Purpose that she most likely fulfilled one way by skating, but now she has to find another way of expressing it. She has a larger purpose that transcends any individual goal she may set for herself, and so do you.

What You're Good At (Your Skills and Aptitudes)

Some people think that their ultimate fulfillment lies in doing what they're skilled at, but are then bewildered when this doesn't turn out to be the case. Surely being good at something conveys a sense of satisfaction of a job well done. Organizing things, greeting people, washing dishes, saving money, making money, programming computers, driving taxis, cleaning up, or sensing others' needs are all things you might be good at. But what you're good at doesn't necessarily translate into feeling fulfilled on a larger scale. Before I became a Life Purpose Analyst, I used to work for nonprofit organizations and was very good at it. My role always ended up involving organizational development and project management. It turns out I'm very organized, and this was very valuable to all areas of the organizations I worked for. But even though this gave me the opportunity to shape the places I worked for at a very fundamental level so they could help the world with relatively few resources, I never felt satisfied for long. I always felt like, *Okay, so now what?* and would seek a bigger challenge. But ultimately, on a larger scale, once I got past my initial enthusiasm for the new job or project, I grew bored with doing the same thing. I began changing jobs, thinking that if I just got into the right field I would stop feeling so dissatisfied, but it didn't work. No matter what the organization was up to, no matter how important, I was doing the same thing I was good at—working hard, feeling depressed and bored, and feeling like there was something wrong with me for feeling disgruntled with my life.

What you're good at may not be what gives you a life-scale level of meaning. In other words, what you're good at is often not the same as your Life Purpose.

What You Believe In (Your Values or Principles)

Many of the books out on Life Purpose actually focus on helping people recognize the values they are living by and identify the ones they'd like to live by. A value is a belief about what's important to you. Knowing what you value is of paramount importance. But if your values are to be kind to others, promote peace in the world, and to be generous, do these add up to your Life Purpose? Does living your values give you a deeply pervasive sense of meaning and fulfillment? If having pride in your work is a strong value for you, but the actual work you're doing doesn't push your fulfillment button, then is that your Life Purpose? I know many people who do a good job no matter what they're doing yet still have a nagging sense of dissatisfaction. And what about people with poor values—greed, selfishness, and blaming others—like Scrooge at the beginning of *A Christmas Carol*? Are the values of greed, selfishness, and blame anyone's Life Purpose? Your values are a part of what defines you. You can be spiritual or creative or helpful, and can apply your values wherever you are at any time, but doing these things is not the same as embodying your Life Purpose because your values can change. How many of us have held values that aren't our own (for instance our parents' or a spouse's) for some part of our lives?

So, living your values does not mean you are living your Life Purpose. It's not the same as inhabiting your highest potential self, although your values surely play a supporting role. Life Purpose is something bigger than your values—it goes beyond them. You can change your mind about what you believe is important to you, but you cannot change your Life Purpose.

Your Temperament (Personality Traits)

You may be sensitive or a passionate thinker or extroverted or introverted. You may be a hard worker or a good decision maker, or assertive or super-creative. You may be reserved or emotionally expressive or perennially anxious. You may be an INFP or an ENTJ on the Myers-Briggs or a 4 or a 7 on the Enneagram, but these things are not your Life Purpose. They are aspects of your dynamic and (somewhat) alterable personality psychology. It is vitally important to understand and be true to your core personality traits, and I encourage everyone to take advantage of every means of self-discovery available. But the strength of these powerful and important systems is that of identifying your personality type, not that of directly pinpointing the transpersonal essential self that is your Life Purpose (and which frequently is at variance with aspects of your personality psychology, something we call the "Delicious Dilemma").

When I speak publicly and get to this spot in the talk, a twinkle begins to come into the eyes of the audience members. The understanding dawns on them that when they make individual goals (or their values, aptitudes, or personality traits) the overall purpose of their lives, there will be a big letdown when these things change or are achieved. Many people have been through this sort of crisis of meaning. They got married, had children, made money, bought a house, got a degree, and still there is *something missing*. Many of them have lived their lives according to values that weren't their own or have found that their values have shifted over time. So many have taken jobs that utilize what they're "good at" only to find fleeting satisfaction. At some point, they find themselves asking, "Is this all there is?" And the answer is a resounding *"No!"* Life Purpose, which is each person's specific point of life meaning, is still waiting to be lived and trying to emerge. It's like stories concluding with the phrase, "and then they lived happily ever after . . ." This wrap-up always leaves me feeling hungry because it seems to me that the story has only just begun. There is always the day-in, day-out meat of life to be lived, and there is a purpose to it. Life Purpose transcends our bundle of personality traits, and its attendant skills, values, and individual goals. It is unchangeable and with you as long as you're alive.

We are each meant to make a unique contribution to the world while we are here by being true to ourselves. Life Purpose is your enduring essence, your core self, your optimal state of being that is always trying to emerge. It is the unchanging part of you that transcends your dynamic personality characteristics. It is the inner purpose of your life that is waiting to be discovered and realized. Life Purpose is the core of you longing to be expressed in every moment of every day. The expression of your particular Life Purpose is as unique and irreplaceable as you are, and when you live it you get a meaningful sense of where you fit into the larger scheme of life, the universe, and everything. You get the big "Aaahhh" of satisfaction and fulfillment that arises from being exactly who you are. You know your place in the world when you wake up in the morning and feel a strong sense of certainty about what steps you need to take to move steadily into your Life Purpose in this moment. What you do becomes a direct expression of who you are. The outer expression of yourself springs from your inner motivations and desires, and there is no division of yourself. You are undeniably yourself when you are living your Life Purpose.

Being and Doing

My savvy colleague Roberta Coker says of your Life Purpose, "It's who you came here to *be* and what you came here to *do*." Her simple phrase points out an essential aspect of Life Purpose, namely that the particular "I am" each of us inhabits is an *internal experience* (being) that requires the support of our *outward actions (doing)*. Your Life Purpose is the state of consciousness you yearn to inhabit. It's the *I am* you wish to align with that determines what you must *do*. For example, if your Life Purpose is Leadership and you are built to feel fulfilled in the conscious state of "I *am* a Leader," then wouldn't it make sense that you must be engaged in leadership *doings* to actually feel like you *are* a leader? To have the internal experience of leadership, you must be engaged in outward leadership actions or doings. Influencing projects and people, expressing your vision of the way things could be at their best, communicating with others, and inspiring them to join forces and work toward that common vision, making tough decisions and standing your ground when others grumble, being willing to take the consequences of your actions . . . these are all leadership *actions* or *doings*.

If you have a Leadership purpose and never take anything on, agree with everyone, refuse to engage in conflict or disagreements, accommodate everyone at your own expense, and generally don't stand up for yourself and what you envision, then how can you have the internal experience of your Leadership Life Purpose? To fully inhabit yourself, it is necessary to take outward actions and set goals that are congruent with your inherent Life Purpose. Your individual and collective actions serve your Life Purpose, but in themselves are not your Life Purpose but the outward expression of it. The goals you set out to achieve need to feed your state of being by being aligned with the "I am" of who you are. There are many different goals in varying arenas that may serve your enduring Life Purpose. This is what it means to live *in integrity* (undivided from yourself) . . . your insides match your outsides and your outsides match your insides. You repeatedly line up your inner *state of being*—that is, your Life Purpose—with your outer *doings*, and life starts to feel deliciously worth living.

Living Your Life Purpose—
The Freedom to Choose It or Refuse It

Destiny, Free Will, and Choice

Though your Life Purpose was carved into your hands in the form of fingerprints, fully formed just sixteen weeks after you were conceived, and you were born with a set of personality characteristics, it is *up to you* to make the decisions and take the actions necessary to move toward the fulfillment of your Life Purpose. You have your own free will and only you have the power to use it or refuse it. Your "destiny" is the Life Purpose and personality traits you were born with, and your "free will" is your willingness to accept and work with what you've got even if it's not what you think you want. Like a card game, you've got a specific hand to play, you've even drawn a joker as one of your cards, but what's really important is the way you accept and work with the cards you've got. It's up to you to turn your seeming disadvantages into advantages, to play your strengths and minimize your weaknesses. This requires you to become aware of what your strengths and weaknesses are in the first place. You make your own decisions and choices about how you play your hand of cards. No one else can play for you. You can strategize, hedge your bets, bluff, and make mistakes. You can sit and refuse to play because it seems too hard or you're afraid you won't "win." You can try different ways of doing things until you figure out what works for you and advances you along. As with any game, it helps immeasurably if you know what game you're playing and what its object is. When you know what you're aiming for and working with, you can make better decisions and take better actions on your own behalf. You can improve your own life skills. When you know what point of the game you're at, while keeping your eye on the big picture, you can navigate more skillfully. You can see where you started, where you are, and where you're headed, and thus greatly enhance your chances of reaching your optimal state of being, which is to be absolutely, undeniably, and blissfully yourself.

You also begin to see that there is no other game in town but your own, and there's nothing better to do than to follow your own rules, the truth of your own unique path. You begin to realize that the more you try to play other people's games, the more you are wasting your precious time and energy, indeed your precious life, and there's no way to win. All of the energy you've got to apply to cultivating yourself gets tied up in trying to be something you aren't and prevents you from reaping the satisfaction of being true to who you are. Besides, the world needs your unique contribution and if you choose not to make it you lose your sense of purpose in life and the world misses out. Just imagine if Martin Luther King Jr. decided that it wasn't okay to be angry about race relations and chose not to speak up about it. Think about the internal and external pressure he faced to keep quiet and not rock the boat. Think about the sense of purpose he must have had every morning when he got up. He knew what to do in a deeply meaningful, inspired way, and it was clear to him that there was nothing else to do with his life. Now think about how the world would be different today if he had not embraced and embodied his Life Purpose. Imagine how much more backward the world would be today, how many more people would still be suffering high levels of racism if he had not chosen to embrace his Life Purpose of Mentorship, which required him to help the world come into integrity with itself, if he had succumbed to the external pressures and not played his own game nor been his true self.

It is no different for you. Although you have a destiny you also have free will. You can choose to discover the inner purpose of your life, your Life Purpose, and choose to realize it . . . or not. As human beings we all live in the realm of free will and have the capacity to shape and create our lives through the choices we make. When you work to create a life in line with your Life Purpose it may not always be easy, but it's always extremely rewarding. As Nietzsche said, "If I have a *why*, I can live with any *how*." And in psychology there is a saying, "Insight plus ten cents buys you a cup of coffee!" Knowing your Life Purpose isn't enough to just make it happen, you must choose to do something about it and gain experience, one step at a time.

Choosing It

So, once you know your Life Purpose and decide to embody it, what does it take to live it? Once you've accepted the Life Purpose you've signed up for, it doesn't automatically follow that everything is just a piece of cake, although a deeper sense of gratification is sure to emerge rapidly. We live in a culture that constantly promises instant gratification (or presents the illusion of it). Everyone desires "instant" and effortless everything; instant prosperity or riches, effortless romantic relationships, weight loss without physical exertion or personal restraint, painless personal growth, and every other form of "happily ever after." And who can blame us? Planet Earth, with its beauty and endless possibilities, also has its harsh challenges and hardships. I, for one, wish I didn't have to do half the work necessary to run my own business and overcome my various fears of failure (and success), and I ache with the desire that everyone would be able to fulfill their highest potential. I wish that no one was starving, that war was unnecessary, and that everyone had a happy childhood. But wishing alone doesn't make any of this so. In order to inhabit your Life Purpose, you need to be willing to engage and embrace the following rules of life:

COURAGE AND RISK

You must be willing to get out your courage. As Lady Macbeth in Shakespeare's *Macbeth* says, "But screw your courage to the sticking-place, And we'll not fail." You have to be willing to try new things, be willing to be uncomfortable in stepping out of your familiar (inner and outer) places and routines, and take risks. There is no ultimate guarantee of success, but if you don't give it a shot then you've failed by default. Remember when you were a child and you wanted something badly but were afraid to ask for it because Mom or Dad could say no? Well, if you didn't ask, then you'd already told yourself no and shut down the possibility of getting it. So what's the big risk? You might as well ask for what you want. Same with your Life Purpose—you might as well go for it. There really isn't anything else to do. Much of the satisfaction of living your Life Purpose comes from the process of doing what it takes to step into it. There is unparalleled satisfaction in owning the fact that you are the choice maker in your life, and also in taking the risk to make decisions, put yourself on the line, and see what happens. "No risk, no return," and "Failing to risk is risking to fail!" both become obviously true when stepping into your Life Purpose.

PATIENCE, PRACTICE, AND PERSISTENCE

As adults, most of us expect to be instantly good at things and give up too easily when we are unable to do something perfectly right away. I have heard so many clients with the Artist Life Purpose painfully say, "I think I'm creative, but I tried to paint once and wasn't any good at it." Usually, they do literally mean that they tried to paint *one time* and were discouraged when they did not paint a masterpiece the first time out. What strikes me is that my clients who say such things are deadly serious, convinced that they really are not truly creative (or powerful, or communicative, etc.) based on only one brief experience. Repeatedly I hear myself asking, "What would you say if I asked you to put on a pair of ice skates, get on the ice, and do a double jump—right now?" Their eyes get big or the phone line is silent for a moment, and then they reply, "I'd tell you I don't know how to do that. You're crazy!" It *is* unreasonable of me to ask someone to do a complex physical task with no prior experience or practice, and I always ask my clients why they expect themselves to be expert at doing things that they haven't practiced. Realizing your Life Purpose requires patience with yourself as you learn how to inhabit it more fully through persistent practice over time. Just because you have a Life Purpose doesn't mean you are automatically masterful at it, but inhabiting your Life Purpose—even (and especially) the parts that are hard to learn—is what makes your life feel meaningful. You must patiently persist at practicing the various elements of your Life Purpose so you can inhabit it more and more fully over time. Be like the skater who learns how to stand on the skates, then walk on them, then stroke on them, then spin, then jump, and who then works very very hard to do it all to the highest level he or she is capable of (with many falls expected on the ice along the way). Be patient and practice with persistence!

Learning from All the Life Purposes

Everyone has something to learn about all of the Life Purposes—after all, most of us have eight fingers and two thumbs, which all have fingerprints. But the state of consciousness denoted by *your* fingerprints as *your* Life Purpose is where you want to spend most of your time and attention. It is your particular *Zone of Fulfillment* and it permeates all aspects and arenas of your life—your family experience, your relationships, your career, how you feel about yourself, and how others see you.

You will find it useful to read about all the Life Purposes (after reading your own first, of course!) both for yourself and in the case of reading about other people. Gaining an understanding of all the Life Purposes helps you understand your place in the world as well as how the people in your life are different from you. Through looking deeply at your own Life Purpose and others', you can gain a deep appreciation for all the different kinds of people in the world and the fact that it "takes all kinds to make the world go 'round." You will increase your ability to be appropriately supportive of yourself and others. When you are aware of the core being in each of us, constantly struggling for expression, your own and others' behaviors become more understandable, and your compassion and patience with everyone's life processes can deepen remarkably. It is quite amazing when you begin to realize that *we are all the same* in terms of wanting to feel like we each have a place in the world, that we belong to it, that we each wish to feel both happiness and a deeper sense of sustaining meaning and fulfillment, and that we all wish to avoid suffering and the causes of pain. *And we are all different* in how we each interact with ourselves and the world around us in trying to find and live out that deeper meaningful life. If you choose to decipher other people's fingerprints, you too can gain a much larger view of what it means to be human and how precious each person's singular life truly is, starting with your own.

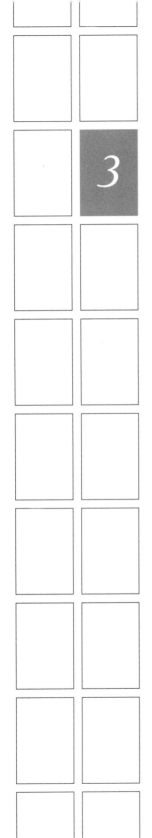

3 Decode Your Fingerprints, Discover Your Destiny

I've come to believe that each of us has a personal calling that's as unique as a fingerprint.

OPRAH WINFREY, *O Magazine*

If there is one question I am asked over and over again, it's this one: "How can I discover my life purpose and make a difference in the world?"

CHERYL RICHARDSON, *Stand Up for Your Life*

Start Here!

Now it's time to learn how to look at your own fingerprints and translate your own Life Purpose from them. Before we "take off" to look at your fingerprints, there are a few pre-flight instructions you need to follow. Together we will embark on learning the language of the fingerprints, along with the terminology you need in order to identify and translate this language. The following is a summary of the steps we'll go through together:

Step #1: Learn the Four Basic Fingerprint Types and Subtypes

First you have to learn what the "letters" of this language actually look like and what they're called. You need to acquire some basic visual identification skills in order to be able to see what type of fingerprint you're looking at. You'll first learn the "regular verbs" (the four basic fingerprint types), then we'll move into the "irregular verbs" (combinations of the four types). Once you start to look at the fingerprint types, you'll see that they are each a fascinating world unto themselves. Unlike spoken languages, this language has just four "verbs" to work with, which can then combine to make other "irregular verbs." When you know the four basics, you can easily figure out any combination you may come across.

Step #2: Identify Your Own Fingerprints

Next, you'll take a look at your own fingerprints and identify them. This is where you'll discover that each one of your ten fingers can have any of the fingerprint types on it. Do you have all ten of one type of fingerprint? Or two of one type and eight of another? Or three of one type, four of a second type, and three of another type? You'll also find that the fingerprint pattern over the five fingers of one of your hands does not necessarily mirror the pattern of the fingerprints on the five fingers of the other hand. You can have any combination of fingerprints over your ten fingers. Which ones do you have?

Step #3: Fill in Your Fingerprint Chart

How do you write down your fingerprint pattern so you can begin to make sense of it? In this step, you will learn the simple "shorthand" for the fingerprints so you can write them down on paper. This is necessary so you can compare them to see which fingerprints "rise to the top" and which fingers are your Life Purpose fingers. This is the symbolic part and it's very easy. You'll learn the symbols for the fingerprints and write them down for translation.

Step #4: Assign Points to Find Your High-Ranking Fingerprints

Who's the fairest of them all? Now you will learn how many points each fingerprint is worth so you can assign points to each one and see which ones rise to the top. The finger or fingers with the most points "win."

Step #5: Decode Your High-Ranking Fingerprints for Your Life Purpose

Here's the exciting moment when you'll translate your high-ranking fingerprints/fingers into your Life Purpose. Each finger means something, and now you will see what that something means—for you. Once you've decoded your Life Purpose, you can turn to the in-depth chapter on each one that is yours and read all about . . . you!

Overview of the Life Purposes

Let's take a bird's-eye view by looking at the structures underlying the meaning of the fingers and how they work together. Once you've determined which of the ten fingerprints are your Life Purpose fingerprints, you will then be looking to the meaning of each finger (or fingers).

- Each **finger** means something. If you take a look at the chart on the next page, you will see that both thumbs signify *results*, both pointer fingers signify *power*, etc.

- Each **hand** means something. The right hand is your "public" or outer-world hand, and your left hand is your "personal" or inner-world hand. Note that almost everyone shakes with the right hand (even if left handed). Think about how, for most of us, no one will touch your left hand unless that person knows you very well or there are unusual circumstances around it. (For instance, a doctor examines it, it's during a massage therapy session, or someone like me prints your hands . . . these are all situations in which you have decided to trust others to be closer to you even though they are not normally part of your inner circle.) If you are uncertain of this logic, try this: in a public social situation, offer someone your left hand to shake without saying anything about it. Watch what happens . . . utter awkward confusion. When you offer your right hand, everyone knows what to do. I have a friend who cannot use his right hand; I've watched him try to offer his left hand repeatedly over the years, and it's always an uncomfortable and frustrating situation.

- Add the meaning of the finger to the meaning of the hand, and voilà! Right (public) + pinkie (communications) = public communications = Messenger. See how easily you can figure out the Life Purpose for each finger? A couple of the Life Purpose combinations will not be perfectly clear to you until you read their longer descriptions. In the chart, I'm giving you a single word for each Life Purpose. Later in the book, you can read about each of them in depth. If you're someone who wants to read others' Life Purposes, I recommend you commit these few basic concepts to memory. It's very organic and doesn't take long to grasp. Each of the Life Purpose names gives you a seed concept to expand upon very quickly.

	Thumb *Results*	Pointer (Jupiter) *Power*	Middle (Saturn) *Responsibility*	Ring (Apollo) *Creativity*	Pinkie (Mercury) *Communications*
Right Hand Outer or "Public"	Public + Results ——— SUCCESS	Public + Power ——— LEADER	Public + Responsibility ——— "BUSINESS"	Public + Creativity ——— ARTIST/ INDIVIDUALIST	Public + Communications ——— MESSENGER
Left Hand Inner or "Personal"	Personal + Results ——— "FAMILY"	Personal + Power ——— PASSIONS	Personal + Responsibility ——— MENTOR	Personal + Creativity ——— INNOVATOR	Personal + Communications ——— HEALER

- **Mythological archetypes.** For those who want to "know it all" (me!). Each of the fingers (not including the thumbs) has a name based on the mythological archetypes—Jupiter, Saturn, Apollo, and Mercury. You will come across these names in the overviews of each Life Purpose. *But be forewarned!* While the nomenclature (naming system) used for the fingers goes back to a common origin with astrology (way back to the mists of time), *the meanings of each finger are not identical to the* *meanings assigned to the planets in astrology*. They are similar, but some differ in significant ways. It is more accurate to rely on your understanding of the Greek and Roman mythological gods. If you are one of those people with an insatiable thirst for knowledge, and you want to deepen your understanding of the mythological archetypes, I highly recommend Jean Shinoda Bolen's well-written book, *Gods in Everyman*. (*Goddesses in Everywoman* is equally wonderful.)

With that groundwork in mind, let's get to the fingerprints so you can find out your Life Purpose!

Step #1: Learn the Four Basic Fingerprint Types and Subtypes

Now it's time to learn to identify your fingerprints, the keys that decipher the code of *your* Life Purpose. Take a good first look at these four basic fingerprint patterns and their names. These are your four basic "verbs." These patterns, carved into your skin (dermatoglyphs), are what you are looking for on the palm side of the entire upper section of each of your fingers. We'll start with drawings of the basic types and then look at the combinations (known as subtypes) that make up the most common "irregular verbs."

As you begin to look at the fingerprints, you will notice how organized and elegant they are. They're like ripples in the sand created by water or by the wind in the desert, or the swirling repeating pattern of the clouds you can see from an airplane and sometimes from the ground. Fingerprints are formed, like these other patterns, by the imprinting of a lighter energy wave on a heavier medium. If you want to see this happen for yourself, take a cup of liquid (tea, coffee, water), blow consistently across the top of it, and watch the orderly concentric ripples form for as long as you blow. The air you blow out is a lighter medium in energetic motion, and the liquid is the heavier medium being acted upon. Since the heavier medium is liquid, it doesn't hold the pattern, but when the medium gets denser than this (sand, wind-carved rocks, water vapor in the sky) the pattern holds longer. The same is true for your fingerprints, which were formed by an energy wave imprint when you were just sixteen weeks old and in utero. You can think of this phenomenon in whatever way suits you, whether it's genetics, karma, the hand of a divine creator, or some combination of the three. Our fingerprints seem to identify us on both the physical and metaphysical level.

WHORLS

Whorls make a full circle. In their nicest "textbook" form, they look a lot like a bull's-eye or a spiral. Notice from the *Schematic* drawing in the following chart that the whorl is flanked by two tri-radii or T-shapes where the ridges of the fingerprints flow together (drawn as triangles on the *Diagram*). Notice in the *Examples* that when you fingerprint a whorl, these tri-radii often don't make in onto the paper, but the circular pattern clearly shows up. We will use the points and symbol for the fingerprint when you are ready to identify your own fingerprints. For now, just note that the symbol is a circular figure that looks like the key characteristic of the fingerprint. Approximately 25 percent of all fingerprints are whorls.

whorls

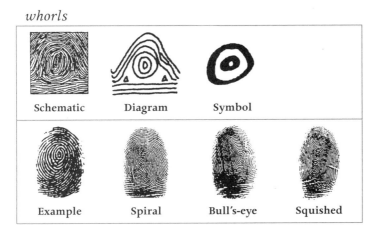

| Schematic | Diagram | Symbol |
| Example | Spiral | Bull's-eye | Squished |

Points: 4

LOOPS

Loops come in from one side, make a U-turn, and fly right back out. They look a bit like a wave that hasn't crested yet. Notice, from the *Diagram* in the following chart, that loops have one tri-radii (drawn as a triangle) *opposite* the side where the pattern enters and exits. Most loops enter and exit from the pinkie side of the hand. These are called *ulnar* loops, after the bone in the forearm on the pinkie side of the hand/arm. Most loops are ulnar loops. Occasionally, you may come across a *radial* loop, a loop that exits and enters from the thumb side of the hand (named after the other forearm bone on the thumb side). Note for now that these radial loops have a slightly higher ranking number than the common ulnar loops. We will use the points and symbol for the fingerprints when you are ready to identify your own fingerprints. For now, just note that the symbol is simply a shorthand figure that looks roughly like the key characteristic of the fingerprint. Approximately 70 percent of all fingerprints are loops.

loops

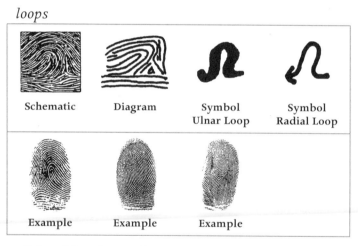

Schematic	Diagram	Symbol Ulnar Loop	Symbol Radial Loop
Example	Example	Example	

Points: Ulnar loop = 3
Radial loop = 3.1

TENTED ARCHES

A **tented arch** looks like a tent with a pole holding it up at or near the middle of the pattern, or like a steep-sided volcano, or like two hands in the position of prayer. Notice, from the *Schematic* drawing in the following chart, that tented arches have one tri-radii located at or near the center of the overall fingerprint pattern and that the "tent pole" extends upward from the tri-radii. It's important to understand that the "tent pole" can be taller or shorter. Look closely at the *Diagram* for the position of the triangle representing the tri-radii. It's the central (or near central) position of the tri-radii that's the identifying characteristic of the tented arch. This becomes very important when we look at the subtype where the loop and the tented arch combine. We will use the points and symbol for the fingerprint when you are ready to identify your own fingerprints. For now, just note that the symbol is simply an upside-down T figure that looks like the key characteristic of the fingerprint. Approximately 2 percent of all fingerprints are tented arches.

tented arches

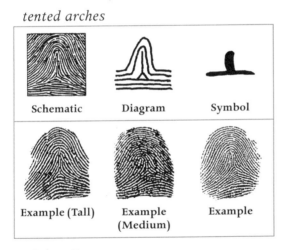

Schematic	Diagram	Symbol
Example (Tall)	Example (Medium)	Example

Points: 2

ARCHES

Arches are the simplest fingerprint pattern and the closest of the four types to a 180-degree line. They arc up and over like a gentle rolling hill. They have no tri-radii and do not make any twists or turns. We will use the points and symbol for the fingerprint when you are ready to identify your own fingerprints. For now, just note that the symbol is simply a stick figure that looks like the key characteristic of the fingerprint. Approximately 3 percent of all fingerprints are arches.

arches

Schematic	Diagram	Symbol
Example	Example	Example

Points: 1

"Irregular Verbs" or Fingerprint "Subtypes"

Now that you've taken a good look at the four basic fingerprint pattern types, let's take a look at what happens when any of these four types combine to make *subtypes*. *Remember that fingerprints do anything they need to do to say what they have to say.* Many people have individual fingerprints that are a combination of two or more of the four basic fingerprints. If you seem to have an "irregular verb" fingerprint, relax. Now that you know the basic types, these combinations are fairly easy to figure out. Here we go to take a look at the most common fingerprint *subtypes*. All are uncommon and some are rare. I joke with my students, "This fingerprint is uncommon/rare, but given that I've just said that, you'll probably come across one next week!"

Note: The points for subtypes are easily calculated. Just add the points for each regular fingerprint type and divide by two.

ARCH + TENTED ARCH

In the **arch + tented arch** combination, you'll notice that the "tent pole" of the tented arch is shortened significantly by the arch on top of it. Notice, in the second *Example* in the following chart, that there are also two strands of loop to the right of the tri-radius—not enough to do anything with. The tri-radius and its very short tent pole are clearly near the center. When it's time to assign points, you will give this fingerprint 1.5. Rare.

arch (1) + tented arch (2) = 3, divided by 2 fingerprint types = 1.5

arch + tented arch

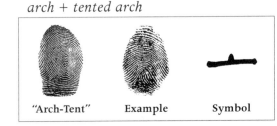

| "Arch-Tent" | Example | Symbol |

Points: 1.5

These are loops that are very short. There is an arch sitting on top of them, "squashing" them so that they are about half their normal height or shorter. Rare.

arch (1) + loop (3) = 4, divided by 2 fingerprint types = 2

arch + loop

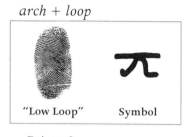

"Low Loop"   Symbol

Points: 2

LOOP + TENTED ARCH

The key to identifying what's going on with the combination of loops and tented arches lies in finding the tri-radius (the upside-down T-shape where the ridges flow together) and determining how centrally located it is in the overall fingerprint. The more centered the tri-radius, the more tented-arch energy is involved. Remember that a loop has one tri-radius off to the side of the overall fingerprint pattern. The tri-radius must move over and effectively reduce the loop, as if it's successfully pushing the loop over. When the tri-radius is dead center with only a little looping (see the first *Example* in the following chart, "Loop-Tent"), go ahead and assign the 2 points of the tented arch (ignore the looping). Uncommon.

loop (3) + tented arch (2) = 5, divided by 2 = 2.5

loop + tented arch

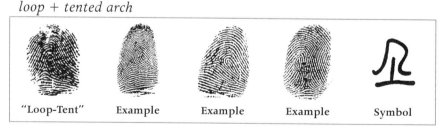

"Loop-Tent"   Example   Example   Example   Symbol

Points: 2.5

Entwined loops are loops with a slight amount of whorling curling them over like a wave breaking. Can't you just see a surfer riding the left side of this fingerprint? Rare.

Entwined loops get just a little boost in points above a plain loop to 3.1.

entwined loop

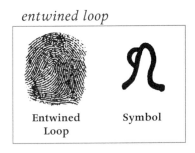

Entwined   Symbol
Loop

Points: 3.1

Peacocks are a mix of loops and whorls. The key to identifying them is noticing that the loop has some amount of whorl within it, whether the loop has pinched its center closed just a little bit (basic peacock) or there is a full whorl within the loop. Peacocks got their name because they look like peacock feathers, which are topped by a pattern that looks like an eye. I think they look like "pregnant" loops. An added method of distinguishing peacock loops from full whorls is to notice that peacocks still originate on one side, make a U-turn, and fly back out. They are not fundamentally symmetrical like whorls. Uncommon.

basic peacock = loop (3) + whorl (4) = 7, divided by 2 = 3.5

basic peacock

Basic   Example   Example   Symbol
Peacock

Points: 3.5

baby peacock

| Baby Peacock | Example | Symbol |

Points: 3.6

super peacock

| Super Peacock | Symbol |

Points: 3.7

WHORL SUBTYPE

The **composite whorl** is an entwining of two loops around each other, flanked by two tri-radii. This is a subtype of the whorl. They look much like yin-yang symbols and have two tri-radii, one on either side, just like regular whorls. Their core makes an S shape. Sometimes the S shape is very small and tight, at other times it is so loose you might first mistake it for a loop. Since the composite is a whorl, but not a complete bull's-eye or spiral shape, its points are lowered to 3.9. Uncommon.

composite whorl

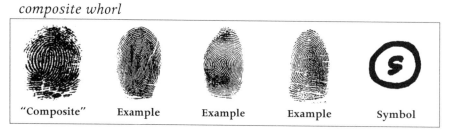

| "Composite" | Example | Example | Example | Symbol |

Points: 3.9

GAMUTS

Gamuts are rare conglomerates of three or more of the basic fingerprint types. They are their own creatures, and they break all the rules by squeezing many print type characteristics into a single fingerprint. Do not count them toward Life Purpose . . . unless they have a component fingerprint that is obviously higher ranking than the other nine fingerprints. For starters, give them 0 points if you come across one (they are rare). Once you've looked at a lot of fingerprints, it becomes obvious how you might work with them in the context of the other fingerprints. Very rare.

gamut

| Example | Example | Example | Example | Symbol |

Points: 0

Step #2: Identify Your Own Fingerprints

Now it's time to take a look at your own fingerprints. At the end of the book, there is a summary sheet you can copy for yourself and others.

Look at the entire top section of your fingers in good light until you are able to discern the patterns carved into your skin. In general, it is much easier to see your fingerprints in good daylight. Otherwise, get under a strong lamp. I've also used a flashlight under low light conditions. Don't be shy about using a magnifying glass if you need one. Most drug stores carry them, they are inexpensive, and some have lights integrated right into them.

Be patient. It takes a little time to train your eye to see the fingerprints. It's probably been a long time since you used your pattern-recognition skills . . . for most it may be as long as since you learned to recognize the letters of the alphabet.

Remember, you can have *any combination* of the four fingerprint types (including all of one type or all four types among your ten fingerprints). And your fingerprints do not necessarily mirror each other from one hand to the other.

If you have a hard time actually seeing your fingerprints:

- *Your eyes ain't what they used to be.*

- *Lines are obscuring them or they are faint.* Use a magnifying glass in good daylight or look at your fingers under a strong lamp. You can also coat your fingertips lightly with a dark lipstick to highlight them and then look. You can try finger-printing yourself according to the directions below. Another effective trick is to take a piece of clear tape and place it over the entire top section of your finger, then look through the tape at the fingerprint. Then take your best guess from what you see. Look for the tri-radii to help you discern your print types. Don't think you don't have fingerprints or that they are unreadable and give up. Some people have been fingerprinted for official purposes (employment, security, etc.) and have been told that their fingerprints were difficult or impossible to print or read. The police and other law enforcement agencies look at the tiny lines that make up the fingerprints at a microscopic level (called "pattern minutiae"). You do not need to look at your fingerprints through a microscope. If you truly have a finger where the print is so faint or obscured by lines that you can't read it, go ahead and leave the chart blank and work with your other fingers. (On the rare occasions when this happens, it's usually on the pinkie finger.) *To identify your Life Purpose, you need only to discern your overall fingerprint pattern.*

  Fingerprinting yourself: Print each finger one at a time. Use a water-soluble ink pad (or even a lipstick) to lightly coat the full face of the upper section of each finger, and then carefully roll each finger gently from one side to the other on a piece of paper placed on the edge of a table. Do not push down hard or you will blot out or smear your prints. Label each one (right thumb, left thumb, right pointer, left pointer, etc.).

- *A fingerprint has been badly obscured by scars or you happen to be missing the finger or fingertip.* Unfortunately, these things happen. Go ahead and fill in what you can of the print chart and interpret what you've got. My experience is that this works perfectly. I had a client whose hands were malformed at birth, and she has just three fully formed fingers. When I first met her and analyzed her fingers/fin-gerprints, I had no idea what she did for a living. I read her Life Purpose accord-ing to the three fingers she had (Successful Creative Communications), and then she told me that she was a paid writer and writing teacher and had always felt the need to express herself. Voilà!

Step #3: Fill in Your Fingerprint Chart

Now it's time to fill in the **symbols** for each of your fingerprints. **Start** by looking at your right thumb, then write down the symbol for its fingerprint into the chart. Work your way across, one finger at a time, to the right pinkie. Then move to the left thumb and work your way over to the left pinkie. I earnestly advise you to build fingerprint charts this way right from the start because it is very easy to mix up the right hand and the left (especially when you start looking at other people's fingerprints and they are facing you so right and left are switched) or to mix up the fingers if you start jumping around. Once you've filled in the symbols for your fingerprint chart, go back and **double-check** yourself!

The correct interpretation of your Life Purpose depends on you making an accurate identification of the fingerprints and getting the print chart right. Notice right away that the print chart structure aligns the fingers of the right and left hand (both thumbs together, both pointer fingers together, etc.) with the right hand on top and the left hand on the bottom. Once you are practiced, you will not even need to draw the chart itself, but can simply write down the fingerprints according to this structure on any piece of paper you have handy (if you keep reading others' prints, you will be able to interpret most people's fingerprints without even writing them down, like being able to verbally translate what someone is saying on the spot).

There is a one-page summary sheet in the appendix at the end of this book that you can photocopy for repeated use once you learn all the steps of decoding your own fingerprint chart. The summary sheet is also available online for free download at www.DestinyAtYourFingtertips.com.

Here are the basic types again, to reduce page flipping.

the four basic fingerprint types and their ranking points

Whorl	Loop	Tented Arch	Arch
4 points	3 points	2 points	1 point

my fingerprint chart

	Thumb	Pointer	Middle	Ring	Pinkie
Right Hand					
Left Hand					

Step #4: Assign Points to Find Your High-Ranking Fingerprints

Next, you need to assign the appropriate points to each fingerprint. The fingerprints worth the most points will determine your Life Purpose. You can have any number of your ten fingers/fingerprints as your Life Purpose. You may have one finger out of ten for your purpose, two out of ten, or all ten. **Write the number of points for each fingerprint in the bottom right corner of each box in your fingerprint chart.** Take your time and double-check yourself.

RANKING POINTS FOR SUBTYPES

If you have subtypes, look up their symbols and ranking numbers in the section beginning on page 39. If you have a subtype not listed, no worries! Just take a look at the component fingerprint types within the subtype fingerprint, use them as guidelines, and do your best to assign points to the print. For example: Do you have a small whorl in the middle of an arch? Make up a symbol combining the two for your chart. Add the points for a whorl (4) to the point for the arch (1) and divide by 2 (the number of print types involved) and give the print 2.5 points. Remember that the ranking numbers are determined for the subtypes by adding together the ranking numbers of the basic types involved and then dividing them by two.

sample chart #1 (with fingerprint symbols and points filled in)

	Thumb	Pointer	Middle	Ring	Pinkie
Right	⊙ 4	⊥ 2	⊙ 4	⊙ 4	♌ 3
Left	♌ 3	⊥ 2	♌ 3	♌ 3	⊙ 4

sample chart #2 with subtype fingerprints

	Thumb	Pointer	Middle	Ring	Pinkie
Right	♌ 3	⩕ 2.5	℘ 3.7	℘ 3.7	℘ 3.7
Left	♌ 3	— 1.5	☈ 0	♌ 3	℘ 3.7

Step #5 Decode Your High-Ranking Fingerprints for Your Life Purpose

Identify which fingerprints have the *most points* . . . those with the highest ranking. In sample chart #1 on the previous page, the highest-ranking prints are the right thumb, right middle, right ring, and left pinkie. In sample chart #2 on the previous page, the highest-ranking prints are the right middle, right ring, and double pinkies.

Go slow at first and double-check yourself.

You may have a single high-ranking print, two high-rankers, or even all ten.

Circle your high-ranking fingerprints/fingers from your chart:

	Thumb	Pointer	Middle	Ring	Pinkie
Right	Right Thumb	Right Pointer	Right Middle	Right Ring	Right Pinkie
Left	Left Thumb	Left Pointer	Left Middle	Left Ring	Left Pinkie

NEXT! #1: If you have **fewer than six** fingerprints tying for high rank, circle your high-ranking fingers on the chart below, then continue on to check for "doubles," and then decode.

#2: If you have six or more fingerprints tying for high rank, skip to the section **"Do You Have Six or More High-Ranking Fingerprints?"** on the next page to determine your Life Purpose.

EACH FINGER'S LIFE PURPOSE

Circle your high-ranking fingers and read on!

	Thumb	Pointer	Middle	Ring	Pinkie
Right	Successful (Master of Results)	Leader	Business	Individualist	Messenger
Left	Family/ Community	Live My Passions	Mentor	Innovator	Healer

DO YOU HAVE "DOUBLES"?

If you have "**doubles**" (for example, *both* thumbs or *both* pointer fingers have high-ranking fingerprints), how do you know which one (right or left) reveals your Life Purpose? Use the following rules. It is possible to have one or more "doubles" plus one or more "singles."

Both ("double") thumb = Master of Results (the right-hand purpose)

Both ("double") pointer = Leader (the right-hand purpose)

Both ("double") middle = Mentor (the left-hand purpose)

Both ("double") ring = Artist/Individualist (the right-hand purpose)

Both ("double") pinkie = Healer (the left-hand purpose)

Put the names of your Life Purpose fingers together to make a name you can remember. (For example: "Successful Passionate Artist," "Healing Mentor," "Artist in Business.")

My Life Purpose Is: _____

DO YOU HAVE SIX OR MORE HIGH-RANKING FINGERPRINTS?

When you have six or more high-ranking fingerprints, the focus of your Life Purpose is the essential nature of the *type* of the predominant fingerprint (whorls, loops, tented arches, or arches).

Depending on the arrangement of the six or more high-ranking fingerprints, it is often possible to decode your Life Purpose according to finger placement as described (especially if there are doubles) and the ten individual Life Purposes. In addition, you will want to read the overlay of your Group (Aggregate) Life Purpose. **Some people have a Group Life Purpose and not an Individual Finger Life Purpose.**

For those who have **six to ten** of the same type of high-ranking fingerprint, the following **Group Life Purpose** is your Life Purpose.

Ten arches = Master of Peace/Balance

Six or more tented arches = Master of Wisdom

Six or more loops = Master of Love/Relationships

Six or more whorls = Master of Service

In the following pages, you can read all about *your* Life Purpose. If you have a multiple-finger Life Purpose, read each one that applies. If you have a Group Life Purpose, turn to the pages on the Master of Peace/Balance, Master of Wisdom, Master of Love/Relationships, and Master of Service just beyond the Individual Life Purpose chapters. Whatever your Life Purpose, each has its high potential/fulfillment point, challenges, and everyday expression for you to become aware of and inhabit in order to live with conscious awareness in your Zone of Fulfillment. Congratulations! You now know your Life Purpose. Are you ready to live it more fully? Read on to see how you can consciously live your most satisfying life!

If you'd like to practice decoding some sample fingerprint charts, turn to the appendix at the end of this book. Add ranking points and decode! Answers follow the charts.

PART II

THE LIFE PURPOSES, AT LAST!

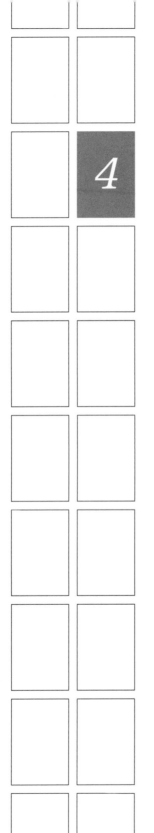

4 The Ten Basic Life Purposes

Not to take possession of your life plan is to let your existence be an accident.

IRVIN YALOM, *When Nietzsche Wept*

Thumb: Results

Tangible, Measurable Material Results

Your Ability to Produce/Capacity for Doing/Accomplishment

Determination/Persistence

Success

Will Power/Control

Decision Making

Effort

Opposability/Grip/Manipulation

Independence/Dependence/(In)Competence

Ability to Shape Your Material Environment (Including Care for Your Physical Body)

Quitters never win, and winners never quit.

> NAPOLEON HILL, *Think and Grow Rich*

The bond that links your true family is not one of blood, but of respect and joy in each other's life.

> RICHARD BACH, *Illusions*

Winners keep score.

> UNKNOWN

Pray like it's up to God, work like it's up to you.

> UNKNOWN

Talent is cheaper than table salt. What separates the talented individual from the successful one is a lot of hard work.

> STEPHEN KING

Thumbs Overview
(The <u>Results</u> Life Purposes)

As human beings, most people haven't thought of or heard about the special properties of their thumbs, and have simply taken them for granted as long as they've functioned properly. Your thumbs can oppose the palm and fingers and therefore have the ability to grip, manipulate, and shape the world. Because of your opposable thumbs, you can manipulate and enact your will upon the material world and create tools to achieve the bigger results you want to get. These tools include everything from pencils—which allow you to write down your intangible ideas and stories in a durable, tangible form—to very complex tools like cars, printing presses, and cell phones. Your thumbs represent your ability to get things done, to literally and figuratively get *results*.

As I write this out, one word at a time, on the tool of my computer at my favorite café, and as my tablemate first maps onto paper a complex computer program interface, we are both doing what those with the thumb Life Purpose do at our best—taking our intangible ideas and, through practical actions, making them tangible in the real world where they can be transmitted and used for some actual purpose. The knitter takes two sticks, some yarn, and a creative idea and builds something stitch by stitch. The stock investor looks over all the information available about the markets, the money to be invested, and the risk involved, and makes a series of intangible decisions and actions that (hopefully) result in a net gain of money (the ultimate tangible result in our modern world). The pregnant woman eats carefully so the physical baby her body is producing has the proper building blocks to be born into the world healthy and whole. And family, ideally, supports and nurtures its members in a safe environment.

When you apply your thumbs, you achieve results to help provide the foundation for some other aspect of life to happen in an ever-expanding, interdependent chain of actions, which create further results. Across the street from the café, there are lights decorating the stores for the holiday season. Someone first imagined the lights (an intangible idea), then drew them on paper (the first step in bringing them into tangible form), then had them manufactured (now they exist as a tangible product), and then sold them (for tangible money, which supports everyone involved in producing the lights). The store owners bought and hung the lights on their store awnings and in windows in order to attract customers. The lights make a nice environment for shoppers, and when the store makes sales, the owners get the result of making money to support their own livelihoods. Shoppers benefit as well when they purchase the tangible goods they need for their lives.

Thumbs represent the foundational supportive building blocks of your life—and your ability to make a solid foundation for your life—starting with your own body and need for emotional and psychological nurturance. They extend out to the physical support of your body (food, shelter, and clothing), a process that requires money of some sort in most places in the world today. When you have one of the thumb purposes, you have the higher potential to be particularly good at creating the different types of supportive results necessary to live a successful life—one that goes beyond grappling with issues of bare survival into a life of true thriving.

MASTER OF RESULTS (SUCCESS)

(Right Thumb and Double Thumb Life Purpose)

Keywords:

Material Results in the World (Money)	Practicality
Doer	"Make" Money/Things Happen
Accomplishment	Competence
"Manifestation"	Independence (Make My Own Living)
Taking Intangible Ideas to Tangible Results	Doing What Works (Dropping What Doesn't)

If you have the Master of Results Life Purpose, you are here to get results in the tangible, measurable material world. You have the potential to become highly successful and have a deep desire for independence, particularly when it comes to being able to make money and succeed on your own terms. As the Master of Results, you reap meaning from making your own living and generally being competent at managing all aspects of living in the physical world. This is not to say that you are meant to focus on money for money's sake, but that you want to accomplish appropriate independence in the world by making a successful, supportive living for yourself. With this Life Purpose, you are primarily here to *determine your own life* and succeed on your own terms, rather than being inappropriately dependent and allowing others or your circumstances to make your decisions and control your life.

Key to living this Life Purpose is pursuing the entire process of taking an intangible idea and turning it into a tangible, usable result. You must first have an idea of what you want to accomplish, then you must set your intentions, and then decide to take practical action until you get results. This process is also known more widely as "manifestation," but I want to be very careful in explaining what this means. The current popular notion of it is that you can simply think about something, and *poof!*—it will appear before you like magic. Many people believe that if they only wish hard enough, what they want will be handed to them without any effort of their own. Witness the popularity of all forms of gambling, including the state lotteries. Our society is saturated by the promise of "instant" and "effortless" everything (instant prosperity, effortless weight loss, painless relationships). Most people place their bets and wait around for something to happen, and they are desperately disappointed when nothing does. These people make excuses by telling themselves, "It just wasn't meant to be," rather than *deciding* what result they want in life and then consistently *doing* something about it until they get there. So many people rely inappropriately on something outside of themselves to determine what they do with themselves. They take the "path of least resistance" as soon as the going gets rough and end up drifting aimlessly through life.

To be the Master of Results, you must first *decide* what you want to accomplish— what you want to get done—then take *determined action* to move toward the desired result. You must also be able to *measure* your progress along the way to make sure you're focused on doing the things that keep you moving toward your intended result, rather than wandering off-course. In other words, you must *make* things happen. When you are inhabiting this Life Purpose, you understand that you must begin with an idea of what you want to *accomplish* (get ready); *assess* in practical terms where you actually are now and make plans to get from here to there (aim); and then start *doing*, taking consistent, steady action to move toward your intended result (fire!). Without a definite target, you have no guidelines for making good decisions or taking the right action. Next, this process must be repeated while regularly assessing what works and what doesn't, and readjusting course as necessary until you get your intended result. You can still buy a lottery ticket, but don't wait around passively for it to pay off! Get busy doing what it takes to determine the life you want and you'll have the best chance of getting there. You have to be willing to do what you can to make things happen. One of my clients put it this way: "God isn't going to do anything for you that you can do for yourself."

This particular Life Purpose happens to be one of mine, and when I held my first successful workshop I had one of those moments of enlightenment about what it really means to be the Master of Results. First I had an idea to conduct a workshop that was a cross between networking for entrepreneurs and a seminar on some aspect of succeeding in your own business. After it percolated for a while in the back of my brain, I sat down and outlined my intentions on paper to begin the process of making it real. It would involve six bi-weekly meetings with dinner and casual networking followed by the seminar topic, limited to twelve participants. I set the dates and the times, designed and created a flyer, and mailed it out to everyone in my database. At this point I'd already learned (by failing more than once) that mailing people was not enough to ensure the success of twelve paying participants, so I printed out a phone-calling list, in order of those who might be most interested, and made ten phone calls per night until I had twelve participants and a short waiting list. Believe me, I didn't want to have to call people and face the possibility that they'd be unhappy that I called, or handle the inevitable rejection from those who weren't interested. But I was *determined* to do whatever it took in practical reality to get the twelve people for a successful workshop, and I knew that twelve was the number by which to measure the extent of my success. Every night I could see how many people had signed up, and I knew exactly where I was on my path to success. I did everything under my control to deliver an event that was valuable for the participants.

At the end of the first meeting, after everyone left, excited about themselves and the connections they'd made, I sat down with the stack of checks I'd been paid and it hit me that *I had made money where money didn't exist before*. I took an intangible idea all the way through to a tangible result . . . I turned an idea into money by making all the decisions and persisting in taking every necessary action until I got the result I wanted—money to pay my rent. Something crashed into place for me at that moment, and I felt perfectly aligned with myself and the world around me. It was *me* who decided, independently, what *results I wanted to get* and who then used my will power and decision-making abilities to *make* it happen! Despite the work involved, it felt like magic. And it gave me a piece of the independence I craved, as I wanted to be self-employed and be in control of my own material well-being.

People who succeed make plans for their success . . . they determine their own lives. Competitive figure skaters have an overall result they aim for: winning a world-level title. This enables them to work backwards to where they actually are and set up all the intervening strategies and goals, all the stepping stones that can lead, in time, to the big result. They have something they're aiming for with measurement points along the way. They don't just do or not do what they feel like doing on any given day. To get to world-level competition, they must first compete locally, regionally, and nationally, and win. To compete locally and win, they must be able to complete two full performance programs with as few mistakes as possible. To complete a full program, they must master a large number of individual jumps, spins, and connecting moves, all orchestrated to music. To do this, they must practice a certain number of times per week, work with a coach, take lessons, eat right, engage in off-ice training (dance and weights and stretching), and time their training to peak during the times of the competitions. They must persist, and there is constant measurement along the way to keep adjusting course. Are the individual moves being mastered or not? Are aerobic and anaerobic stamina high enough to complete the programs or not? Can they compete with strength and elegance under the pressure of being judged, even if they wake up on the "wrong side of the bed" on the day of the competition? In this sort of scenario, it is impossible for the skaters to lie to themselves about whether they are succeeding or not. They are clearly winning or losing competitions along the way.

In other circumstances it can be easier to fudge on this process for a long period of time. I've known many people who have started their own businesses and failed because they did not hold themselves to standards of measurement along the way and because they had no firm result in mind. They had no solid financial goals (I will make x dollars per year or month), so they never clearly knew if they were succeeding or failing—they didn't know what they were aiming for and whether or not they were on course to reaching their goal. Invariably, I watched most of them go out of business in less than five years when their financial resources ran out or when they went into debt they could not repay. Approximately half of all businesses fail in less than five years due to lack of a determined result to work toward and/or an inability to adjust course when things aren't working according to the expected plan.

When the Master of Results consciously begins to learn and engage in the realistic process of success, and achieves results, it can look like absolute magic to others, but actually, *you* know that you have learned the way the material world works and are simply operating consistently by its rules to produce the results you want. A friend of mine calls it the "hard-work miracle." She experimented with how to find clients and retain them, and she notes that it was difficult at first, but as she persisted through her failures, corrected her mistakes, and attained an understanding of what worked and did it consistently, she began to succeed more and more easily. She was willing to determine what she wanted, work with reality, keep her eye on her bottom line, and persist through failure to get to the success she knew she could create in time.

If you are a Master of Results, your deepest fulfillment arises from determining all aspects of your life, whatever your circumstances, and realizing you are in a position to do so, whether you're self-employed or working within an organization, deciding whom to marry or where to go on vacation. Life doesn't always make self-determination easy, but it's absolutely possible. Ultimately, success is about determining your own life so you have the level of independence you desire by generating the money you need to sustain it.

Challenges

Just because you are a Master of Results doesn't mean that it's always easy to inhabit your purpose all the time and in all circumstances. You are here to grow into your being and what it requires you to do. Two types of challenges help you gain the broad experience you need in order to live the Success Life Purpose.

Internal Challenges (Being)

These are some of the challenges you have within yourself, the negative beliefs you may hold about yourself and about Success, which need to be brought to consciousness and worked with so you can do what is necessary to create the results you want.

"I DON'T UNDERSTAND MONEY OR THE MATERIAL WORLD"

Many with this Life Purpose start off with a poor understanding of how making money or making a living works. Notice that the phrase we all use is "make" money—not "win" money or "find" money or "get" money. You may have grown up impoverished, or, conversely, very well-off. Either way, there was a lack of practical training in how money is made or how things get done, or how material results are actually achieved, all due to an unbalanced relationship to money. The environment was one of fighting to survive, fearing a lack of money, and being caught up in poverty mentality, or of everything being too easy in a way that dependence and incompetence was fostered and self-reliance discouraged.

"MONEY OR SUCCESS IS BAD"

Many with this Life Purpose feel that it's not okay to succeed because money is bad or because people with money are ruthless or arrogant or gain their wealth illicitly. Some with this purpose feel it isn't okay to achieve higher levels of success, of any kind, than their families of origin.

"FAILURE IS BAD"/"MONEY IS ALL THAT MATTERS"

Some people with this purpose are succeeding very well materially, but feel a lack of meaning around *how* they are making their money. They are afraid to risk failure at doing what they truly want to do with themselves. The possibility of experiencing failure is frightening to them, so they do the safe, secure thing they hate in order to avoid the risk of feeling like a failure. And who can blame them? Who wants to feel like a failure? These people can feel like their worth is determined by how much money they have. But there are always failures on the way to true success and self-determination . . . it's part of learning how to succeed. Usually these people are limiting the larger success or true independence they can have at the expense of being secure. Their sense of meaninglessness comes from not being truly self-determining. These people also have a hard time sticking to the process of measurement, because if they are falling short they feel like failures and want to avoid feeling this way, instead of redoubling their efforts to succeed.

INDEPENDENCE/DEPENDENCE ISSUES

Those with this Life Purpose commonly struggle with issues of independence and dependence (or competence and incompetence). When you have the Success Life Purpose, you are learning how to be appropriately independent, which means that you know when to ask for help and when to do things for yourself. As you learn the balance between the two (appropriate *interdependence*), you may make the error of doing *everything* yourself because you feel incompetent if you allow others to help you (or feel that other people are too incompetent to help you). Or you may be completely dependent on others for your material well-being, and lazy about doing things for yourself. At a certain point, to expand your ability to succeed, you have to engage the help of others because you are only one person with twenty-four hours in a day. You limit your ability to create success if you believe that getting help makes you incompetent. On the other hand, if you are overly dependent, you need to start determining and doing things for yourself. You need to cultivate self-reliance in order to achieve appropriate independence and feel a sense of fulfillment, and not be left in the lurch if the person or money that provides for you disappears for any reason. Taking the path of least resistance will leave you feeling out of control of your own life. If you have this Life Purpose and rely on someone else for your living, when you are capable of making it for yourself, you're in trouble.

External Challenges (Doing)

When you begin to succeed, various obstacles are likely to arise in the external world to challenge you and help you develop strength in your ability to determine your own life. Remember that having the Master of Results purpose doesn't guarantee your success. You have to work as skillfully as you are able with the times, the circumstances you're living in, and the people in your life, and all three are likely to confront you in many ways. Here are a few possible external challenges.

OTHERS ARE THREATENED BY YOUR SUCCESS OR YOUR FOCUS ON SUCCESS

Various important people in your life may actually discourage you from succeeding due to their own insecurities. Your parents or siblings or good friends may be afraid to lose you or may be jealous of your success. Your spouse or children may not like the ways in which their lives, by being tied to yours, have to change because of the demands of your success (though they often do not want to give up the fruits of your success that they enjoy!). Others' resistance to your success may catch you by surprise and cause you to hold yourself back or sabotage yourself. These important people can threaten (in subtle or obvious ways) to leave you, reject you, or disapprove of you if you do too well and trigger their fears of the unknown. One of my favorite bumper stickers declares, "Those who defer their dreams, discourage yours." When you succeed, others in your life may feel their own failure to determine their own lives and may not be happy about what they see about themselves in the mirror of your success.

PERSISTENCE #1: *EXPECT* OBSTACLES!

The road to success is usually strewn with rocks—you lay your best plans and then hit the road and see what happens. "Man proposes, God disposes" feels all too true as you come up against the obstacles that can stand in the way of succeeding. One of my favorite successful people humorously rephrased this saying as, "Man plans, God laughs!" He wasn't suggesting that God is mean spirited, just that as humans there is no way to know everything that might happen in advance. You need to expect that there will be obstacles and face them head-on as they arise, rather than avoiding them and giving up when you stumble upon them. A large part of whether you succeed or fail lies in how you accept and persist through obstacles, while staying on course, until you achieve success.

PERSISTENCE #2: LEARNING FROM FAILURE, LEARNING FROM SUCCESS

Just ask anyone who's successful, and that person will tell you that the road to success certainly has its ups and downs. Many highly successful people went through the depths of failure, often more than once, on the way to their notable success. Success is an *ongoing process* when you have this Life Purpose, not something that you achieve and then it's over and done with. I often have clients who say, "I tried and failed, now what?" They haven't learned that you can't let a single failure stop you in your tracks, no matter how severe it seems. You can find stories of failure and success in many places, and it's useful to study them in order to learn from them and be inspired by them when you're in the midst of failure or feeling like a failure. You almost certainly will fail in small ways and large ways, so it becomes pertinent that you learn from both failure and success. What works? What doesn't work? To succeed consistently over time you have to learn what works and *do it* as well as learn what doesn't work and *drop it*. You must persist through your failures and learn from them to find your success. Sometimes it means pushing harder, sometimes it means waiting, sometimes it means throwing in the towel for a while when something you set out to do flops entirely. Success requires learning "when to hold 'em and when to fold 'em." You can watch the poker channel on TV for an incredible education in this. It's fascinating to watch those with poor hands drop out to minimize their losses in a single game and the ways in which those who have something to work with strategize to use it to best effect. Overall, you don't want to quit entirely. One of my favorite books about what is means to succeed, called *Art & Fear*, by David Bayles and Ted Orland, states, "Basically, those who continue to make art are those who have learned how to continue—or more precisely, have learned how *not* to quit." Or, as Napoleon Hill, author of *Think and Grow Rich*, succinctly puts it, "Quitters never win, and winners never quit." And then there's the old adage, "If at first you don't succeed, try, try again." Keep trying and learn from your failures and your successes.

WAITING ON THE WORLD TO CHANGE

These excuses for a lack of self-determination tend to center on waiting for some external circumstance to change. "I'll do what I really want after I retire, or my kids or grandbabies grow up," claim some. Others are waiting to meet a mate who will "pay the rent" and make things happen for them, or are waiting to win the lottery. Still others have a hard time moving into what they really want to do because they are supporting families and fear material failure when they are the sole breadwinners. We need dedicated parents when children are very young, and sole breadwinners may have to rearrange things very carefully over time (and, if married, get spouses to help out with supporting the family to mitigate the risks of making a change). But while some of these "excuses" are perfectly legitimate, most times the versions of these excuses I hear make little objective sense. One client said mournfully, "I can't do what I know I'm called to do because my son needs me." When I asked the age of her son, she replied, "Sixteen." It was all I could do not to sputter out loud that her son is a healthy teenager and, like most sixteen-year-old young men, absolutely does not need or want his mother to be around constantly. Another client's excuse, exclaimed in front of twelve people, for not going out and promoting the books she'd already succeeded in getting published was an emphatic, "But I have grandbabies!" I looked her directly in the eye and said, "You can't be serious!" and the entire roomful of people (including the client) almost fell out of their chairs, hooting with laughter at the absurdity of her self-sabotage. Many of these excuses stem from a misdirection of will power, which disallows them from making plans for their own success and accomplishing it. Some are truly dealing with difficult life situations requiring extra strategizing to make changes. But all need to be doggedly determined to make change for themselves instead of waiting for the world to do it for them . . . or not.

Being It, Doing It, and Faking It (Attitude to Adopt)

Since success is the state of being you wish to live in, where life feels meaningful to you, you can ask yourself the following questions when you're working on adopting the attitude of your Life Purpose in order to more fully inhabit it and then *do it.*

When you feel like a *frustrated failure*, ask:

- How do I *feel* when I succeed? Can I stop and step into this version of myself?

- What do I need to *do* to succeed? What actions do I actually need to take to succeed?

- Am I allowing or depending on someone or something else to determine my life for me? Am I inappropriately dependent? Am I generating my own income? In what ways am I taking the path of least resistance?

- Am I succeeding already and not stopping to measure it so I can acknowledge and enjoy it? Am I falling short of my success and do I need to adjust course?

Do I need to aspire to a higher level of success for myself? Or, when starting out, do I need to aspire to a more appropriate, practical level of success?

• What would I *do right now*, in this situation, if I were *already* successful?

> "I determine what I want to accomplish then set out and do it,
> no matter what it takes to get there."

Practical Everyday Expression/Steps

To build up your ability to get results, you must *practice* the actions that create success!

• *Practice determining what result you want before you start.* Ask yourself, "What do I want to get out of this?" Then *work backwards*, step by step, to where you are now to see what you need to do to get the result. Make a list of tasks. Once you begin taking action, stop frequently and evaluate whether you are actually moving toward your intended result so you can work with unexpected obstacles and challenges.

• *Write down the result you want and put it somewhere you can see it constantly.* Start it with "I will . . ." or "I am . . ." I know that many success gurus emphasize this, but I'm surprised at how few people actually do it. Writing down the results you want on paper is an obvious first step of taking your intangible wish and pulling it into the tangible. *How much* money do you want to make this year? *How much* weight do you want to lose? *How many* students do you want in your workshop? *How many* people do you want to reach this year with your message? *By when* do you want to run a marathon? Remember the famous Depression-era saying, "A chicken in *every* pot!" This clear declaration of a seemingly difficult result inspired and motivated many people in hard times to do whatever they could to get food on the table and to persevere when it seemed impossible. You must have something concrete and measurable to aim for in order to make it happen.

• *Practice completing everything you start.* The dishes, folding your laundry, washing the car, keeping track of your income or savings. Becoming a Master of Results means being a master of all aspects of your material life. The same basic process that applies to successfully cleaning up the kitchen applies to getting more complex results in your life. You must initiate then continue all the way through to completion. Take a look around your life and assess how many incomplete projects (of any size) you have and determine to get them done. Make a list of what you want to complete. If you want a clean glove box in your car, start there. Competency with small tasks quickly and reliably builds your sense of being successful and helps you feel like you're up to larger projects. When I'm feeling out of control with my larger business, I stop and do something small that can be accomplished quickly and easily, like filing my expense receipts, mopping the kitchen floor, or making a single phone call I've been avoiding. I *immediately* feel like I can tackle my next steps because I get a hit of fulfillment from my Life Purpose by succeeding at something, however small, and I want more of that feeling.

Positive Feelings Associated with This Life Purpose

- Successful

- Competent/effective

- Self-sufficient (and can ask for/allow help when needed)

- You're the one determining your life, you're in control of your actions, you're in the driver's seat of your life

"I get things done!"

Questions to Ask Yourself

- What do I *do*?

- How do I *decide*?

- What *results* do I want to get?

- What am I good at getting done myself? What do I need help with?

- Am I aiming my actions at the result I truly wish to achieve?

- When do I have a hard time enlisting the help of others?

- Do I quit when the going gets rough, or do I push through to accomplish what I set out to do?

- At what point do I tend to drop the ball?

- When do I tend to take the path of least resistance when I should take action?

- Do I know when to push (control) and when to wait (not control)?

- When do I feel incompetent and like a failure?

- When do I feel competent and capable?

- Am I choosing to determine the aspects of my life that are under my direct control?

- Am I paying my own way through life?

MASTER OF "FAMILY" BONDS

(Left Thumb Life Purpose)

Keywords: Personal Material World = The Body/ Root Chakra

Physical Foundation of Life ("Family")

Nurturance and Support (Giving and Receiving from Self and Others)

Belonging to Groups without Selling Out

"Ties That Bind"

Family/Community/"Tribe"/ Society/Groups

Your Physical Environment as an Extension of Body

Kinship

If you have the Master of "Family" Bonds Life Purpose, you are here to participate in mutually supportive ties with other people, whether they are your blood family of origin or the nurturing network of friends, colleagues, and acquaintances you surround yourself with in your adult life. You have the potential to be the "glue" or connector linking people together in such a way that they become foundational for one another and feel they can look to each other for caring support when needed. At your best, you are the person who can gather people together into inclusive groups, communities, tribes, and societies with just enough structure so the members can associate and connect, without being so rigid that they have to efface their individuality to belong. As the Master of "Family" Bonds, you garner meaning through nurturing yourself and others and, in turn, allow others to nurture and support you, without being overbearing yourself (the "Italian" mama pushing others to "Eat! Eat!"), allowing others to smother you (eating another serving when you're already stuffed . . . and hating it), or opting out of groups entirely due to fear of this possible dynamic.

Key to living this Life Purpose is engaging fully in the process of appropriate control over your personal material world. This process includes your relationship to your own physical body, the physical and emotional environment you provide for yourself (as an extension of your body), and the sustaining relationships in your life. With this Life Purpose, you have the potential to truly "make a home for yourself in the world" and to provide the resources for others to do the same by being the "hub" of an interconnected family, community, or group. You are here to embody the true healthy meaning of "family" in its most positive sense—an interconnected group of people who care for each other and offer ongoing nurturance, and who "have each other's backs" if something goes wrong in life and material and/or emotional support is needed. Until fairly recently, it was said that "blood is thicker than water," meaning that your relationships with your family of origin were the strongest bonds you have in your life over your entire life, whether it's "bad blood" or truly loving bonds. In these days of familial decentralization, where members of traditional blood families choose to part ways and live in different communities, many are struggling personally with the definition of what "family" really means. (You may be in search of personal identity away from the expectations of blood relatives and a narrow definition of who you have to be, or you may be in the pursuit of a more materially secure life for yourself and the family you are creating.) Most do not stop to think of what "family" signifies in the broader sense of *belonging* within the context of groups of people—it is not solely your blood relations, but also your family of friends, colleagues, community, and your broader society. With the "Family" Life Purpose, your potential is to inhabit and model what it means for people to be "like family" or kin to one another, whether they are members of a blood family or participants in a larger support group, community, or tribe.

To be the Master of "Family" Bonds, you must start by being self-governing. You must be a good family member *to yourself* by taking proper care of your own physical and emotional needs. What do you need to do to nurture your body so that it can be the solid foundation for living the rest of your life? For each of us, health and basic physical condition are the bedrock from which the rest of life is lived. We all live in the material form of a body and can't live life without it. If you are tired (not enough rest), improperly nourished (underfed or overfed), temporarily or chronically ill, or you otherwise abuse your body in some way, then it is difficult to feel solid enough to do the things you want to do each day. It's as if the foundation of the house of your life is collapsed or missing and, therefore, cannot support all the other aspects of your life. With this Life Purpose, you are here to be a master at caring for your body in a loving way . . . the way good parents take care of the physical and emotional survival needs of their own children.

How do you express your love for yourself through taking care of your body and your environment? Next, you can become a foundation for other people. As you embrace yourself, make yourself feel welcome in the world, support and properly nurture yourself, give yourself room to be yourself, make a safe space for yourself (literally by creating a safe, nurturing home and working environment for yourself), and know that *you* will always be there for *you* no matter what, then you begin to be a model for others. You can reach out and bring the supportive people you want and need into your life to create an emotional support network for yourself and them. You begin to relish "the ties that bind" by having healthy interdependent relationships with other people and help foster their connections to one another. This is what gives you the deepest sense of satisfaction—knowing that you have yourself to rely on and a "tribe" where you can be yourself *and* belong, both offering and receiving the fundamental sustenance of human relationships.

A friend of mine, Chris Zydel, is a wonderful example of this. She leads ongoing painting-for-self-discovery workshops wherein members are "guided and supported in an environment free of critique and full of warmth, safety, and encouragement." Many participants have been together as groups for many years and have supported each other through many life changes. They have stuck around when friction arises among group members—they work their relationships out over time and have built a strong trust, which binds them together. My friend is the hub of it all. She creates the groups by carefully bringing new people in, providing basic guidelines for group membership, and making the space for everyone to connect into a supportive web, which, in turn, supports each individual's search for his or her own individuality.

People who reap the satisfaction of their "Family" Life Purpose involve themselves with groups of people over time. They choose to participate in networks and clubs, their communities or associations, support groups, and, yes, their families, whether of origin or created. They know that "no man is an island," "everyone needs a helping hand," and "there is strength in numbers." They naturally enjoy bringing people together and helping them connect or bond to the mutual benefit of everyone involved. Others turn to them as a resource because they are well connected and know who does what and who knows whom. The Master of "Family" Bonds is good at opening up the conduits for giving *and* receiving, and understands that being able to do both is what ties the knots in the safety net of connections we all need in order to feel a sense of belonging in the world. We each have a place among our fellow humans from where we can get the help we need and offer help to others. Taking in nurturance helps us feel we belong, feel accepted by others, and feel safe. And giving connects us to others because we realize we are naturally resourceful and have a place in the world when someone needs what we can offer.

If you are the Master of "Family" Bonds, you need to watch out for the various ways you can look like you're doing your Life Purpose but are actually a bit off center. Being a "master" does not mean that you have everyone under your control. It does not mean that you should be overbearing in trying to force connections to others or expect others to "be like you" to belong. The "Italian" mama stereotype who tries to force people to eat is a classic negative example of this, as is the father who is the dictatorial head of the household, expecting everyone in the family to do as he says without question. Many with this Life Purpose embody its opposite and "go it alone"; they shy away from interacting with groups because of having grown up in a family where they felt they had to give up what was important to them in order to fit in, belong, and survive. These "lone wolves" can have a hard time being true to themselves when in a group so they ditch it entirely, when actually, with this Life Purpose, they are meant to work on this conundrum rather than avoid it. True belonging is about being able to be yourself *and* belong to a group, to maintain your individuality *and* offer and receive support from others. Being a member of a "family" does not mean the members are carbon copies of one another.

Another common mistake with this Life Purpose is to be someone who pulls groups together from a position of authority (like a workshop/support-group facilitator or community leader—both are excellent expressions of this purpose), but who does not engage in *peer* relationships because of not being in the control seat. When engaged in peer relationships, we have to connect with people by being appropriately vulnerable and on an even footing with them, in regard to giving and receiving. I once read an interview with the actor Tom Hanks and really appreciated an honest admission he made about enjoying coming home because his kids didn't know him in his professional capacity. To them he was "just Dad," and they treated him like a regular person and weren't constantly deferent to him because of the powerful professional connections he could offer.

When Masters of "Family" Bonds consciously begin to learn and engage in the process of nurturance of self and others, it is clear that they have a place within a tight-knit group or community where they are accepted and accepting of others. Within this group, each member has a sense of healthy obligation to the other members. In big-wave surfing, it takes a three-member team for one person to surf—one drives the Jet Ski to tow the surfer to the wave and then watches the surfer's back from the shoulder of the wave, another is in the channel below the wave ready to retrieve a wiped-out surfer from the water, and the third person surfs. Big-wave surfing is extremely dangerous, and the Jet Ski driver is also there to pull the surfer out of harm's way in the event of a wipe-out. The Jet Ski driver is willing to put his (or her) life on the line in order to rescue a downed surfer, and within the big-wave surfing community, *any* Jet Ski driver will literally risk his or her own life to aid any surfer *even if they don't like each other*. The attitude within this "family" is that any individual could need life-or-death help at any time, so each member is willing to offer help in the event he or she may need it in return someday. It's okay to be different and even dislike each other, but at the end of the day, everyone who surfs is a member of the tribe, and all are bonded together by their love of surfing.

If you are a Master of "Family" Bonds, your deepest fulfillment arises from a profound sense of feeling safe in the world due to your mutually supportive connections with others. You are able to take care of yourself, your physical world, and your life in such a way that you feel like you can truly thrive and enjoy living, because you are firmly grounded and deeply present in the here-and-now with yourself, other people, and the world around you. Ultimately, "family" is about having a conscious sense of positive interconnectedness and interdependence (close bonds) with yourself and others based on your ability to give and receive. This helps you feel that you are not alone in the world, but an equally nurtured and nurturing part of the human family, and perhaps all of nature.

Challenges

Just because you are a Master of "Family" Bonds doesn't mean that it's always easy to inhabit your purpose all the time and in all circumstances. You are here to grow into your being and what it requires you to do. Two types of challenges help you gain the broad experience you need in order to live the Master of "Family" Bonds Life Purpose.

Internal Challenges (Being)

These are some of the challenges you may have within yourself, the negative beliefs you may hold about yourself and about "Family," which need to be brought to consciousness and worked with so you can do what is necessary to create true nurturance in your life.

"IT'S HARD FOR ME TO BE AWARE OF AND PRESENT TO MY BODY AND THE ENVIRONMENT"

Many with this Life Purpose start off having a hard time staying connected to what their bodies need and want. Some have been physically or emotionally abused, others grew up with a lack of supportive material resources (food on the table, clothes to wear, roof overhead—for whatever reasons) or the *fear* that things could fall apart at any minute and security could be lost (poverty mentality despite the presence of material security). One of the ways to cope with this is to ignore the needs of the body and numb out its sensations. Others grew up without the model of good care of the body (for instance, the entire family overeats, engages in substance abuse, or clamps down on the expression of feelings to survive). The emphasis here is on taking proper care of your body and being able to rely appropriately on others for nurturing support.

"FAMILY IS MORE IMPORTANT THAN I AM"

Some with this Life Purpose believe they have to give themselves up in order to be connected to their families or a social or cultural group. Examples of this include the classic story of being expected to become a doctor because your father is a doctor or fulfilling the family's expectation of taking over the family business. I find that many children of immigrants have parents who sacrificed and worked hard to give them a better chance in life, but absolutely expect them to go into a narrow range of secure professions rather than truly choosing what to do with their lives . . . or be shunned by the family. Many female children are still told what professions are (un)acceptable for women and are trained not to aim too high (because, after all, their job is to get married and have children and grandchildren). Other families try to dictate whom their children can marry (or not marry—for whatever reasons). Families can have many rules about what "we" do and don't do as a group that discount individual group members' preferences and inappropriately try to dictate their lives in order to be a member of the group. Groups *do* need to have guidelines around which the members bond (all the way up to large groups, such as societies), but where is the line drawn between individual freedom and the group's security needs?

"I'M AFRAID GROUPS WON'T SUPPORT AND ACCEPT ME"

Those with this Life Purpose commonly struggle with whether to join groups or not due to a fear of the group requiring them to sell themselves out to belong, or the fear that they will be unable to maintain their own autonomy in the face of a group's bonding dynamics. When those with the Master of "Family" Bonds Life Purpose "go it alone," rather than joining forces with others, it's often due to their fear of interacting with a group, rather than the reality of the experience they might have if they did join a group.

REPEATEDLY SIGNING UP TO FORCE ACCEPTANCE BY THE WRONG "FAMILY"

I regularly see those with this Life Purpose trying to force a group of people (often their blood family of origin) to accept them as they are (and it isn't going to happen), rather than recognizing the limits of the closed group and seeking to create true support for themselves by bonding with other people. Over the years I've watched many students, who had their classmates as their supportive tribe, pour all their energy into trying to get their blood families to accept them. Unfortunately, their families often continue to see them as the "black sheep" and are repeatedly unsupportive. It's understandably painful to accept that your family of origin may not be your biggest fans, but this can be a vital adjustment to make so you can see who *is* in your life, offering you what you so badly need, so you can receive it. Someone I know describes this as learning how to "tend to your garden by pulling the weeds and watering the flowers." This, of course, is more easily said than done, but it is vital to know where to put your emotional energy so you do not, eventually, deplete your physical body.

External Challenges (Doing)

When you begin to get connected to yourself and others, various obstacles are likely to arise in the external world to challenge you and help you develop strength in your ability to give and receive nurturance. Remember that having the Master of "Family" Bonds Life Purpose doesn't guarantee close bonds with others. You have to work as skillfully as you are able with the times, the circumstances you're living in, and the people in your life, and all three are likely to confront you in many ways. Here are a few possible external challenges.

"IT'S HARD FOR ME TO *DO* WHAT MY BODY REALLY NEEDS"

My clients often tell me that it's hard for them to eat right, get proper sleep or an appropriate amount of exercise, maintain the outer physical aspects of their world (home, car, office space, etc.), or just plain relax. As you gain awareness of what your body needs to feel nurtured, sustained, and safe, you may next find it challenging to *do* the things that create a sense of self-governance and appropriate self-control for yourself. Can you stay on your diet? Stick to your exercise regimen? Go to bed on time? Maintain your house? Beyond these sorts of maintenance issues, can you also relax and enjoy life? Smell the flowers? Can you go beyond feeling anxious to savoring the pleasures of life?

JOINING IN VS. HOLDING SELF APART

Once you join groups, what happens when you (disappointingly) come up against the same dysfunctional group dynamics? This is when things get really interesting, if you can observe closely how you interact with the group and its members and seek feedback from others about your own behavior. This is what various types of support and therapy groups focus on and explore, so that all members can learn the difference between the way they *think* they are acting and the way they are *actually* behaving. Do you *join in*, express yourself, ask the group for support, offer what you have to others? Do you stick with it and do your best to stay present and grounded, even when it becomes uncomfortable for you or other group members? When I work with groups over time, I often have members confide in me that they don't feel like a part of the group, or that the group doesn't like them, or they don't know how to relate to the group and they're uncomfortable. Usually these members are holding themselves out and not participating in the group because they're afraid to express a dissenting idea or opinion, or they're just plain afraid to be rejected if they don't agree with the group consensus. Sometimes the opposite is true and they are participating, but they have a hard time when others don't agree with them about something or if they struggle with holding their own opinion when others have differing ideas.

CONTROL ISSUES

As a Master of "Family" Bonds, you must learn that you cannot force others into a connection with you. Watch to see if you have a hard time letting others be themselves instead of being like you. Do you feel threatened because others don't like what you like and don't want to let you tell them what they should like? Are you finding that you want to leave a group because others don't agree with you on every point? Be careful that you don't expect others to sell out inappropriately to be a part of *your* "family" or group. Although groups must have some basic rules or have something in common to get along (even if it's just a common task like working together or having a common hobby), being a "family" or community is not about the members being carbon copies of one another. You must allow others to have their own opinions, and likes and dislikes, and respect their individuality.

"FAMILY" THREATENS DISCONNECTION

When you really get going with holding your own within your family or a group, the group can threaten to cast you out. I just saw the movie *Miss Potter,* which is about the life of children's author Beatrix Potter. When she finally finds love, her family threatens to disinherit her because people of their social standing don't mix with those of the "trades" classes. (It's 1902 England when she and her book publisher fall in love, and his working for a living makes him a lower-class person in her mother's eyes—despite the fact that the Potters' wealth originally came from a printing business and a cotton textile business.) Fortunately for Beatrix Potter, she makes enough money to support herself, but she still acquiesces to her parents' request that she keep her engagement secret and go away for the summer with them to see if her feelings for her beloved remain the same. In the meantime, he dies of tuberculosis, she is too late for his funeral, and the precious time they could have had together is lost. Beatrix then realizes that she has to get out from under her family's control if she is to live life on her own terms.

You can expect, as you grow into being true to yourself in the context of groups, that the boat will get rocked. It is your challenge to work over time with your connections to other people and to make the hard decisions about who you have in your life—who gets to be closer to you because they are truly supportive of you? Who do you need more distance from?

Being It, Doing It, and Faking It (Attitude to Adopt)

Since having a connected sense of "Family" is the state of being you wish to live in, where life feels meaningful to you, you can ask yourself the following questions when you're working on adopting the attitude of your Life Purpose in order to more fully inhabit it and then *do it*.

When you're *struggling with your (physical or emotional) connection to self or others*, ask:

- What is causing my sense of disconnection? What do I need to do to *nurture* myself or others?

- In order to stay connected to myself, do I need to limit my exposure to those who are trying to control me inappropriately?

- Do I need to *join in* rather than wait to be asked to join?

- How can I *belong* to groups *without selling myself out* or expecting others to sell themselves out to be connected to me?

- How can I belong to groups and have a "family" I can rely on, and who can rely on me?

"I can give and receive nurturance as an accepted and accepting member of a group."

Practical Everyday Expression/Steps

To build up your ability to connect to other people, you must *practice* the actions that create "Family"!

- *Practice nurturing yourself by being good to your own body, feelings, and environment.* Take an inventory of how well you're taking care of your *basic physical needs.* Do you treat your body as your wonderful vehicle for your journey through the rest of your life? Do you listen to and accept your own feelings? Do you treat yourself like your own precious child (not too indulgent with yourself, not too strict)? Then take a look at your physical environment. Do you have a safe, nurturing home? Work environment? Do you take good care of your car, clothes, etc.?

- *Assess your relationships with others.* Stop and consider the relationships you have with others. Do you offer your accepting support to the people in your life and allow them to be themselves (rather than trying to change them)? Do others offer you their caring help when you need it (and allow you to be yourself)? Do you ask for what you need from other people? Are there people in your life who try to control you? Do you allow them to do so? What kind of emotional environment do you place yourself in by associating with these people? Do you expose yourself to people who expect you to squash your individuality to belong?

- *Join groups for support and to offer your support to others.* Your Life Purpose is about being the hub of families, support groups, associations, communities, or other groups of people, so form them or join them so you can find the fulfillment that comes with being a part of a clan! When you practice being a member of a group, you discover over time that it is very satisfying, and that others will look to you as a wellspring of support and will be willing to support you in turn.

Positive Feelings Associated with This Life Purpose

- Supported and nurtured (by self, others, and the world)

- Supportive and nurturing (of self and others)

- Belonging while maintaining your unique identity

- Safe and comfortable in your life and in interacting with groups as a peer and a connector of people

"I can belong and be myself."

Questions to Ask Yourself

- How comfortable am I with belonging to groups or engaging in all types of relationships?

- How do I nurture and support myself and others?

- How do I care for my body?

- What do I do to stay anchored and present in my body and my environment so I can be present with others and enjoy life?

- How do I create a supportive, secure environment for myself?

- Are my physical body and environment the foundational structures that can support the rest of my life?

- Do I allow myself to be controlled by others so I can belong?

- Do I control others as a requirement that they be part of my life?

- Can I have supportive, close relationships with peers?

- Do I connect people together into networks/groups (both personally and/or professionally)?

- Do I feel safe and secure in my life and in the wider world?

Pointer Finger: Power

(MYTHICAL ARCHETYPE: JUPITER/ZEUS)

Desires/Wants/Appetites/Internal Agenda

Role You Play/Choices

Independent Action/Initiative

Confidence/Decisiveness

Boundaries/Turf/Stand Your Ground/Protection

Respect

Authority/Assertiveness

Ideals/Principles/Big Picture/Vision

Impact/Influence/Command/Achievement/Status

Politics/Power Issues

Often wrong, never uncertain.

UNKNOWN

God grant me the serenity to accept the things I cannot change; courage to change the things I can; and wisdom to know the difference.

REINHOLD NIEBUHR

Make it so.

CAPTAIN PICARD, *Star Trek: The Next Generation*

Pointer Fingers Overview
(The <u>Power</u> Life Purposes)

The pointer fingers are named after the Roman mythological king of the gods, Jupiter (in Greek mythology, Zeus), and they represent your use of power—both your personal sense of empowerment and the wielding of your influence out in the world. Stop to think about the gestures associated with the first finger: you can point it at someone; turn it the other way, crook it, and beckon someone to "come here"; or point it straight up in victory to say, "I'm number one!" These motions indicate that the person performing them feels in charge, on top, or is imposing authority on others.

Living high atop Mount Olympus, Jupiter was able to see everything going on down below; he could see the big picture and make informed decisions as the leader of the land. When you have one of these purposes, a large portion of your work is about keeping an eye on the larger picture in order to gain some objectivity and understand your role in your own life and in the wider world. Both purposes are about dreaming about the way the world *could be* and then connecting with the inner desire to "make it so."

The CEO of a company keeps an eye on the competition as well as what the market needs and what the company wants to achieve. The captain of a hockey team formulates a strategy based on his or her own strengths and weaknesses, as well as those of the other team, and on the overall desire to win the game. Jacques Cousteau's passion was to explore the oceans and show the world that they aren't vast wastelands to pollute. An artist tries working with glass and loves it so much she devotes her life to it. The man who loves children decides to become a teacher.

The basis of true power is a having a deep connection to the way your personal world or the larger world *could be* and then *taking initiative* to do something about it, without being inappropriately swayed by others' opinions about it—or you. The fulfillment of these purposes is associated with being firmly connected to your own desires and knowing that *you* know what you want and that *you* can then make the decisions and take the initiative necessary to take charge, achieve your dreams, and have a positive influence within your own life—or on the larger world around you. Knowing the central role you play in your own life and the ways in which you impact the world, as well as understanding the limits of your power, is what the Power Life Purposes are all about.

When you know what you want, and you connect with the world to work toward getting it, another aspect of this purpose gets activated: boundaries. This means knowing the difference between self and other, being respectful of your own desires and the desires of others, and working with the interplay of the two when they conflict. If I want Chinese food for lunch and you'd like Mexican, how do we each express what we want and then negotiate to reach agreement? Who is in charge and how do we reach consensus? And when we are in a longer relationship together and go through this negotiation repeatedly, how do we make sure we are compromising appropriately and one person (or group) isn't constantly taking advantage of the other? Becoming adept at going through conflict and confrontation in order to find appropriate compromise while standing up for your life, for (and within) your family, your team, your country, etc., is the order of the day. Knowing what you want and working it out in your life and in the world is the foundation of the Jupiter Life Purposes.

LEADERSHIP

(Right Pointer Finger and Double Pointer Fingers Life Purpose)

Keywords: Power in the World
Authority/Command
Impact/Influence
Inspire Others with Vision/The Way
Things Could Be

Lead the Way
Politics
Being Respected by Others
Achievement

If you have the Leadership Life Purpose, you are here to wield influence and authority and call the shots. This Life Purpose is about using your power out in the world. You have the potential to envision the way things *could be* and then inspire others to get onboard to assist in achieving a larger vision. As the Leader, you reap meaning from being in charge and inhabiting the chief position to supervise a territory or turf that is your own. This is not to say you are meant to be a dictator who gains the respect of others by ruling through force or arrogance, but rather you are someone who wishes to lead by empowering and encouraging others to step up to themselves in the service of a larger constructive vision. With this Life Purpose, you are primarily here to dream a better world, make the decisions, and take the actions necessary to achieve it, rather than relying indecisively on other people's opinions about what you do with yourself.

Key to living this Life Purpose is engaging the entire process of envisioning what you want, making practical plans on how to attain it, prioritizing the steps and intermediate goals along the way, putting the plan into action, then keeping your "eyes on the prize," *and* the bigger picture, *and* the implementation of the action plan until you *achieve* the vision—whether it's a large long-term aspiration (world peace) or a more finite goal (running a marathon, losing five pounds, cleaning out the garage). As a good leader, you must be willing play a leading role in your own life and the lives of others. Leaders must, well, *lead*, which implies that you've got a direction to follow and have decided what you would like to achieve. Think of a general leading troops into battle, crying, "Charge!" with a pointer finger directed straight ahead with absolute certainty. You must be willing to guide others, direct, go before, and be in charge. Leaders must be good shepherds of their "followers" (whomever they are in the position of influencing) and be able to rally others around a common cause, inspire them to join forces and cooperate, manage the politics, and coordinate to keep everyone on course toward the goal.

To be the Leader, you must formulate a vision (ideally about something that is important to you), hold the big picture in the face of obstacles and challenges, and stand your ground with "followers" who would take things in a different direction than you (beware of mutiny). You must also protect your "turf" by fending off challengers who want a piece of your action, your position of power, or who are opposed to your vision (the KKK didn't like Martin Luther King's vision and vice versa, and cell phone companies are always trying to take a bite out of each other's market shares), and see beyond your own personal agenda to manage the agenda required by the vision. Ask any leader and that person will tell you that at its best, leadership is demanding. As the Leader, you are the only one in the ultimate role of trying to look at (and see) *all* of the aspects of your enterprise (internally and externally) so you can steer it in the right direction. At the end of the day, there is no one standing behind you to take the heat . . . it's you! Hence the phrase, "it's lonely at the top."

Leaders must accept the role of standing alone at times to make the tough decisions. A business-owner friend of mine recently had to demote an employee he'd placed into a management position because the employee couldn't see the forest for the trees—the big picture—to such an extent that the manager plotted to get rid of a staff member he personally disliked. Short-sighted and stuck on his own private agenda, he trumped up reasons to fire the top salesperson, who was generating the lion's share of the enterprise's income (and his own salary). My friend does not particularly enjoy the conflict inherent in being a leader (demoting someone is not an easy task), but it is imperative that he keeps an eye on the big picture and does what's necessary to not lose money, which would destroy the business and put everyone on staff out of a job. End of vision. My friend has to keep an eye on what's good for the *entire* business and everyone in it in order for it to survive and thrive.

I was fortunate to work for an excellent leader years ago. He is someone who has a vision for healing the environment through energy conservation and smart energy policy choices. He felt so strongly about his vision that he put together a plan to start a grant-making foundation, persuaded several large foundations to fund it, hired staff, and began soliciting proposals from other nonprofits doing work on energy efficiency in several well-defined sectors of the energy economy. His strategy was constantly one of looking hard to create win-wins—outcomes beneficial to both sides of a seeming conflict. He and the staff were exceptionally good at finding strategies that were both environment preserving *and* business enhancing. As a leader of an organization, he was excellent at seeing staff members' potential and then assigning projects to each of us, requiring that each of us to step up to the challenge of learning new skills, take on more responsibility, and own a piece of the foundation's vision with pride in our own capabilities. He is a person who constantly sees *potential* everywhere—in the world and in people—and he has enough confidence in himself to take action and hold everyone and everything to a higher standard, encouraging everyone to achieve more, individually and collectively, in order to save the natural environment we all rely upon to live.

There is no end to the impact a leader such as this has on the world. Personally, years later, I am still inspired and empowered to be the best I can be, to believe that *I can* achieve my desires and dreams and effect change if I just apply myself to it and take initiative. I know I can learn what is hard for me and face things that scare me in order to do what *I can* to create a better world . . . whether it's picking up trash at the park when I'm walking along, or getting up in front of people and speaking to them about what's possible in their lives. He helped me understand that I have an impact and that it's important to be aware of it and to use it wisely. The legacy of his influence continues on indefinitely through the many people whose horizons he expands through his own vision of the world and what the people in it are capable of.

People who lead effectively know how to impact others within their sphere of influence. They insist on controlling and protecting their sphere of influence in order to produce the highest impact possible for the greatest good of everyone involved. Conductor of the Boston Philharmonic Orchestra, co-author of *The Art of Possibility*, and motivational speaker Benjamin Zander has an exceptional understanding of this. He controls *every* aspect of his performance when speaking, and audience members have a deeply empowering, inspirational, and unforgettable experience in his presence. His influence begins *before* audience members actually enter the speaking hall (he's already thought about the state of mind he wants his audience members in from the get-go). The doors or curtains are closed, dramatic classical music enticingly booms within the hall, and doorkeepers do not allow anyone in. As people gather, they become excited and start talking amongst themselves—the energy level comes up and connection among people starts to happen, rather than people wandering in and floating around in a large hall, engrossed in their own thoughts. When the doors open, everyone is enthused and rushes into the hall to grab seats because they can't wait to see what comes next. When Zander comes out, he speaks frankly about everyone staying committed to the entire program and how the people who want to hang out, standing in the back of the room, won't get the full benefit of being there if they're considering slipping out (so they might as well leave before he goes any further and not adversely affect everyone else's experience). He goes on to engage the audience in singing "Happy Birthday" in fresh new ways and actively listening to live classical music being played, and he eagerly persuades the audience to use their heightened senses to understand that something more is possible in every moment of life if they would only open up to the world around them and participate more fully. When his presentation is over, no one is in a hurry to leave and the general air is charged—everyone is exhilarated by being more awake to the way things could be in their lives if they would only stop and take a look around. After an encounter with a true leader, people feel empowered and motivated to see a bigger picture and an expanded view of their own role in life. Good leaders inspire others by presenting them with a vision and showing them how they can take initiative on it, instead of being passive bystanders who believe they are stuck. Leaders are people who achieve much and lead the way by showing us that we can too!

Now, many with the Leader Life Purpose start off with absolutely no interest in rocking any boats and err on the side of timidity. Yesterday, a client with this purpose put two and two together and exclaimed, "Oh! If I really know what I want, then I'll have to do something about it, and it will probably stir up my life!" He's absolutely right. Leaders have to be willing to change things. In fact, good leaders are agents of change. If you're someone with a vision, it implies that the status quo is insufficient and change is necessary. You can't inhabit leadership if you feel like you're stuck with what you've got and are unwilling to take initiative to change it. Others with this Life Purpose go the other direction and try to force change on others. These are people who give unsolicited advice, tell others what to do with no explanation whatsoever, and who do not see the need to inspire others, empower them, or let them in on the vision. This kind of leader dictates and is often surprised and frustrated when other people resist them or do not cooperate with them. They end up in unnecessary power struggles with their own "followers" (staff, family, co-workers), and movement toward a larger vision gets bogged down in in-fighting, petty politics, and active sabotage by the leader's constituents.

As a Leader, when you consciously begin to learn and engage in the process of empowerment, you become a center of influence and find that other people eagerly hop onboard to be influenced by you. They look to you for direction because you have a direction to follow and can get others to see your vision and how it is beneficial to work for it. They see that you yourself are willing to take action and put yourself on the line for your vision, and they are inspired by your readiness to act even when it ruffles feathers. As you become more certain about where you want to go, you inspire certainty and others trust that they can get into your boat and row along with you. They are willing to take direction from you, make their own contribution, and follow where you lead.

If you are a Leader, your deepest fulfillment arises from moving toward achieving a vision and empowering others to participate in fulfilling it, rather than passively playing the role of the victim. The more you realize that there is no one else out there who can tell you what you want—you're truly *it*—the better you feel about yourself and your role in the world. You are a person of action, a mover and shaker, who eagerly takes life into your own hands and doesn't wait around for someone else to make the world the place you'd like to live in. You stand up to be counted, take on the challenges and responsibilities of playing a leading role, focus on achieving something, earn the cooperation and respect of others, and take appropriate initiative to forge a path to a better world.

Challenges

Just because you are a Leader doesn't mean it's always easy to inhabit your purpose all the time and in all circumstances. You are here to grow into your being and what it requires you to do. Two types of challenges help you gain the broad experience you need in order to live the Leadership Life Purpose.

Internal Challenges (Being)

These are some of the challenges you have within yourself, the negative beliefs you may hold about yourself and about Leadership, which need to be brought to consciousness and worked with so you can do what is necessary to become truly influential.

NO VISION/ASPIRATION

Many with this Life Purpose start off without a larger vision they would like to move toward, much less inspire others to follow . . . even in their own personal lives. "I'm setting my expectations low and I'm meeting them," "I can't dream a bigger dream," "I just can't imagine things being different (even if I don't like the way they are)," and "I'm trapped" are common thought patterns. Because of these thoughts, it feels scary to step into a role where you are leading others, and it is difficult to effect change in your own life.

"I DON'T LIKE CONFLICT"/"CONFLICT EQUALS POWER"

It's common with this Life Purpose to have grown up in a crisis- or strife-filled family, when all you wanted was peace and harmony. In this scenario, stepping into your Life Purpose and standing up for yourself feels uncomfortable, and you may believe that to be powerful you must step on others as you were stepped on—and hate the idea. After all, if power struggles are the only known model for working things out, then you may avoid conflict at any cost instead of looking for a more positive and cooperative way to be powerful (why would I want to be a dictator like my father or my boss?). These experiences are actually meant to push you to say, "There's gotta be a better way and I'm going to find it!" They train you to stand up for yourself, instead of allowing yourself to be mistreated. Others with this purpose believe that being powerful is all about jerking people around, and being a leader means creating dissent or uproar, or ordering others around. If you are on this side of the fence, it is hard, if not impossible, to pull people together to move toward a unified vision.

"WHO, ME? LEAD?"

Many with this purpose simply can't see themselves as leaders. It seems like too much responsibility, too many hassles managing the "people factor," too much politics, and too egotistical. I've had many a leader protest on any or all of these grounds, but most, at heart, fear that taking a leadership position requires an attitude of arrogance or superiority and that self-assertion automatically equals being aggressive or dictatorial. I like to tell them, "You're right! Becoming a leader requires an appropriate amount of small-*e* ego, also known as *confidence* in yourself and your abilities . . . what's so bad about that? Who are leaders you admire? Aren't you glad they are/were confident enough to get up and lead? The Dalai Lama is a fantastic recent example of a great leader . . . why not you? Don't these people lead with confidence without being dictators?"

IT'S LONELY AT THE TOP

It's true, it *is* "lonely at the top." Many who strike out on the path to their vision look around and find that they are the only people with their particular view of things and are daunted by having to stand tall and enlist others to hop onboard. Even when there are others aboard, you are required to be the person who holds firmly to the principles and ideals of your vision for the way things could be. My business-owner friend says that the hardest thing for him is knowing that he has to maintain strictly professional relationships with everyone who works for him (even his top lieutenant) because he may have to fire people for various reasons—whether they irreversibly screw up or a business venture doesn't take off and he has to reorganize or pare down to stay afloat. Another example of this is the speaker, trainer, or teacher who gets up in front of people. When you lead (or co-lead, etc.), it's *you* who's holding the space, the vision, the container, and the territory because it's yours to protect, manage, and expand. You are the torchbearer who cares most deeply that the vision gets transmitted and perpetuated for the betterment of the world and people's lives. For comradeship and friendship, find other bold souls who are engaging in leadership so you can share stories, advise one another, and talk shop.

External Challenges (Doing)

When you begin to get connected to your Leadership, various obstacles are likely to arise in the external world to challenge you and help you develop strength in your ability to impact and influence others. Remember that your Leadership purpose does not automatically guarantee authority. You have to work as skillfully as you are able with the times, the circumstances you're living in, and the people in your life, and all three are likely to confront you in many ways. Here are a few possible external challenges.

TAKING INDEPENDENCE OF ACTION

Once you have an idea of what you'd like to do (a vision), your challenge is to *do* something about it and not be excessively concerned with the opinions of other people. Can you imagine Gandhi asking friends, indecisively, if they thought it was a good idea to work for Indian independence? When you are a leader, your job is to solicit appropriate advisement—when you can't see the forest for the trees or you need to gather information before you make a decision and to continuously adjust course. You also have to know that what you decide to do is *your decision and yours alone—even when you decide* to let someone else make the decision or go along with what someone else thinks is the correct course of action. Good leaders never imitate Bart Simpson, crying, "Don't look at me, I didn't do it!" over anything that is within their turf. They take responsibility, stand tall, and face the consequences. When something goes wrong, good leaders find out what led to the problem and seek a solution to prevent its recurrence. They see it as their responsibility to do so.

POWER STRUGGLES ("OTHERS IGNORE MY AUTHORITY/TRY TO USURP IT/MAKE ME PUPPET TO THEIR OWN AGENDAS")

A delightful client of mine relayed a perfect example of this just last week. While in a meeting on a project given top priority by her work group, a subordinate co-worker interrupted and asked for something he needed for a lower-priority project he was working on. My client was polite and told him she would get it to him as soon as her meeting was over and no later than a specific time that day when the information was formally due. The co-worker immediately ran to their supervisor, complaining that she *refused* to give him what he needed. My client was called on the carpet by the supervisor, but rather than just letting this outright lie slide, she provided an explanation of what had transpired. To her shock, the boss ignored her, indicating that he didn't want to hear any excuses; she was to give the co-worker what he asked for immediately. My client told me she felt good about standing up for herself (and the prioritized project), and through doing so, she realized she works for someone who does not respect her or her judgment. She indicated that this experience caused her to re-evaluate her position, and she decided to quit and return to consulting, so she could have her own territory, independence of action, and be in a higher role of authority, commanding more respect (and pay) for her area of expertise. As you step up to your leadership, be on the lookout for those who try to jerk you around disrespectfully—by ignoring your authority, attempting to usurp your leading role, or trying to turn you into a puppet for their own agendas.

POWER BEHIND THE THRONE VS. SITTING ON THE THRONE

Many with this Life Purpose are occupying the "Power Behind the Throne" role, either professionally or personally. They are in supportive positions to a leader (or a powerful spouse), pulling all the strings behind the scenes to help someone else achieve his or her agenda. The "executive assistant" and the "senator's wife" are two archetypal examples of this. I've had many female clients who have the Leader Life Purpose who do whatever is necessary to advance their husbands' careers and have no agendas of their own, or who abandon their own life agendas repeatedly as their spouses' careers demand. Gender-wise, this can go the other way, of course. If you are contending with "executive assistant syndrome," there's nothing wrong with this position for a certain amount of time—it can be an excellent apprenticeship role—but eventually you need to step up, get a throne of your own, and be the person setting an agenda, rather than following someone else's the majority of the time.

PRIDE OF OWNERSHIP/EXCELLENCE

Leaders are the sorts of people who take appropriate pride in what they do. At their best, they strive for excellence in all areas of working toward their vision, and they inspire others to take ownership of their individual roles and acknowledge the achievements of those individuals. When you embody excellence, you strive for the best while realizing that the world is imperfect. You can hold suitably high expectations for yourself, your "followers," and the world. You help others see how the world *could be*—to see your vision and step up to the more empowered version of themselves in the service of the vision. As a Leader, you need to be a model of excellence and to surround yourself with people who want to take initiative and pride in a job well done. Your challenge is to empower others to be up to their tasks, to make sure they have the resources to do their jobs, to get out of the way and let them have the authority to do their jobs, and to offer acknowledgement and respect for a job well done. You also need to bravely weed out those who don't want to row on your boat, who don't take ownership and pride in the vision and their accomplishments ("I just work here"), and who are disrespectful of others.

Being It, Doing It, and Faking It (Attitude to Adopt)

Since Leadership is the state of being you wish to live in, where life feels meaningful to you, you can ask yourself the following questions when you're working on adopting the attitude of your Life Purpose in order to more fully inhabit it and then *do it*.

When you feel *powerless*, *overwhelmed*, or *trapped*, ask:

- How can I step back and take in a larger, more objective view? What are all the factors involved in what's going on? How can I pull myself up out of the box I'm in to peek over the side? Will what I'm currently overwhelmed by matter tomorrow, or six months, or five years from now?

- What do I believe I am powerless to change? What decisions am I ignoring or delaying that are holding me up and creating a sense of powerlessness?

- What initiative do *I need to take* that no one else can take for me? (What do I secretly wish someone else will do for me? How can I step up and do it for myself?)

- Can I recognize the limits of my power and stop trying to change people and circumstances that are not truly under my influence and focus on the choices I *can* make for myself?

- What would I *do right now*, in this situation, if I were *already* an authority?

"I can envision a better world and take action to bring it into being!"

Practical Everyday Expression/Steps

To build up your ability to use your power in the world, you must *practice* the actions that create leadership!

- *Stop and look at the way things <u>could be</u> and the way things <u>are</u> before making decisions.* Leaders are excellent at holding two pictures at once: the ideal picture of the way things *could be* and the practical picture of the way things *are*. This enables leaders to make the plans and to take the practical steps necessary to bring reality up to higher standards, rather than be daunted by the work to be done. Leaders set their sights on a goal and then work out the logistics to figure out how things *can* be done. Work with this in your everyday life! Decide what you want, then consciously work out how to achieve it, and then do it! I regularly have people who want to take my classes, who tangle themselves up unnecessarily with the practical logistics (they think about how they *cannot* get to the class, rather than how they *can* achieve their goal of attending). I am always shocked when someone in Houston can't envision driving to Austin for the class. (I happily fly 1,628 miles, then drive from the airport to get to class . . . it is possible! I often have students, who have to make all kinds of life rearrangements, who fly to class as well.) Last week I even had someone who was worried about driving *across* Houston to get to class! On the other hand, some can be challenged to see the way things *are* in reality, in contrast to their vision of the way things *could be*. Many people stay in relationships because they see the way their partners *could be* (they put them on a pedestal) instead of who their partners *really are*, and they get into various sorts of trouble this way. Leaders strive for a balanced view of both sides of the equation, and they try to look at how things *can get done* rather than ignoring reality or being daunted over the practical work to be done.

- *Take initiative/be proactive.* One of my clients with this Life Purpose expressed frustration with her staff. She took a position directing a daycare center, and many of the caregivers refused to take initiative over taking proper care of daily problems at the center when they arose. If a toilet backed up, they didn't report it, much less grab a plunger, and then they complained to each other about their working conditions. It's as if they couldn't even see that they would come to work the next day and the problem would still exist. This was unimaginable to my client, who does not hesitate to find solutions to problems when they arise (hence she's been hired as the director to turn the place around). "Who do they think will handle the problem if they won't?" she asked in bewilderment. Leaders do not wait around for someone else to solve problems, make decisions, or take action in the hopes that what they want will somehow magically happen. Practice taking appropriate initiative, and be proactive to take the steps to bring your life, your workplace, and the world closer to the best it can be. If you don't make a difference, who will? Practice saying, "I'm it!" and remember the concept of "pride of ownership" to take care of your world as if it is your own, while showing consideration for others. Leaders are women and men of well-directed action.

- *Make executive decisions.* Leaders make "executive decisions" all the time—they are willing to make decisions and take action on them, whether lots of input is first required, or very little. This doesn't mean they disregard the opinions or desires of others—just the opposite. Practice taking the entire picture into account and making as objective a decision as possible, one weighing the benefits to everyone involved, while ultimately serving the larger goal or vision being strived for. Also recognize when you are the only person who should be making a decision, especially with all the everyday things in your life that, properly, are not up to anyone else. Realize when you're "it" and it's time to stand and deliver, and face the consequences—good, bad, or indifferent—of your actions. Don't wait for others to make decisions for you and then blame them when you are unhappy with the results.

- *Take pride in your achievements.* When you achieve something, don't just toss it off as unimportant. What if you stop and actually congratulate yourself for what you did? Are all your diplomas, trophies, or awards in the bottom of a drawer somewhere? Many with the Leadership purpose feel that taking appropriate pride in what they've done (and in themselves) is overly egotistical, and so they duck their heads and say, "Gee, shucks, it wasn't anything," and actually believe it. (Of course, some Leaders *do* need to stop and temper their arrogant superiority.) Try to stop and enjoy your achievements, large and small—after all, you need just enough small-*e* ego in order to believe you can take action and make a difference in the first place. It takes confidence to be a leader, and it's important to respect yourself and your own accomplishments in order to build your basic certainty in yourself. Without it, how can you get up and influence others?

Positive Feelings Associated with This Life Purpose

- Influential/authoritative

- Respected

- Certain/decisive

- Confident

"I can!"

Questions to Ask Yourself

- Do I know what I want?

- Can I make plans to achieve my dreams? Or do I just dream?

- Can I hold my boundaries with others? Stand my ground for what I want?

- Do I know the limits of my power?

- Am I comfortable with conflict?

- Do I strive for excellence in all I do? Do I take pride in myself and my achievements . . . or discount them as unimportant?

- Am I in charge of something and/or seen as a leader or authority?

- Am I in a position to impact and influence other people?

- Am I respected by others . . . rather than feared?

- Do I have "independence of action," the power to make independent decisions and be respected?

- Do I feel pride in my own achievements?

- Can I be open to the opinions of others *and* stand my ground appropriately?

- Do I think about the way the world *could* be and then do something about it?

LIVE MY PASSIONS

(Left Pointer Finger Life Purpose)

Keywords: Personal Power   Boundaries
             All-Consuming Interest   Self-Respect
             Desires/Personal Wants/Appetites   Unbridled Enthusiasm
             Intense, Fervent Focus

If you have the Live My Passions Life Purpose, you are here to tap into your deepest desires and be true to them. You have the potential to live life to the fullest according to what is of utmost importance to you. This Life Purpose is about harnessing your personal power to live an intensely passionate life centered on something you feel deeply ardent about. When you are living your passions, you reap meaning from engaging your passions as much of the time as possible. Ideally, you want your work and your life to be one and the same—to make your living from what you're passionate about. If it truly isn't possible to pay the rent from your passion, you need to consciously arrange your paid work to fund it and spend as much time as possible doing it. When I first read someone with this Life Purpose, they often ask, "Isn't *everyone* supposed to live their passions?" And the answer is no. Not everyone is built to be fervently involved with something 24/7/365. Many people (who do not have this purpose) are just fine with pursuing their hobbies after hours, not as the centerpiece of their lives. Not everyone is built to zealously pursue something as if it is a personal crusade and live constantly in the strong emotional states associated with true passion. With this Life Purpose, you are here to know what you want and become personally empowered enough to connect to and express your desires.

Key to living this Life Purpose is engaging in the entire process of knowing, from within yourself, what you truly desire, and then devoting yourself to it as many minutes of the day as you can manage. This process begins with being rooted firmly in all your own everyday wants and choosing to express them so you can take care of yourself. From "What do I want for breakfast?" to "What do I want to wear today?" Live My Passions is very much about owning your own life and choosing to stand up for it. My favorite question to ask someone with this purpose is, "Whose life are you living anyway?" As a Passionate, you must be able to say, "Mine!" and know exactly what that means for you—even if it isn't easy to work out the logistics of living it. To be personally powerful, you have to understand that it isn't anyone else's job to tell you what you want or to get it for you. You must be able to stand your ground for yourself and not give up what you want in the face of others' desires. Conversely, you must not always get what you want at others' expense. Ultimately, *you* are the only one who can know what you want and then take action on your own behalf to get it.

To live your passions, you must be in touch with your various mundane desires: "What do I want for breakfast?" "What movies do I want to see?" "Where do I want to live?" "How do I want to spend my free time?" "Where do I want to go for vacation?" Then you must stand up for yourself and do something about getting what you want. Sometimes this means making the effort to get it for yourself, and at other times it means interacting with other people because they are involved in what is being eaten or the way time is being passed or where we're living—what you desire has an impact on them. Living your passions requires that you be able to discern what you want from deep inside you and then take appropriate action to get it, while being mindful of your impact on others.

I'm in New York right now with my business partner and friend, Roberta, and we want to do different things with our limited "play" time. We added two days to our trip, before our work schedule begins, so we can see some things in this incredible city, but I then realized I still have to write because I'm under deadline with my publisher. I'm happy to have the writing-in-a-café-in-New-York experience (which is only marginally different than the writing-in-a-café-in-the-San-Francisco-Bay-Area experience), but naturally, Roberta wants to get out and see things. What to do? I feel bad leaving her on her own (who doesn't want a companion to go sightseeing?), but I clearly want to buckle down and stay on my own writing agenda. We each desire different things and don't want to disappoint each other. So I'm here writing, then we'll see a matinee Broadway play together, then I'll write some more tonight. Tomorrow I've decided to write all day since I won't get pages done while working over the weekend, and I'll leave Roberta on her own for the day. Not easy for me. But vital. Living my passions begins with such seemingly mundane matters . . . everyone I know is saying, "But Ronelle, you're in New York City! You can let your writing schedule go a bit and just make it up later!" But I know it isn't true (given the number of pages to go and the number of days I have left), and only I can know this and stick to what is of utmost importance to me. If you are meant to reap deep fulfillment from living your passion, you need to be tapped into *all your desires* in order to be connected to what it is you are fervent about and be able to make the space for it in your life until it can take over your life and inhabit you fully.

For some, passion shows up and bites them and won't let go. Many wish for this to happen to them, but living your passions can be very challenging. Erin Brockovich, in the movie of the same name, is a well-known example of this. Struggling financially as a single mother with three children, she finally gets some administrative work at a law firm where some documents catch her eye. She investigates further, something seems fishy, and before she knows what's hit her, she is obsessively researching apparent malfeasance on the part of the utility company—contamination of the local water supply with a highly carcinogenic toxin. Brockovich becomes all-consumed with getting to the bottom of the problem and eats and breathes and sleeps the case. She pushes her boss about it, demands funding from him to go after it, and puts herself (time, energy, resources, and her actual *life*) on the line to find the truth and help the people of Hinkley, California, who are suffering in great numbers from various forms of cancer due to the utility company's negligence and malfeasance. In short, Brockovich becomes passionate about something and rearranges her life to accommodate *it*. She may have won or she may have lost, but she felt compelled to pursue things. She was overwhelmed by her desire and stuck to it when everyone around her urged her to use her "common sense" and quit.

Others are passionate in a quieter way, like the character Schultze in the gentle German film *Schultze Gets the Blues*. Schultze is retired early from his mining job in a small German town and is at loose ends. He's played the accordion (polkas and marches) for years. One night when he gets up for a drink of water, he turns on the radio and flips channels and comes across a station playing Cajun accordion. He listens for a few seconds then tries to head back to bed, but he keeps returning to the radio to listen some more with sleepy interest. He finally grabs his accordion and picks out the Cajun tune, and that's it, he's hooked. The rest of the movie is about Schultze playing his new song to his flummoxed aging music community and his ardent quest to get to the United States to have a direct encounter with Cajun music, an adventure he eventually achieves through taking part-time jobs to raise money and a "scholarship" from his music club.

When you live a life of passion, you allow yourself to want what you want and then respect yourself enough to heed what your insides are telling you. It is then your job to express your desires and take appropriate action to fulfill them. This can be tricky, as it can be difficult to discern how to work with your circumstances to meet your desires and to understand that you might not always get what you want—but it is important to know what you want for yourself. When other people are involved, you must take a look at the larger picture to consider your personal impact on them and decide judiciously on how to proceed. When you live your passions, you are constantly negotiating the boundaries between yourself and other people—balancing consideration for yourself with consideration for others. You are particularly working with your internal boundaries with yourself: How well do you know your own feelings? Which feelings do you yield to and which ones are overwhelming in ways that are destructive for you? With this purpose, it can be quite difficult to get a balanced handle on your feelings and take appropriate action on them. You are figuring out how to take full responsibility for yourself and your own desires, and not blame anyone else for how you feel or for attaining what you want. You are learning how to "make things work" for *you*, without stepping on other people's toes (disrespecting them) along the way. You are aiming at taking appropriate charge of your own life and recognizing that *you* are the ultimate decision maker for yourself. When you let others decide for you, this too is *your* decision . . . don't blame them later if you don't like the decision they made! Only you can know what you want and choose it and, therefore, live your passions in all the small details of your life, right on up to knowing what you desire to do on a life scale.

On the way to living your passions, you may slip on one of several banana peels along the way. The first is living a life of numbness: if you aren't in touch with what you're enthusiastic about on a daily level and stand up for it/yourself, how can you be in deeper touch with the larger passion you want to embody? If you let all your "smaller" wants slide because you feel like it isn't okay to want anything, or to rock the boat with others because you want something different than they do, you just get stuck because you're constantly slamming the door on your own deeper feelings. You shut yourself down and rationalize away your own desires and have no idea what they are. Or, you'll allow yourself to know what you want but make a lot of excuses for why you don't do anything about them . . . another form of avoiding conflict. My life-coach friend and hand analysis colleague Stacy Davenport calls this the "I want to want to" zone. It's the place where people get stuck when they finally want something but are afraid to take the necessary actions and make the necessary changes to go after it. They blame others or their circumstances instead of pointing the finger at themselves.

The second sidetrack is creating the wrong kind of passion—intense emotion through playing the victim and victimizing others. Having affairs, stirring the pot, or generally creating trauma and drama through poking at others and then blaming them for everything are all negative expressions of this purpose. Your life looks like a melodramatic soap opera, and it constantly appears as if someone else is at fault for your crisis-filled crazy life. People on this track often relish telling dramatic stories about what is happening *to them* and how they can't do anything about it. They are victims of their circumstances, or their parents, or their intimate partners. It's always someone else's fault, and this person seems incapable of seeing their own role in *choosing* the never-ending "why is this happening to me?" saga. Once you're an adult, and not truly powerless, you must own your role in your own life, even when it isn't easy because it entails leaving familiar relationships (abusive or not) or a secure job.

When you live your passions consciously, you learn to respect yourself and others. You engage in the process of taking care of your own desires and truly taking charge of your own life. You realize that no one else can tell you what you desire—it's *you* and only you. No one else can read your mind. As you begin to make your own decisions and stand up for yourself, you gain self-confidence. You enjoy your life more fully and radiate a contagious enthusiasm for being alive. As you better discern your everyday wants with more clarity, you open up to the part of yourself that can find and recognize what you are passionate about pursuing, because you are emotionally awake and able to heed your own feelings, rather than being numb to them.

If you are a Passionate, your deepest fulfillment arises from taking charge of your own life and everything happening in it that is under your power. You don't sign up to be a victim of others, and you don't step on others. When you are feeling trapped or paralyzed, you can step back and take a look at your life, make different choices, and honestly say you are living a life of *your own choosing*. You feel personally empowered by owning your decisions and actions, respecting your own feelings and those of others, and working out compromises when appropriate. Because you live a life of choice, you know what you can do and that you can always make another choice if you don't like the status quo—even if you can't change some things, you can choose your relationship to them and whether to involve yourself or not. You become inspiring to others for using your personal power to live the life you want to live—and loving it.

Challenges

Just because you are meant to live your passions doesn't mean it's always easy to inhabit your purpose all the time and in all circumstances. You are here to grow into your being and what it requires you to do. Two types of challenges help you gain the broad experience you need in order to live the Passions Life Purpose.

Internal Challenges (Being)

These are some of the challenges you have within yourself, the negative beliefs you may hold about yourself and about personal empowerment, which need to be brought to consciousness and worked with so you can do what is necessary to become truly Passionate.

"I'M NUMB"/"I DON'T KNOW WHAT I WANT"/"I HAVE NO PASSION"

Many with this Life Purpose have shut themselves down and feel numb. They may have had childhood experiences where they learned it isn't okay to know their own desires, much less have them fulfilled. Recently, at the coffee stand at a convention center, I watched as a mother asked her young son what he wanted. His eyes lit up as he spotted a chocolate cupcake, and he politely told her he'd like it. She scornfully said, "You don't want that! It's too messy to eat. You want M&Ms or some Skittles." When he protested, she shamed him about what a mess he was sure to make with the cupcake and repeated, "Do you want M&Ms or Skittles?" The little boy knew what he wanted and then was discounted by his mother. This type of experience is common for those with Live My Passions purposes and, rather than perpetually blaming your parent for not knowing what you want now, the challenge is to rediscover what it is you desire and to practice giving it to yourself. You need to "un-numb" and not let others tell you what you want anymore (and stop asking them to know for you). A challenging part of this process *is* about waking up to your feelings of anger or frustration with your parent and yourself, and anyone else past and present, for overriding you, so you can get down into your "I wants" again. You need to realize that it's okay to want things and practice expressing what you want rather than "smiling while your heart is breaking" to keep the peace.

VICTIM MENTALITY—"POOR ME"/"ONLY MY DESIRES MATTER"

Some play the "victim game" and enlist others to feel sorry for them. They desire intensity and want things, but don't want to be responsible for their own desires. They tell a lot of sad stories about how they can never get what they want or rant about how someone else is keeping them from what they yearn for. Everything is about "poor me," or how "no one cares what I want," or about "how I tried and failed to get" something. "I wanted to do *x*, but someone or something wouldn't let me" is a common refrain. "It's everyone else who's to blame for my life, not me." If you are a "poor me," stop and ask yourself what you can do for yourself, and get conscious of how you play the role of victim so you can stop. Remember that when you point the finger of blame, there are three fingers pointing back at you. What's *your role* in your drama, and how can you take responsibility for *your actions* and *your life*?

TIMIDITY/CONFLICT AVOIDANCE/LACK OF CONFIDENCE

Many with this purpose have to work with feeling underconfident, timid, and trapped. Even when you know what you want, you may feel very uncomfortable expressing it to others. You don't want to "bother" anyone, and you tend to go without and go along with what other people desire, or even jump in to help them get what they want as a substitute for knowing your own desires. Living your passions requires making space in your life for what's important to you, even when it rocks the boat and "bothers" or bewilders others. You must grow your confidence in yourself so you can stand up for your passion in your life.

"I DON'T WANT TO FEEL SOME OF MY FEELINGS"

It is vital to recognize that you cannot feel passionate about anything if you are not willing to feel *all* of your feelings. If you shut down *any* of your feelings (and some people are as uncomfortable with feeling happy as others are with feeling angry), then you're shutting the door on your desire department entirely. What you feel and what you desire are inextricably linked.

External Challenges (Doing)

When you begin to get connected to your Passion, various obstacles are likely to arise in the external world to challenge you and help you develop strength in your ability to stand up for your desires. Remember that with the Passion Life Purpose, feeling passionate about your life isn't automatically guaranteed. You have to work as skillfully as you are able with the times, the circumstances you're living in, and the people in your life, and all three are likely to confront you in many ways. Here are a few possible external challenges.

GENERATING PASSION, EXCITEMENT, ENTHUSIASM/THE "WRONG PASSIONS"

With this purpose, you want to feel passionate about something, and in the absence of knowing your inner desires you may *generate* enthusiasm for things that are important, but not to you. How can you tell if it's your passion or you're just hitching a ride on someone else's train? Usually the biggest giveaway is that you start things with a lot of energy and then lose interest as they progress. And when you achieve something around this interest, you feel let down rather than enthused. If it's your work, you don't feel like you want to go as far as you can go into it. Moving up or going deeper doesn't appeal to you. Another common form of generating passion or "stirring the pot" is having love affairs. They're intense, passionate, fervent, and all-consuming—a very popular form of sidetrack from sitting with the discomfort of not knowing what you want until you find it, of occupying yourself for a while to distract yourself from your inner "I don't know." So many affairs go nowhere because, eventually, the intensity wears off and you're back where you started with yourself; the affair didn't solve your basic problem of not knowing what you want in your life. When you *generate* passion in any form, it makes a lot of dramatic and traumatic noise and takes you out of yourself, out of your own inner territory, making it even harder to figure yourself out.

"FINDING MY BOUNDARIES" (LEARNING THE DIFFERENCE BETWEEN
YOU AND ME)

When you are passionate, you are personally powerful—you know what you want for yourself and know how to express it and get it. But as you grow into this, you are likely to make errors because you are unsure of where the boundary is between yourself and others. How forceful should you be about getting what you want? What if it means someone else has to give up on what they want? There is a lot to be learned about negotiation. What do you fight for and what do you give up? When are you selling yourself short and when are you compromising reasonably or just being realistic about what's possible? How do you prioritize your desires? When do you fight for your principles, and when are you "cutting off your nose to spite your face"? How do you balance respect for yourself with respect for others? If I want Mexican food and you want Chinese, how do we decide on where to go today? How do you assert yourself and when? When does confidence cross over into arrogance? Remember that it's all practice, and keep on practicing.

"OTHERS DON'T LIKE IT WHEN I EXPRESS MY DESIRES"

You can just expect that as you start to want things, and let others know, they may not be thrilled about it. They're used to you "going with the flow," meeting their expectations, supporting their agenda, or not having an agenda of your own. Your job is to go ahead and express what you want and stand up for yourself so others will learn to respect you and your desires. If it is not emotionally or physically safe to do so, and you're an adult and free to choose for yourself, then you need to take a hard look at why you are staying in the circumstances you are in (signing up for victimization).

"OTHERS DON'T UNDERSTAND MY ENTHUSIASM"

Once you begin to live life more passionately, others don't always understand. Schultze's community, from the previously mentioned story, just didn't understand his newfound love of Cajun music. In *Erin Brockovich*, Erin's boyfriend feels left in the dust (and justly so) by her passionate advocacy. He didn't sign up to be with someone who was passionate about something, so it's hard for him to be understanding about her enthusiasm. If you are a Passionate, realize that it isn't always easy to live with someone who's on a crusade about something. But know it's even harder to live with a Passionate who is numbed-out, unenthusiastic, and not living his or her passion.

Being It, Doing It, and Faking It (Attitude to Adopt)

Since Passion is the state of being you wish to live in, where life feels meaningful to you, you can ask yourself the following questions when you're working on adopting the attitude of your Life Purpose in order to more fully inhabit it and then *do it*.

When you feel *numb* or find yourself asking, "Why me?" ask yourself:

- How do I feel when I'm deeply enthusiastic about something?

- What would I want/do if no one else was around?

- How do I feel when I do things I don't want to do? Do I "disappear" or space out? When does this happen? Can I come back to the present to know what I want?

- How do I feel when I stand up for myself?

- Do I expect other people to know what I want and give it to me?

"I know what I desire and stand up for myself!"

Practical Everyday Expression/Steps

To build up your ability to know your desires and own your personal power, you must *practice* the actions that connect you to your Passions.

- *Ask "What do I want?" and "What's in it for me?"* Off the top, this will sound selfish to the conflict-avoiding types who don't want to be seen as narcissistic or egotistical. But if you're over-sympathizing with what everyone else wants and forgetting about yourself, how can you inhabit yourself enough to know what you deeply desire? How can you get in touch with your passions? I call this "playing with other people's toys." If you're playing with everyone else's toys, how can you know what toys you want to play with? How do you know what you'd rather be doing with yourself, your time, your energy? When you forget about yourself, it's as if you become an anti-advocate for yourself—you're advocating constantly for why others should get what they want as a substitute for knowing what you want. Practice catching yourself thinking first about others' welfare and completely forgetting about your own. It certainly is uncomfortable to stop and ask, "What do I want?" or "What's in it for me?" because the answer at first may well be "I have no idea." It's important to stick with yourself when you find these numb spots and to be willing to explore them, to wonder why you don't have an agenda for yourself first. Ask yourself why it isn't okay to want anything. Keep realizing that no one else can tell you what you want—it can only come up out of you.

- *Notice when you numb out.* When you do numb out, stop and see if you can "come back into yourself." Is there something you can do to get present again? Breathing deeply, doing a focused task (running, gardening, washing the dishes), taking a walk, jumping up and down to get grounded and centered? Even if you don't know what triggered your numb-out, acknowledge it and pay close attention to it. What emotion are you blocking? Can you name it, get in touch with it, and express it? When you numb out while interacting with others, try to tell the other person that something isn't right for you even though you're unsure of what it is, and ask for some time and space to come back to yourself before making a decision. Remember, you can't know your passion if you've got pieces of your emotional system shut down, so be willing to sit with your numb places so they can thaw out. Know that most people, at their core, numb out around their anger.

- *What role am I playing? Am I disappearing or "stirring the pot"?* When you don't like what's happening in your life, stop and take a look at the role you're playing in creating the situation. Are you being too passive or timid and not speaking up for what you want and feel? Are you poking at others to stir the pot to create some (negative dramatic) excitement? Or overriding what someone else wants to get what you want?

Positive Feelings Associated with This Life Purpose

- Passionate/excited/enthusiastic

- In charge of your life/you know what you want

- Free to choose

- Self-respect balanced with respect for others

"I feel enthusiastic about life!"

Questions to Ask Yourself

- Am I so passionate about what I do that it feels like I have a cause? Am I working for/with something that matters to me?

- What is in my life that really isn't working for me?

- Is what I do with myself all-consuming for me?

- Do I allow myself to want things? Do I remember that I matter too?

- Do I see it as *my job* to get what I want for myself?

- Do I stand up for what I want with the people I know best?

- When I don't know what I want, do I just go along with what others want?

- How do I respect myself? In what ways do I disrespect myself?

- When do I feel like and play the victim and blame others for my circumstances when I need to stand up for and act on behalf of my own desires? When do I find myself asking, "Why me?" and throwing my hands up helplessly? What can I do about it instead of giving up too easily?

- What do I feel trapped about?

- Do I expect others to know what I want? Do I expect them to get it for me?

- Do I get what I want at the expense of others? In what ways am I disrespectful of other people?

- Do I know the difference between myself and others?

- Whose life am I living anyway?

Middle Finger: Responsibility

(MYTHICAL ARCHETYPE: SATURN/CRONOS)

Value/Worth

Security/Resources/Money/Work

Responsibility/Accountability/Discipline/Reliability/"Right and Wrong"

Appropriateness/Doing the "Right" Thing

Commitment/Contracts/Promises/Follow-Through/Practice

Faith and Belief in Self and Others/Others' Belief and Faith in You

Structure/Rules/Laws/Systems of Life/Reality/Integrity

Time/Death/Maintenance Factor

Organization/Governance/Efficiency

Shoulds/Needs/Musts

Balance

For discipline is the channel in which our acts run strong and deep; where there is no direction, the deeds of men run shallow and wander and are wasted.

URSULA K. LE GUIN, *The Farthest Shore*

You've got to learn your instrument. Then, you practice, practice, practice. And then, when you finally get up there on the bandstand, forget all that and just wail.

CHARLIE PARKER

Discipline is freedom.

UNKNOWN

Save your pennies and your dollars will take care of themselves.

UNKNOWN/MY GRANDFATHER

And this is why you come to a Guru: with the hope that the merits of your master will reveal to you your own hidden greatness.

ELIZABETH GILBERT, *Eat, Pray, Love*

Middle Fingers Overview
(The <u>Responsibility</u> Life Purposes)

Named after the Roman mythological god Saturn, the middle fingers are representative of your ability to work with the practical realities and structures of life (the *rules* of life) in order to maintain your precious existence and feel as if you have a sense of direction. The Greeks called this god Cronos, the god of time and death, which are the two ultimate limitations of human existence. Your human life is restricted to a certain amount of time that makes it valuable—truly precious. If you live to be eighty years old, you have 4,160 Saturdays to live—a very finite, comprehensible, and unsettling number.

Within the limits of your human lifespan, you have basic needs requiring regular attention in order to sustain your life physically and to go beyond mere survival to live a life that feels good. You *must* eat, sleep, and make money to buy what you need, as well as fulfill more complex needs such as love and appreciation—and you must get a balanced amount of these things so life feels steady and safe and valuable (i.e., worth living). There are many details to living life and maintaining things so that both yield what they are capable of yielding. The Saturn fingers represent the regular maintenance factor of life that is absolutely required to keep things going: brushing your teeth so they don't rot, changing the oil in your car so it doesn't break down, washing the dishes so you can eat the next meal, working regularly to literally "make a living" by earning money, filing your taxes, following the rules of the road so you don't have an accident while driving. Everyone has to be appropriately disciplined to work within the rules of life in order to stay alive, get things done, and feel rich and secure.

Steady, responsible commitment to yourself and life's requirements provides a sense of internal reliability, value, and self-esteem. When you know you can take care of the "business" of life, you know you can rely on yourself and believe in yourself over time. The more advanced forms of this involve doing work that feels good to you to make money ("proper pay for proper work"), and being careful about what commitments you make so you can keep them. You feel worthy of *being*, of existing, because you take proper care of yourself as well as your commitments to others. When you know from the inside what you *should* do for yourself (and *do* it), and balance it on the outside with what you promise to do for others, then you convey to yourself and the world that you are reliable and valuable, and you find that others value you as much as you value yourself. You come into *integrity* with yourself and the world around you, which is all about balancing your commitment to yourself with your commitment to others, as well as lining up who you really *are* on the inside with what you *do* on the outside.

It is through commitment that value is created and the structures of things work efficiently. The Olympic figure skater is dedicated to rigorous, disciplined practice over many years in order to perform and compete. The businessperson learns about how money works in order to earn it. The accountant tracks all the details of a business to ensure more money is coming in than going out. An organizational consultant assesses the structures of a company to make sure it's efficient. Jockeys monitor their weight so the horses they ride can run as fast as possible. Students study so they can pass an exam. Coaches structure the lives of their students so they can be the best they can be and have faith in themselves. Judges uphold the law and decide what's right and wrong. And Ann Landers helps us understand appropriate behavior in the context of our societal interactions. You must take committed, structured action over time, as long as it takes, in order to reap the full value from life. Remember the story of the Little Red Hen? She wants to have something to eat and she asks her animal friends if they will help her grow the wheat, and they all reply, "Not I!" The responsible Little Red Hen goes ahead and plants and tends the wheat until actual wheat is ready to be reaped. Then she asks who will help her take the wheat to the mill, and again all her lazy friends reply, "Not I!" But the Little Red Hen persists through every step, she does the necessary step-by-step *work* in a timely manner. She is committed to having bread to eat and, in the end, all her animal friends show up to eat her bread, but she, appropriately, eats it all to sustain her own existence. She did the work and recognizes that she is worthy of the reward.

Those with Saturn purpose are at their best when they are working with the necessary details of life in a structured fashion so full value can be reaped—whether it's in dollars to pay the bills or in encouraging some aspect of precious human potential.

"BUSINESS"

(Right Middle Finger Life Purpose)

Keywords: Proper Pay for Proper Work
Worth in the World/Money
Contracts/Agreements with Others

Following Through on Details until
Value Is Attained
Time and Money Management

If you have the "Business" Life Purpose, you are here to engage in "proper pay for proper work." This means you want to create security for yourself by making money from working in alignment with who you are, offering something of value to others, and being valued for it in return. Being in business is about being someone with high integrity who is excellent at taking care of the *business of life*, i.e., making sure your practical material needs are met by being accountable to the outer world in order to make the money necessary to meet your needs. You find meaning in figuring out how to make things work out in practical reality so you can create security for yourself from your "right" work and from interacting with others in a socially appropriate and fair manner. With this Life Purpose, you are here to figure out how to be responsible to the spoken and unspoken contracts you make with others rather than breaking your contracts or allowing others to break their agreements with you.

Key to living the "Business" Life Purpose is engaging in the entire process of *social accountability*. You must be willing to make a contract (an agreement) and be accountable to others to do the work to provide something of value in exchange for monetary payment in return. At a basic level, being *socially accountable* simply means making good on your contracts or agreements with other people, whether it's one person or many people at a time (and whether money is involved or not). You promise to provide your time or services or a product and receive "payment" in return, in accordance with what you and another party have agreed upon. At your best, you constantly practice delivering on your commitments with others and make sure you are valued in return— in money, when appropriate, but also in other ways (like being thanked). You mind your contracts to make sure they are fair, and you know exactly what you are agreeing to do, so you know you can keep your promises. You make sure that a fair exchange of resources is happening, that both parties are benefiting according to the value offered and the value received. You cross the t's and dot the i's, or get help in making sure that the contracts you enter into are fair to all parties involved and enforceable. If you take a moment to think about it, spoken and unspoken contracts are being made and kept (and broken) all of the time on every level of life. If you are employed, you have a contract with your employer to provide work for pay. If you are married, you made vows to your partner. Businesses make promises to those who buy their products and services. When you go into a café and order a coffee, it is tacitly understood that you are paying the posted price for a cup of coffee (not for a cup of tea or for a pastry) and that the coffee will be hot (unless otherwise specified and agreed upon). If you receive something else, then there's been a misunderstanding about what you agreed to pay for (or someone has been dishonest), which must be settled. In general, when you get in line at this café, there is an unspoken social contract among patrons that each person will order according to who arrived first and that everyone will line up and not take cuts to speed up their own ordering process at the expense of everyone else (time is one measure of valuation after all). So, when you are inhabiting your "Business" purpose, you practice staying in alignment with all your contracts with others, with a particular focus on your work or career agreements through which you receive monetary compensation.

To embody your "Business" purpose, you want to be engaged in "proper work," work that is in alignment or integrity with who you are and utilizes your special gifts. This purpose is not simply about taking care of your needs by getting yourself a secure livelihood (though this isn't a bad place to begin to focus yourself if you're new to working for pay or you're having trouble being responsible enough to hold down a job). Your proper work ultimately has to do with the contract you have with yourself to be who you are and then to be valued by the world as that person. If you do work that is meaningless for you but get paid well, you are not inhabiting this purpose fully. This is the purpose most directly related to the marriage of *meaning* and *money*. Your challenge is to *do something meaningful* and then *make it pay* enough to take care of your needs. Many with this purpose have one or the other—a secure job (with good pay or not) or a meaningful occupation they can't figure out how to get paid for (whether it's just tricky or they're not particularly practical about these things and need some help with it from an agent, a broker, a business mentor, etc.).

This purpose also happens to be another of mine, and my career history is one typical example of the process of the "Business" purpose. As one of the overly responsible types of people, I started working under the table when I was fifteen because my single mother had a chronic illness and money was tight. At sixteen I was working above board as many hours as the law permitted (thirty-two hours per week) while in high school full-time. I started out making money to take care of many of my own needs out of necessity. Now, even I don't pull out any tiny squeaky sad fiddles about this. I *liked* working! It felt so good to make my own money and to discover so early on that I could do so. It gave me a strong sense of security, that at my best I could work and make money, even in (or because of) less than ideal circumstances. I found out I could rely on myself. I put myself through college by applying for local scholarships, and other grants and loans, and by . . . working.

Now, here's the catch many with this purpose snag on—debt. When I got out of school, I had loan debt (for yourself, if you have debt, you can insert here: mortgage debt, medical debt, family to support, etc.), I was unsure of what I wanted to do as a career (no direction or strong sense of what was meaningful for me), and I had to start making more money, so I found a well-paying nonprofit job trying to do good (proper work) for the world. I was getting by, steadily paying down my loans, but my sense of daily satisfaction started draining out of my life, a little at a time. I made a job change (to another nonprofit sector) and that lack of meaning only magnified. I was selling out for security, and had proper pay but not *my* proper work. This second job was so bad for me I left it, went through a time of financial and emotional crisis, and came out the other end with my own business, as a fingerprint and hand analyst, both excited and scared to death (who would think anyone could make a living doing *this?*). But I remember thinking, *If I can be as dedicated to providing something valuable for people and learn how to "mind my own business" in as disciplined a fashion as when I worked for others, then I may just have a chance at making money for myself.* It hasn't always been easy to make what is meaningful to me pay, but I keep at it, keep following through, keep learning the rules of how "business" works, and keep doing the work it takes to make money. And it's literally and figuratively paying off. My life is an ongoing marriage of meaning and money. I provide something of high value to others and they value me in return by paying me.

Now, I would be the last person to say that doing this or following any Life Purpose is a piece of cake. Like all the purposes, there are so many hurdles to trip on and banana peels to slip on. If this is your purpose, you specifically want to watch out for being off balance in how you make contracts with others and the world at large. An organizational example of intentionally messing up with this purpose is exemplified in Michael

Moore's latest film, *Sicko*, which is in part a scathing account of how health insurance corporations in the United States (and many individuals who work for them) are receiving *improper pay for improper work*. These companies promise their buyers medical and health services and then look for every way they can of backing out on those promises—of breaking the contract they entered into with their buyers. These companies misrepresent themselves as being dedicated to providing medical care to their customers and then routinely deny them the services they paid for—all in the interest of increasing the company's profits. They are actually in the business of providing as little value as possible for each dollar received. There is particularly poignant footage of an individual medical doctor trying to set things right by publicly confessing that she repeatedly denied patients care (even when the results were their deaths), because she would receive *more* pay for *not* providing services. In other words, in a gross example of being sold out for security, she was paid *not* to doctor. Individuals and businesses engaging in such practices are blatantly breaking their social contract and are out of integrity with the world.

When you consciously begin to learn and engage in the process of being appropriately responsible to others by being careful about making promises and then following through on all of your agreements in a fair and timely manner, you find others learn they can rely on you and begin to value you for it. When you are reliable, it is natural that others want to do "business" with you—in other words they want to work with you. And as more people want to work with you (i.e., pay for your services or products), what you are offering becomes more valuable. Of course, this requires that *you* know what you are offering is valuable and that you ask others for appropriate compensation. It is the fair exchange of value and creating your own security that makes your life satisfying.

If you have the "Business" purpose, your deepest fulfillment arises from being paid appropriately for your proper work. You reap deep satisfaction from making agreements with others, keeping those agreements reliably, and finding those in the world who value what you have to offer and will pay for it. Life doesn't always make it easy to figure out what you're worth in objective terms. But the more secure you are in the value and benefits of what you have to offer, the more you will find others value you in return, and the easier it becomes for you to handle the "business" of your life.

Challenges

Just because you have the "Business" purpose doesn't mean it's always easy to inhabit it all the time and in all circumstances. You are here to grow into your being and what it requires you to do. Two types of challenges help you gain the broad experience you need in order to live the "Business" Life Purpose.

Internal Challenges (Being)

These are some of the challenges you have within yourself, the negative beliefs you may hold about yourself and about being responsible to others, which need to be brought to consciousness and worked with so you can do what is necessary to become truly valued and valuable.

"I DON'T KNOW WHAT I'M WORTH IN THE WORLD"

Those with the "Business" purpose often start out with little understanding of what they are worth in the world. This tends to result in not knowing what to ask for or expect, whether they are unsure of what they should receive in pay for work performed, or there is money in their lives that is distorting their value in the eyes of others. Many with this purpose simply don't have a sense of what they are worth and take the little offered them, or they ask for too little in exchange for the value they are offering. They have a hard time looking around to see what others doing similar work are being paid to see if what they are earning is in an acceptable range, or just can't manage to ask for what they're worth. And this applies to more than money. Do you believe that what you do for others is valuable and appropriately expect thanks or acknowledgement? For others with this purpose, the issue can be one that sounds like the kind of problem you want to have until you scratch beneath the surface. Imagine you've turned eighteen and have come into a large family inheritance. Sounds good at first, doesn't it? But all of a sudden you are worth a lot, in money, in others' eyes, and you don't know whether someone wants to date you for *you* or for your *money* (or for some other perceived value, like fame). This is not a nice situation.

In the movie *Mumford*, one of the characters is a young man who unexpectedly hits it big with a modem he invented. He is a laid-back and sincere guy who rides a skateboard and treats his company's employees very well, and life seems good, but he's terribly lonely. He incredulously reveals to his therapist that he has been besieged by sycophants—women who suck up to him in the hopes of his becoming their meal ticket—and he is deeply disillusioned about his prospects for finding love. To be clear: I am not saying that money is bad, just that when your worth is distorted in either direction, it's very challenging. With the "Business" purpose, you are working your way into understanding what you have to offer and receiving value in return.

"I DON'T HAVE ANY SENSE OF DIRECTION IN LIFE"

Many with this purpose wrestle with finding an overall sense of direction in life, particularly around career direction. It is as if true north on your personal compass is missing, and you have no sense of purpose over time. The Saturn finger is about work and about the structure of the abstract (our concept of time is a structuring of something that is an abstract idea), which includes being able to project an idea of yourself and what you are doing with yourself into the future, particularly about your own life's work. This is the challenge of what to get committed to "out there" so life feels meaningful and you have something to aim for and follow through to. With this purpose, it is very easy to get sidetracked by the everyday responsibilities and tasks of life so you can't see the forest for the trees. Life is one never-ending "to do" list—washing the dishes, fixing up the house, tending the garden, doing the laundry, running errands, folding your socks—and it can be hard to pull it together and keep track of it all. Bogging down in handling the day-to-day business of life can also be a big distraction from stepping back to look at the bigger picture and direction of your life.

Another variation of this I encounter involves those who have a lot of money (whether inherited, earned, or gained from a successful IPO or by winning the lottery) and have no sense of direction and value in the world because they don't have to work.

GETTING WITH THE PROGRAM OF REALITY (MONEY, TIME, AND MORE)

This is all about the necessity of learning the rules that govern the way things work. Those with the "Business" purpose are those who, at their best, learn enough of the rules so they can shepherd things along to the desired outcome. It is very difficult to work with the "business" of life if you are unwilling to take a look at the way things *are* and at the practical way they actually *work* according to their structure. For instance, let's say you need something to eat and decide tomatoes would be just fine. To keep this simple, let's say you have to grow the tomatoes yourself in order to have something to eat. What do you have to do, *in practical reality*, to get tomatoes? You have to plant seeds or seedlings, in good soil, in a spot with enough sun, and then fertilize and water on a regular schedule, protect the plants from pests, trim them and stake them up . . . and how long do you have to do this for? For as long as it takes to get edible tomatoes! If you quit watering, what happens? If you water too little, then water too much, what happens? So, for growing tomatoes, are there basic practical rules that can't be broken? Yes. And, if you take a moment to think about it, there are rules for just about everything else in life too. Time has rules. Are you aware of the passing of time so you can be punctual when you promise to be somewhere? Or are you always late? Money has rules; saving money creates various forms of security ("A penny saved is a penny earned," said Benjamin Franklin). If you spend beyond what you've got, you end up in an insecure position if you can't repay your debt. As a businessperson, you need to figure out how to make things work out in practical reality (even if you get help with this). Take a look at your own life and see if you can identify areas where things just aren't working, and see if you can learn more about them and how to work with them so you can reap the full benefits of your efforts.

"I DON'T WANT THE RESPONSIBILITY"/COMMITMENT ISSUES

This is the Life Purpose of being appropriately responsible to the outer world. It is about being reliable and accountable for your actions and being conscientious, which means taking something on and following through so others can depend on you. It can be challenging for you to take on full responsibility for tasks, projects, yourself, your life, and others. Ideally, you want to start small and follow thorough, follow through, follow through to build up your belief in yourself and others' belief in you. It is very much about creating security for yourself by providing something of value for others. As a self-employed businessperson, I am keenly aware of my various responsibilities: I must go out and find clients, then commit to an appointment with them at a specific date and time, keep my calendar, then be on time (and require them to be the same), and do my accounting, maintain my website, and on and on. Phew! That's a lot of responsibility, and there's no one telling me what to do or when to do it. I am responsible for the structure and the perpetuation of my business. Those with the "Business" purpose also seek reliable help and consultation when they need it. Being responsible means taking your commitments seriously and personally, in whatever context you find yourself in.

External Challenges (Doing)

When you begin to *know what you're worth in the world*, various obstacles are likely to arise externally to challenge you and help you develop strength in your ability to handle business. Remember, your "Business" purpose does not guarantee proper pay for proper work. You have to work as skillfully as you are able with the times, the circumstances you're living in, and the people in your life, and all three are likely to confront you in many ways. Here are a few possible external challenges.

SOLD OUT FOR SECURITY

This is as simple as it sounds, but not so easy to look at squarely for all kinds of reasons. You may be making good money for what you do (I've had clients report that they are *overpaid* for what they do because their company doesn't want to lose them), or you may be underpaid in a very secure job where you can't be fired, but the real question is, do you have proper pay for proper work? Money *and* meaning? Or do you have yourself roped into your position because it's safe and secure and has benefits and vacation, sick leave and a retirement plan? If you just don't care about what you do, whether you are being paid well or not, and you're afraid to even consider making a move because there's risk involved, you are sold out for security. What I find interesting for many in this position is that they are actually *limiting their earning potential* by playing it safe. They are often (but not always) ironically lowering their potential for security, in terms of money, by staying put. A question I like to ask those in this position is, how much is your *life* worth? Because, at the end of the day, you are exchanging the precious minutes of your life for money, and that time cannot be bought back for all the money in the world. (Time has rules, remember?) There are endless ways to make money, but once each moment of life has passed, it's *gone*. Are you spending your precious time the way you want to spend it? Are you valuing yourself and your own life? Our society tends to overvalue money and undervalue meaning. As Lily Tomlin said, "The trouble with the rat race is that even if you win, you're still a rat." Can you figure out how you want to make money, then understand what you have to contribute that is valuable that you can offer when and to whom you choose? What would it mean to you to *balance* money and meaning?

BROKEN CONTRACTS

You're being careful about what commitments you're making and being conscientious about keeping your promises (contracts), only to find others breaking the promises they made to you! What gives? You're working hard not to drop the ball on your end, but others keep dropping the ball on you without apology (or they may keep apologizing, but keep dropping the ball until their apology is worthless). As you become someone who follows through consistently on what you set out to do, it becomes apparent how others promise things and then flake out. They say they'll meet you at a certain time and then are late *every time*. They say they'll take on a task and then forget all about it and make excuses about why they didn't follow through. They will even make contracts in writing and then try and wiggle out of every clause if it is no longer convenient for them or it turns out that more work is involved than they anticipated. As someone with the "Business" Life Purpose, you will find it is your job to structure things so your time, money, and resources are not put into jeopardy or wasted by others. In fact, you will need to be quite careful about whom you choose to do business with, and you will want to be sharp in seeing when someone is not committed to holding up their end of the bargain. How can you tell if you and they are committed? Look at what is actually *being done*.

"EVERYONE GETS MORE VALUE THAN ME"

Once you are engaged in proper work, you want to watch out for whether you are receiving appropriate compensation for your efforts. Are you charging enough for your product or services? Getting paid and being acknowledged properly for your contribution? Are others getting their needs met through you while your own needs are not sufficiently taken care of? Are you a conduit for "wealth" (this can be money, health, creation of resources, understanding, etc.), but it passes through you to others because you don't reserve enough of it for yourself? A client of mine had this issue going on in more than one way. She is successful in her own business of consulting for other small businesspeople about how to set up their accounting (income and expenses and business planning) so they can become successful, but she's undercharging for her services and doesn't do for herself, in her own business, what she does for them! Collectively, her clients are benefiting more from her business savvy than she is. We had a good chuckle about it (she is doing well enough to make her living after all, and she was insightful enough to catch her own mistake), and she made some plans to redress this imbalance.

Raising her rates would afford her the time to do her own financial and business planning and to take more time out to attend to her personal needs.

SOCIAL INAPPROPRIATENESS

At its best, you feel good with your "Business" Life Purpose when you "make things right." This translates into how you interact with others and the world in a socially responsible way. The question is, how do you value other people and the wider world? Inappropriate behavior can range from *faux pas* (making honest embarrassing social blunders) to outright devaluation of others (behavior that says, "I'm more valuable than you!"). Larger social inappropriateness consists of things like companies knowingly polluting (devaluing) the environment or making mortgage loans to people who can't afford them, which is currently destabilizing the real estate market and the larger economy. Examples of everyday inappropriateness abound: people talking loudly on their cell phones when they know they're disturbing others, cutting in line at the store for whatever "reason," being consistently late when they've agreed to meet others and always having an "excuse" (what's really being said is, "My time is more important than yours, you can wait for me"). I read an article in the paper recently about single drivers clogging up the carpool lanes here in the San Francisco Bay Area. I was amazed at the people who agreed to be interviewed, with their photo and name, admitting unapologetically that they regularly drive in the carpool lane. They all had "reasons," but the bottom line was they all had terribly selfish excuses for why they *had* to use the carpool lane and why it was okay for them to inconvenience actual carpoolers. They were personally socially irresponsible and inconsiderate. If you've got this purpose, see if you can take an honest look at how you are balancing your self-value against how you value others, and see what you can do to "make things right."

Being It, Doing It, and Faking It (Attitude to Adopt)

Since "Business" is the state of being you wish to live in, where life feels meaningful to you, you can ask yourself the following questions when you're working on adopting the attitude of your Life Purpose in order to more fully inhabit it and then *do it*.

When you feel *worthless* or *impoverished*, ask:

- How do I *feel* when I am properly *valued* for doing my proper work?

- What do I need to do to make sure others value me properly?

- Am I allowing anyone to undervalue me? Can I look around to see how others are valued and make sure what I offer is valuable and appropriate to the situation?

- Can I ask others to value me when they aren't? Do I undervalue others?

- What would I do right now if I valued myself properly for my work? Valued others properly for theirs?

"I know my own worth and am properly valued by others."

Practical Everyday Expression/Steps

To build up your worth in the world, you must *practice* the actions that create accountability!

- *Cross your t's and dot your i's.* Practice minding the details of things. What steps are necessary to follow all the way through to giving and receiving full value? Do you need help taking care of the practical details? I had a client with this purpose who was so good at anticipating and taking care of the details of her business that she comfortably ran a multimillion-dollar import business on her own. She was meticulous about whom she worked with and in making sure all the fine points of the contracts she entered into were fair and enforceable. In your everyday life, can you focus attention on all the practical steps and tasks it takes to follow through into the future? Be willing to do the work it takes to create value and get yourself valued.

- *Keep your commitments.* If you agree to do something, practice following through and getting it done in a timely manner. The businessperson, at best, is known as someone who can be relied upon. Be careful to consider what commitments you make, because you are going to keep them and expect others to keep their promises to you. Take a moment to look around your life and see where you tend to break your commitments to others, whether large or small, and see what you can do to keep your word and keep things fair.

- *Mind what you're worth.* This means being aware of the balance of what you offer and what you receive. Do you expect too much or too little? Give too much or too little? Remember that this does not apply only to money. Are there ways in which you are spending any of your resources—time, money, energy, etc.—and depleting yourself (too much going out and not enough coming in)? Or are you are receiving too many of the rewards of someone else's efforts while they go lacking?

Positive Feelings Associated with This Life Purpose

- Secure/valuable/valued

- Directed/consistent

- Resourceful

- Disciplined

"I do my proper work for proper pay!"

Questions to Ask Yourself

- How am I valued by others?

- Do I keep my commitments/agreements/promises to others?

- Do I make what I'm worth? Do I ask for what I'm worth (in money as well as thanks and acknowledgement from others)?

- Am I sold out for security?

- Am I reliable? Do I follow through on what I set out to do?

- Do I mind my contracts and agreements with others and make sure they deliver on what they promise in return? Do I make sure I deliver on what I promise?

- Do I know what's socially appropriate and inappropriate?

- How do I manage my finances? My time?

- Do I have my proper work?

- Is my sense of direction in life clear? Do I stop to think about my future?

- Can I pay enough attention to the practical side of things?

- Are there things in my life I'm pessimistic about? Can I stop to consider my future and believe in my ability to do work that is in line with who I am?

MENTORSHIP

(Left Middle and Double Middle Fingers Life Purpose)

Keywords: Self-Worth/Esteem
Personal Integrity
Appropriate Self-Discipline
Understanding Your Own Needs and
Taking Care of Them

Balanced Commitment to Self
and Others
Understanding the Structure of Life/
Existence/Being

If you have the Mentorship Life Purpose, you are here to assist others in developing the internal structures and discipline necessary to be committed to themselves and their own highest potential. You have the ability to see the value inherent in other people, and you wish to help them develop themselves so they can live in integrity with their own needs and deeper being. You are not here solely to teach something, but to guide others into who they need to *be* in order to do what they want to *do*, to help others to a higher level of responsibility to themselves. With this Life Purpose, satisfaction comes from being in a position to coach or counsel others in some capacity, to be their number one cheerleader as well as the taskmaster who pushes and encourages them to do the step-by-step work required to become the very best they can be.

Key to living this Life Purpose is engaging in the entire process of helping others value themselves and their own talents enough to make the decision to do the work necessary to bring their full potential to fruition over time. Mentors have faith in their protégés, even when the protégés' faith in themselves wavers. (I'll use various words for a "mentee" throughout this chapter, since there is no single word currently in use for this concept. Sports coaches work with "players," gurus have "disciples," teachers have "students," life coaches have "clients," and various professions have "apprentices," etc.) Good mentors are skilled at holding the bigger picture for mentees of *who they can be* when they believe in themselves and follow through to *doing* it. They assist their mentees by guiding them in figuring out *what* they are devoted to. Do the mentees wish to learn to play the piano? Win the Olympics in figure skating? Lose weight? Run a marathon? Move into another line of work? Sometimes the mentors' job is to guide mentees when they don't even know what they wish to learn or who they really are. Having a mentor is like having a good parent in your life who is encouraging when encouragement is needed, tough when discipline is needed, patient when patience is needed, insistent when you need pushing, honest when you are fooling yourself. Always, mentors guide the students toward accountability in order to foster inner alignment between themselves and their highest potential. Always, mentors have an eye on where the students are on the path toward developing into the people who believe in themselves enough to acquire the internal discipline needed to stay the course. The mentors guide the students in developing a strong sense of self-worth or "good enough-ness" so the students' belief in themselves and their own abilities expands through staying committed to all the stages or steps of their own growth.

To be the Mentor, you must first practice being committed to yourself. What does it mean to be committed to self? It means being in integrity with yourself, which means knowing what you *need* and being able to be responsible enough to do the work to get it for yourself, rather than not knowing what you need, or giving up what you need in favor of what others need, or knowing but not following through on doing it. What are your basic needs? How do you take care of them so you build your ability to rely on yourself? When I am traveling to conferences, and meeting hundreds of people in just a few days, my introverted self needs to go back to my hotel room and get in the bathtub with a book, even if it means I don't see the city I'm visiting (sigh). To be the person who can get up again and be "on," I need quiet, a good night's sleep, and a real breakfast with eggs every morning to keep me going. To be a reliable foundation for other people every day, I need to pay attention to my own foundation in order to keep it solid. I have to keep the promises I make to me. When I do this, I feel good about myself and experience deeply that self-esteem that comes from being committed to my needs. It truly is an inside job. Self-esteem comes from being good enough for *yourself*, from being able to rely repeatedly on doing what's right by you. You are the only one who knows what you really need and who can judge how to balance what you do for yourself with what you promise to others. Mentors are constantly looking at what it means to be responsible to themselves so they can help others be responsible to themselves. Mentors have to walk their talk to stay in integrity. They have to be as honest with themselves as possible in order to help others do the same. Instead of being a "good girl" or "good boy" in accordance with what others or society expects, mentors must look into themselves to see who they *are* and then be able to rely upon themselves to do it.

One of my favorite movies about mentorship is the movie *Miracle*, about hockey coach Herb Brooks, who put together and led the 1980 U.S. Olympic hockey team to victory over the formidable Russian team whose members had played together for more than ten years. As a coach, Brooks carefully selects the members of his team, catching flack for not focusing on picking celebrity players. "I'm not looking for the best players," he says, "I'm looking for the *right* ones." Despite pressure to compromise himself and do his job the way others believe it should be done, he maintains his integrity by sticking to what he knows is right from his own experience, and he repeatedly has to remind those who hired him to let him do his job. He's as solid as a rock in his belief in himself and in his players' ability to step up to their highest potential. To get them to own their potential, he has to discipline the arrogant team members who don't believe they have to work hard to have a chance of beating the Russians. Brooks makes them work harder than they ever thought possible, pushing them to their limits and then beyond them so they can discover the real work required and what they're really made of. He emphasizes that they are all talented, but that talent alone is nothing without serious work. To be *the best* they must be willing to honestly face themselves and the ways in which they are not good enough so they can improve those areas to become the best they can be. "The important thing is those twenty boys knowing in twenty years they didn't leave anything on the table. They played their hearts out. *That's* the important thing." Good mentors want to help others take themselves as far as they can go so they have no regrets about what they could've, would've, or should've done.

People who are mentors have to possess a strong sense of self-esteem to put themselves into the position of being like a good parent to others. This strong sense of esteem derives from reliance on the wisdom of the mentor's own life experience. Herb Brooks was a top-level hockey player himself before becoming a coach. Real mentors know things that other people, who haven't done what they've done, know nothing about. Others may have ideas about what it takes to become something, but until they've traveled the road of experience those ideas are not rooted in reality. Good mentors are those who have already pushed themselves up to their highest potential. They know what work is to be done and what sacrifices need to be made. They know how hard it is to believe in yourself enough that you can keep yourself on track toward what seems impossible. They make the unreachable seem attainable so you are willing to follow through with yourself. Mentors hold themselves up as examples of what is possible. "If I, a mere human being, could do it, so can you."

On the path of mentorship, one of the most common stumbling points is placing your confidence in teachers or gurus who are not trustworthy. I just heard an awful story of this involving a religious community where the "gurus" expect people to give significant amounts of money to the organization (and encourage them to make considerable personal financial sacrifices to do so), but they themselves are dipping into the organization's bank accounts for personal use and refuse to be accountable to their donors. They criticize anyone who questions what they are doing. Since mentorship is the purpose most directly requiring personal accountability, any form of advising others to do what you yourself have not done is not true mentorship, but a form of dishonesty. *Mentors have to walk their talk*. To hold others accountable, you have to be accountable and know what it takes to be responsible to your higher self, even when it gets hard and temptations show up.

It is also common for mentors to advise anyone and everyone around them and then discover that people don't want their "advice." Mentors need to hold themselves accountable by getting into an official coaching or teaching or counseling position where the people they advise *want* what they have to offer and ask for it, rather than running around telling others how they should do things when those people are uninterested in finding out. Mentors need to find "students" who sign up for the mentors' wisdom and guidance. In the movie *Miracle*, the coach questions and challenges every player's commitment . . . they are free to leave at any time they wish if they don't want to be held to task by Brooks. The *Karate Kid* movies have a tagline that is a perfect statement of what mentorship is all about: "He taught him the secret to karate lies in the mind and heart. Not in the hands." The main character, Daniel, *asks* and begs Mr. Miyagi to teach him karate. Miyagi at first refuses, but then decides to teach the willing Daniel, carrying him through many life lessons along the way. Mentees have to be willing to learn from a mentor, because they have to put their faith in their teacher's experience and methods, often without fully understanding the reasons for those methods until they have gained their own experience. The scene where Miyagi sets Daniel up to wash his car is classic. Daniel doesn't understand why he should wash the car, but Miyagi is training Daniel's body movements, building his strength, and fostering his willingness to *work* at the level he is at—that of a beginner. And Miyagi wants Daniel to *learn for himself* from having this experience of work rather than just tell him everything about what he is doing. If you watch *Miracle*, look for the main thing Brooks is trying to *teach* his team rather than *telling* them what to feel and do. Good mentors set their mentees up to gain their own experience, all with the aim of helping them strive for their best and learn from their own mistakes, while avoiding the disastrous mistakes that could cut their potential short.

When the mentor consciously begins to learn and engage in the process of appropriate self-discipline, which builds integrity, other people begin to recognize the mentor as someone they would like to learn from. "You've been where I'd like to go, what can you tell me about it?" "Can you guide me to being my best?" "Can you be my role model?" For mentors, being in integrity with yourself and leading a meaningful life ultimately requires that you be willing to take on the responsibility of guiding others. Generally, this Life Purpose tends to flower later in life, once you've lived enough of it to gain experience at some aspect of it.

If you are a Mentor, your deepest fulfillment arises from helping others find out what they are made of. You take joy from seeing your students become *who they are meant to be* and taking their best shot at living life to their fullest personal capacity. In *Miracle*, Brooks gives a rousing speech to his team before playing against the Russians. He tells them, "Each one of you was *born* to be a hockey player. You've *earned* your opportunity to be here, and now it's *your time*, so go out there and take it." Whether your mentees win or lose, ultimately, is not the point. Helping your protégés give 100 percent of themselves, seeing what happens, and living a life without regrets because they live a life in full integrity with their deeper *being* is the ultimate satisfaction. It's not whether you win or lose, but how you play to game [of life] that counts in the end.

Challenges

Just because you are a Mentor doesn't mean it's always easy to inhabit your purpose all the time and in all circumstances. You are here to grow into your being and what it requires you to do. Two types of challenges help you gain the broad experience you need in order to live the Mentor Life Purpose.

Internal Challenges (Being)

These are some of the challenges you have within yourself, the negative beliefs you may hold about yourself and about Mentorship, which need to be brought to consciousness and worked with so you can do what is necessary to create true integrity in your life and the lives of others.

"I DON'T KNOW WHAT I NEED"

For many with this purpose, it can be difficult at first to know what you *need*, much less get it or do it for yourself. An internal voice says that it's not okay to need anything, to be here and take up space, much less be deserving enough to have your needs met. When you stop to think about what you need, guilt tends to come up and derail you, or it seems like there's a big black hole inside of you and nothing is coming out of it in terms of knowing what you need. Feeling undeserving can run your entire life. "Everyone else deserves to get what they need, but not me." It seems easier to latch on to what others need and take care of it, rather than sitting with your own sense of unworthiness to get down to your own true needs.

COMMITMENT ISSUES

Not knowing what you need makes it very difficult to know what to commit yourself to, what to actually *do* for yourself balanced against what you do for others. This can lead to various forms of avoiding responsibility for yourself—*committing to too many things* (the dilettante) and then making lots of excuses for being unable to complete any of them; *committing to nothing at all* and never getting focused enough on anything to become a master of it; *committing to what other people need* so they'll pat you on the back and tell you you're good; or *committing only to what you need* and ignoring the needs of those around you (selfishness). As mentors make these errors they are learning how to balance commitment to self with commitment to others and following through responsibly on those commitments so they don't make themselves untrustworthy liars when they break their commitments. Mentors are careful and realistic about what they commit to because they fully intend to follow through on their commitments.

"I'M NOT GOOD ENOUGH" (GOODY-TWO-SHOES OR LET'S-RUN-WITH-THE-DOGS)

Many with this purpose wrestle with feeling they aren't good enough . . . they have low self-esteem due to not knowing their own needs and, therefore, being unable to meet them. This shows up in one of two ways: some work very hard to be good according to what other people expect (Goody-Two-Shoes) and others say, "Forget it! I'm just no good. Why bother? I'll just run with the dogs and prove that I'm no good so others will punish me to confirm it." The Goody-Two-Shoes are always figuring out what other people need, and they pour their energy into meeting others' needs in order to be told they're a "good girl" or "good boy." They try hard to be perfect. The "bad" boys and girls can be out of integrity in a wide range of ways—overeating, undereating, overspending, using drugs or alcohol, or being outright dishonest in their dealings with others. You can have both going on at the same time and playing into each other. For instance, you're trying to be good for everyone else and this opens up a big, hungry hole in yourself that you literally overfeed, which makes you feel worse about yourself. So you try and be even *better* for everyone else, feel worse, eat more, and on and on in a downward spiral.

RIGHTEOUSNESS AS A WAY TO BUILD ESTEEM

I regularly see people with this purpose engaged in having to be right or correct all the time as a way to feel good enough. Being a Mentor *does* require having a strong sense of right and wrong and knowing what the rules of life are so they can be followed. But insisting on perfection all the time doesn't allow space to make the mistakes that go along with the learning process. And making yourself right and everyone else wrong makes the world a mighty cramped and disappointing place to live. To be a Mentor, you have to give yourself and others room to breathe, to learn, to stumble and pick themselves up, and to move forward again. To learn, you have to be able to admit you are making mistakes in the first place and realize it is (usually) not the end of the world. It's also ridiculous to constantly believe that you are infallible and that you know the *only* way to do something. It blocks your ability to find various means to the end you and/or your mentee are trying to reach and denies others the chance to be "good enough." As one of my favorite writers, Anne Lamott, says, "Perfection is the enemy of the people." I like to add, "Perfection is a goal, not a destination." You strive for it, but there are many ways to get there. Making yourself feel good by making yourself better than others (in your own head) doesn't allow you or a mentee to see what's really needed if it doesn't seem to "look good" to the rest of the world.

External Challenges (Doing)

When you begin to get committed to yourself, various obstacles are likely to arise in the external world to challenge you and help you develop strength in your ability to live in integrity with yourself and others. Remember, your Mentor Life Purpose doesn't guarantee your integrity. You have to work as skillfully as you are able with the times, the circumstances you're living in, and the people in your life, and all three are likely to confront you in many ways. Here are a few possible external challenges.

"OTHERS TELL ME I'M NOT GOOD ENOUGH OR UNDERVALUE ME"

As you progress along the path of getting aligned with your true needs, and increase your sense of self-esteem, you may find yourself being challenged by others or your circumstances to maintain your integrity. The following is an everyday example of this. I had a client who paid for a session and then no-showed twice without apology. She called up (a month later) and said, "I guess it didn't work out, I guess I forgot to call you and you didn't call me, which is not a problem, and I'd like to reschedule with you sometime." What do I do? She was basically telling me that I'm not good enough to deserve her remembering her appointment, that my time is not important, and that it's my responsibility to chase her down, even though the clear terms of my appointment policy are that my clients call me. I rescheduled her once and reiterated that she needs to call me for the appointment. Just a few days later, she no-showed again. Her message again implied that she wasn't responsible for missing her appointment. Should I be "good" for her and "nice" and put her on my books, and potentially lose time and money if she no-shows again? At what point do I simply do what's good for me and be responsible to myself? How do I maintain my integrity and encourage my client to take responsibility for herself? As mentors get aligned with themselves, others behave in ways that challenge their newfound levels of integrity. This challenge can present itself in much more extreme forms as well (being roped into bribery, swindling, and other forms of dishonest conduct). Rebellious types who have reformed themselves can find themselves tempted to slip back into their destructive ways when others don't believe they can maintain their integrity.

PERSONAL RESPONSIBILITY

As you progress on the path of the Mentor, you are challenged to refine your sense of personal responsibility. What are you responsible for and what are others responsible for? What does it mean to take full responsibility for yourself, your actions, and every aspect of your life? Mentors need to be very good at helping their mentees be responsible for themselves. As a Mentor, you need to be personally accountable for yourself, admit your mistakes to yourself and others, apologize when necessary, correct course when you get off track, and walk your talk.

INAPPROPRIATE REQUESTS

As you get dedicated to yourself, and honest with yourself, others can ask you to be dishonest or to engage in questionable activities. I know of someone who is required to lie every day at work if she wants to keep her job. She works for a small business that sells medical equipment, and the owners are in debt they can't repay. Although the business owners have not directly asked her to lie, she has to field calls from creditors and fend them off by lying. The owners say, "Just tell them I'm not in," or "Tell them we sent the check, didn't they get it?" when no payment has gone out. She hates it, but she's afraid to lose her job since they pay her well. Can she get committed to herself and get another job?

In the book and movie *The Nanny Diaries,* the main character finds she is gradually expected to do much extra work requiring many extra hours of work at no pay. She does the extra work in hopes of being paid and because she doesn't want to leave the child who relies on her. Her self-esteem is very low, and she receives nothing, not even thanks. The plot thickens when the husband's mistress sends her a letter and a good chunk of money to set up a weekend with the husband for her (bribery). The nanny feels increasingly bad about herself for allowing herself to be devalued and caught in the family web of lies, while guilt plagues her on the other end at the thought of leaving the child she takes care of who relies on her. How far will she compromise? What does it mean to do the right thing? What is she responsible for and not responsible for? Should she be honest and tell the wife? Watch out for the slippery slope of sly and gradual compromise that can erode your integrity.

I find that mentors are often already advising people. One of two things is usually going on—either people are coming to the mentor asking for advice, or the mentor tries to advise people who don't actually want to be mentored. As a Mentor, you need to be helping to guide people through something *you've been through*, something you've actually had life experience with. You also want to be mentoring people who have signed up to be mentored by you. If you try to advise others and they haven't asked for it, you can find them surprisingly resistant to taking your advice. Reformed alcoholics and drug addicts who help others on the road to recovery are in integrity with their mentorship. Successful authors who have been published and now help other authors understand the practical process of getting published are also aligned with themselves. T. Harv Eker, who made and lost one fortune, then made another and learned from his mistakes, now mentors others about understanding their relationship to money. To be a true mentor, you need to be running off your own hard-won life experience. If you're unsure what your body of experience is, you can set yourself up to learn about counseling others in the meantime, or volunteer through a program like Big Brothers and Big Sisters, or tutor school children to get yourself involved in what it takes to be a mentor while you live your life. I know a Mentor who immigrated to the United States and had to learn English after he was here. He's now looking to teach English to other immigrants and has already been volunteering to counsel young gay immigrants who are in conflict with their families over being gay, as he was.

Being It, Doing It, and Faking It (Attitude to Adopt)

Since Mentorship is the state of being you wish to live in, where life feels meaningful to you, you can ask yourself the following questions when you're working on adopting the attitude of your Life Purpose in order to more fully inhabit it and then *do it*.

When you feel *unworthy and guilty*, stop and ask:

- How do I feel when I keep my promises to myself and others? When I catch myself compromising inappropriately (being out of integrity), what can I do to clean up my act?

- Did I do something wrong? Break my word to myself or others? If so, what was it? What do I need to do to make appropriate amends and apologize? If I feel guilty when I didn't actually do something wrong, how can I acknowledge my feelings and still take care of my needs?

- How do I balance what I need against what others need? Is there a win-win option here if I look more closely at the situation? When do I take care of myself first?

- Am I trying to be good for everyone but me? Can I stop and ask what "being good enough for me" means right now?

- When do I find myself being judgmental and having to be right? Can I stop and see that there's more than one right way to see things and do things?

- Does my life feel like a lie in any way? What can I do to align who I am inside with what I do on the outside?

> "I have good self-esteem by knowing what I need, and I balance
> my commitments to myself with my commitments to others."

Practical Everyday Expression/Steps

To build up the sense of self-esteem necessary to be a Mentor, you must *practice* the actions that create integrity!

- *Practice asking yourself what you <u>really</u> need.* Practice checking in to ask, what will make you feel good about yourself. What feeds your feeling good about yourself over time? Eating a cookie or not eating a cookie? Working more or working less? Buying the latest gizmo or making a payment on your credit card debt? Going to bed on time or staying out late at the party with friends, even if tomorrow is a workday? Having a third drink or stopping at two? As you can tell from these mundane examples, the answer isn't always easy. It depends on whether you've already eaten twenty cookies and whether you're on a diet, diabetic, trying to eat better overall—or not. It depends on what you've promised yourself and how you feel after you eat the cookie or have the extra drink. If you feel bad about yourself, then you (hopefully) learn from experience and try to remember for the next time. Extreme self-denial can erode your self-esteem, as can extreme overindulgence. How can you do your best to walk the path of moderation so you don't have to bounce back and forth between asceticism and gluttony?

- *Pay attention to your guilt meter.* Guilt is a necessary and useful human emotion. It tells us when we are doing something wrong and unreliable so we can correct course. When do you feel guilty? When do you avoid feeling your guilt and how do you shut it down? Do you feel guilty when a police siren goes off, sure that they're coming for you, when you're a law-abiding citizen driving the speed limit (too much guilt)? Are you constantly late when meeting people and unapologetic about it? Or are you apologetic to assuage your guilt, but you continue to be late? Do you prove you're guilty by not taking care of your needs? Do you break your promises to yourself and others? Can you admit you feel bad when you do something wrong and then make amends to yourself and/or others? How can you keep cleaning up your own act so you don't lie to yourself or others or make yourself a liar by not keeping the promises you make?

- *Stop and assess what you are actually committed to.* It's easy to see what you are committed to. Just stop and see what you are actually *doing*. Not what you're *thinking* about doing, or what you *say* you *will* do, but what you are *actually doing* with yourself, your time, your resources, and your energy. I had a client who said she thought she was dedicated to losing weight because she went to the gym three times a week to work out. She promised herself, "I'm going to lose twenty pounds," and kept plugging away at the gym with no results. She felt she was dedicated by going to the gym and sweating, but when she got on the scale, it told the truth—she wasn't losing weight. She made excuses for this ("The scale must be wrong"). One day she decided to hire a trainer. After one session with the trainer, who put the *work* into her workout, my client was amazed to realize that she had been committed to working out, but not to losing weight. To lose weight she had to be personally responsible for *doing* what it actually takes to shed pounds, not just showing up and putting in time at the gym. In fact, she did shorter, more intense workouts and lost weight. Watch out for self-deception about what you are committed to.

Positive Feelings Associated with This Life Purpose

- Knowing your needs

- Life is balanced

- Aligned with self

- Internally structured/directed

"I believe in myself."

Questions to Ask Yourself

- Do I believe in myself?

- Do I know what I need?

- Can I give myself what I need?

- Do I feel worthy? Good enough? Guilty? Undeserving? Unimportant?

- Do I have a good sense of right and wrong without being overly judgmental?

- Do I expect myself to be perfect to be good enough?

- How comfortable am I at apologizing when I make a mistake or break a promise? Do I apologize for the "wrong things"?

- When do I allow others to guilt-trip me into meeting their needs at the expense of my own?

- In what ways do I tend to break my promises to myself? How can I be more reliable for me?

- How do I balance my commitments to myself with my commitments to others?

- In what ways is my life out of balance? Too much work? Too much play?

- When I feel guilty, do I tend to rebel? Or try to be more perfect?

- What life experiences have I gone through that I can now mentor others through?

Ring Finger: Creativity

(MYTHICAL ARCHETYPE: APOLLO)

Individuality

Creative Self-Expression

Artistry

Showing Up, Being Seen

Finding Your Audience/Stage/Spotlight and Owning It

Being True-to-Self

Fame

Originality

Nonconformity/Uniqueness

Exceptional/Unconventional

The world is a mirror of the mind's abundance.

JEANETTE WINTERSON, *The PowerBook*

I think that art is the principal way in which the human mind
has tried to remake the world in a way that makes sense.

J. G. BALLARD

To be nobody but yourself in a world which is doing its best,
night and day, to make you everybody else, means to fight the
hardest battle any human can fight and never stop fighting.

E. E. CUMMINGS

There is nothing more difficult to take in hand, more perilous
to conduct, or more uncertain in its success, than to take the
lead in the introduction of a new order of things.

NICCOLO MACHIAVELLI

Ring Fingers Overview
(The <u>Creativity</u> Life Purposes)

The ring fingers are named after Apollo, the god who drags the sun across the sky every day with his chariot. The sun in its singularity represents uniqueness, creativity, and visibility. There is only one sun in our solar system, and it transforms gas into heat and light, both essential elements for the creation of life down here on planet Earth. The sun is also up where we can see it and benefit from it; it shows itself and its light exposes or illuminates everything on the planet's surface. Life as we know it would not exist without the sun.

Those with one of the ring finger Life Purposes are here to tap the wellspring of their own uniqueness and then express it externally in some form. They are the creators of the world. Take a moment to look around you, wherever you are sitting right now, and notice that *everything* in your environment was created—tables, chairs, lamps, pens, plants, curtains, your clothes, the paint on the walls, the building you're in, your own body, the very planet you live on—all of these things were *made*, they were brought into existence through a creative process. When you have an Apollo Life Purpose, you are meant to be one of the creators of the world, whether you engage literally in making art (painting, writing, singing, drawing, knitting, sculpting, etc.), you invent new things, or you are a person with creative ideas or thinking, or someone who comes up with new ways of doing things or presenting yourself. The key is your uniqueness, your different and subjective view of the world and your ability, and willingness to own it and to let the rest of us in on it.

Picasso painted the world as he saw it through his own eyes, Alexander Graham Bell invented the telephone, and the Wright brothers devised the airplane. An office manager creates the systems for the organization to run smoothly. Computer programmers develop code. Comedians make up jokes. Designers create gardens, graphics, textiles, and furniture. Chefs develop new recipes, public speakers formulate lectures, and quilters weave together unique patterns and color combinations.

On a basic level, being creative is about being true to your uniqueness, the ways in which you are different from others, and being willing to let them show. When creative types are at their best, they are true to themselves and don't worry excessively about what others think of them. It is important for creative individuals to understand that they are nonconformists, and by marching to the beat of their own inner drummer they give the rest of us permission to be ourselves as well.

When you have one of the Apollo purposes it is imperative that you show up as yourself every day with everyone you know so the world can connect with you, benefit from what you have to offer, and then offer you the applause and appreciation you desire and need. Apollo types are not supposed to be invisible wallflowers who work overtime to please others in order to be appreciated; they are meant to be themselves and let others "love me or leave me," and understand that "Not everyone is going to like me, just as I don't like everyone I meet, and it's okay." It *is* a challenge to feel and be different from the rest of the world ("Why can't I just be *normal?*"), and it is common to be sensitive to criticism, but learning to handle criticism and to work with it appropriately is key.

Ultimately, the biggest critic of the creative type is—guess who?—the Inner Critic . . . and those with the Apollo purpose can expect to work first and foremost with the Inner Critic who says, "Who would want to listen to me?" "Don't put that fuchsia paint there, your mother hates fuchsia!" and "Who am I to think I have anything special to offer?" I like to turn this on its head and ask my reluctant clients, "Aren't you glad your favorite singer/musician gets up and performs even though not everyone in the world likes them? Wouldn't you miss having movies to watch if every director gave up in the face of inevitable criticism? Who are you to hold out on yourself and us? Please offer your creative self-expression to us!"

When living their highest potential, creative types leave their signature on everything they do and tend to become known for the way they do things. They know when to be the center of attention and when to yield the spotlight to others. They help us make some kind of sense out of the world by giving us new perspectives—fresh ways of seeing things that illuminate our lives, inspire us, and touch us in deep places. Creative individuals connect us with the spark that is life and enable us all to re-create and reinvent our lives and the world in accordance with being exactly who we are.

ARTIST/INDIVIDUALIST

(Right Ring/Apollo and Double Ring/Apollo Life Purpose)

Keywords: Creative Self-Expression

Offering Uniqueness/Creative Output
   to the World

Being Different

Showing Up/Standing Out

Living in the Spotlight/Finding
   Your Audience

Performance

If you have the Artist/Individualist Life Purpose, you are here to be yourself and let it show. In other words, you yearn to inhabit your individuality, live your life as an expression of your uniqueness, and put yourself in a position to receive applause and appreciation (as well as criticism) from others. As an Artist, you want to figure out what form your uniqueness or creativity wants to take and then express it, offer something unique, and put it out there where others can enjoy and benefit from it. From the way you live your life to creating something unique, you wish to exist on your own terms and no one else's. That little voice whispering "you're special" is right . . . you're special, as in unique, different, singular, but not as in "I'm better than everyone else." At a basic level, you are meant to be an individualist, someone who creates the life you want to live without worrying too much what "they" think. Your job is to be a nonconformist, not necessarily as a statement of rebellion, but simply because you are just *you*, doing your own thing, without being overconcerned about what the world thinks of you.

Key to living this Life Purpose is engaging in the process of figuring out what it means to be *different*, to sort out for yourself how you would like to express that difference in your life and in the world. This involves the ability to stop measuring who you are up against what others expect you to be and to get comfortable with being yourself wherever you go. Can you walk the fine line between being yourself *and* finding where you belong (instead of squeezing yourself into a version of you that looks like everyone else)? Can you learn not to perennially hold yourself apart as a misunderstood "outsider"? In a way, the Artist/Individualist *is* an outsider by definition. At your best you see things in your own unique way, and this requires standing apart from the herd so you can get a different perspective on the world we all live in. But then you need to find your niche—where you belong in the world—by expressing your true self. I like to say that you need to be willing to stand out in order to find where you fit in. You have to show up as yourself in order to find and be found by the people and environments supportive and appreciative of the fact that you are different. In order to do this you must be willing to expose yourself to the risk of criticism and rejection, two things most do not profess to enjoy.

To be the Artist, you must first accept that you are different instead of resisting it (or wallowing in it!) or trying to be "normal." Many Artists have families who were critical of them for being "different" and who "accused" them of being "too sensitive" or asked, "Why can't you be normal (i.e., like us)?" My dear friend, Yoshi, is Japanese, and from early on his father recognized that he wouldn't do well in the highly conformist culture of Japan and encouraged his son to move to the United States. It was true, and even by U.S. societal standards he is deviant. Yoshi works as an accountant for periods of time, saves all his money, then quits and does what he wants for as long as the money lasts, then gets work again, and so on. He's so completely comfortable with himself that all his employers love him, encourage him to return, and he never has trouble getting another job when he needs one. Potential employers don't ask suspiciously, "What are all these gaps in your resume?" Instead, he is very choosy about where and with whom he will work, he is honest about how he lives, and he is highly valued. When I asked Yoshi if I could use his story, with a pseudonym, he said, "I don't care if you use my name!" He is indifferent to anyone else's opinion about how he lives his life as he's created it.

Another example of this is exemplified in a song I love by the Barenaked Ladies called "Box Set," in which the main character of the song, a popular singer, describes his adversarial relationship with his audience. They've loved him more than he could've imagined, but now, when he tries to grow and present new songs, all the audience wants to hear are his hit songs from many moons ago. What's an Artist to do? Give 'em more of what they want to hearty applause and approval? Or forge ahead and present what he wants to offer them now? Bob Dylan, like many Artists, faced mighty resistance and criticism when he moved from acoustic folk guitar to electric instruments. Artists, when filling the shoes of this purpose, choose to stay true to their own creativity, even if their larger audiences drop off and reject them. As individuals with the right-hand creativity purpose, they primarily face the challenge of "living out loud" and not letting the public or society dictate how they live or what they create.

Recently I've read (and re-read) Elizabeth Gilbert's wisdom-packed bestseller, *Eat, Pray, Love,* which openly charts the writer's painful and inspiring journey from conformism to true individuality. As she approaches the age of thirty, married with a house in the suburbs, an apartment in Manhattan, and a successful writing career, Elizabeth discovers that she doesn't want to have the baby she and her husband planned on. In fact, she's realized she doesn't want any part of the American Dream she's lost herself in. No one personally told her specifically what to want for her life or to aspire to, she's just gone along with what society has presented as the way to live the good life. The book chronicles her painful and enlightening search for her authentic self and life over a year of travel. At one point she notes, "I don't even have an address, and that's kind of a crime against normality at this ripe old age of thirty-four," but she doesn't let that stop her. She realizes she is different and has to learn how to "Tell the truth, tell the truth, tell the truth" of her life so she can live it. She wrote this book for others to read, total strangers who might criticize her (for her life, for her writing style, for her beliefs, etc.), which may inspire us to be true to ourselves. Gilbert bravely embodies the Artist purpose by living her own life and by exposing herself to criticism through the creative medium of her written work.

With this purpose, you need to make time and space to cultivate your creative self-expression, then find a way to put yourself and/or your work in the spotlight in front of an audience (remember that, for starters, even one or two people is an audience). Whether you have creative ideas, express yourself through your physical presentation of yourself, or engage in one of the traditional "arts" (painting, acting, singing, drawing, etc.), being an artist means you are here to be a conduit for the universal human creation that is struggling to come into the world through your unique filters, your unique personality.

As the Artist, you need to present yourself or your work in a way that offers others your perspective—just as Elizabeth Gilbert gives us a modern-day view of a very human "dark night of the soul" that can mirror our own and help us reframe our experiences in both universal and completely individual terms. Good "art" enables us to reframe the world, helps us see things we're missing, and assists us in accessing parts of ourselves that we are blind to. When Georgia O'Keeffe painted flowers, she painted them the way *she saw them,* very close up and enlarged, bright, and luminous, as a small insect visiting a giant world might see them. Sensitive to stopping and seeing the world with fresh eyes, she honed her painting craft so she could show the rest of us her view of flowers, and she made a piece of the world new for all of us. As an Individualist, just the act of living on your own terms can inspire others to do the same.

Like all the purposes, there are various ways to goof up and think you're being the Artist/Individualist when you're not. I've come across many with this purpose who "look proper" and "present well," but who are not really expressing themselves. Everything is overly calculated and is phony. I call this the "not-a-hair-out-of-place syndrome." There is an elaborate presentation going on that has very little to do with the real people underneath the façade—they are playing an exquisite defensive game of hiding out rather than using their presentation of themselves to express who they are. Of course, Artists/Individualists need to have a public persona, but though we all wear social "masks," I always recommend that the mask look as much like you as possible. (That is, unless your gig is being a mime or acting in a show requiring costumes to express your creative vision—there's a fine line between pandering to your audience and inviting them into your authentic, subjective world.) This is a form of selling out in order to be "liked" or "loved" or "approved of," and to avoid the possibility of being rejected or criticized. It's about "looking good" instead of actually expressing yourself (which allows others to connect to you). It does require vulnerability, and it is risky and scary. But when do you stop expending your energy trying to be someone you're not so that others will be pleased with you? When do you start being who you are despite potential criticism?

Another common stumbling block is when you make trouble to get attention in order to feel special, rather than spending your energy on *doing* something different. Teachers perennially have trouble with students who are not owning their Artist purpose, who are late to class in order to create a stir, who always want to be the one answering the question asked by the teacher, or who seem not to notice that they are hogging the class's time, attention, and energy by making trouble. These are the squeaky wheels looking for oil to feed their sense of being special because they aren't doing their own thing elsewhere in their lives. I call it "creating the wrong kind of drama" to get attention. We even had a student one year who would not participate during class (hiding out). But during breaks she crept off into the next room to make loud, complaining phone calls about the class, the other students, and the teachers. People talking loudly on cell phones in cafés and on airplanes, who get angry when you let them know that no one is interested in listening to them, are also candidates for the "Negative Artist/Individualist" award. Artists/Individualists want to feel "special" and naturally can make various errors in how they go about receiving their moments of "fame."

When you as the Artist/Individualist consciously begin to learn about and engage in the process of understanding what it means to be unique and to express that uniqueness, you feel like the key of your life has finally found the right lock. There's a more natural and relaxed fit between you and the world around you—even with the tomatoes that fly your way. You find yourself simply being yourself everywhere you go, and discover that when other people don't like you it doesn't matter so much to you. You can take in feedback about how you are presenting yourself and not be anxiously defensive about it, but stop and take a look to see if the shoe fits, and adjust accordingly. You find you can stop the old game of trying to "fit in" and just be yourself. You are willing to seek your place in the world instead of bemoaning that you don't fit in anywhere or forcing yourself into the wrong "lock." What a relief! And how wonderful to offer yourself and be appreciated and enjoy it!

If you are an Artist/Individualist, your deepest fulfillment arises from understanding that you are the creator of your own life and then unselfconsciously choosing to live that life on your own terms. Your *life* is an expression of you, your home is an expression of you, the way you dress is an expression of you. How do you express yourself in all aspects of your life? What form does your creative self-expression want to take? You need to be consciously and actively engaging your creativity, exploring your uniqueness and letting it show in order to reap the satisfaction of your purpose. The best feedback and appreciation you can ever receive from others is when they say, "Thank you for being *you* and for doing what *you do*!"

Challenges

Just because you are an Artist doesn't mean it's always easy to inhabit your purpose all the time and in all circumstances. You are here to grow into your being and what it requires you to do. Two types of challenges help you gain the broad experience you need in order to live the creative self-expression Life Purpose.

Internal Challenges (Being)

These are some of the challenges you have within yourself, the negative beliefs you may hold about yourself and about being creative, which need to be brought to consciousness and worked with so you can do what is necessary to live your life as an Artist.

INNER CRITIC (PERSONAL ENEMY #1)

As I approach writing about the Inner Critic (IC—as in "*I see* you and am watching your every move, so you'd better behave yourself!"), my own is blasting me and I get up to get another coffee and start musing that maybe I'd better pack it up for the day. At this very moment, I am blasting back by putting on some headphones and drowning it out with some very favorite loud bohemian music here in the café. All artists have an IC (and if you write me telling me *you* don't have one—that's very *special* of you—take it as a sign that you *do*, as it will be your IC showing up to socialize with mine). The IC is not to be banished, nor is it to be taken to heart. When your IC shows up to help you improve your presentation, thank it wholeheartedly. But when it shows up to judge you and asks, "Who are you to think you can do *anything at all?*" breathe deeply and reply, "Thanks for your input, but what I'm up to is *none* of your business, and it's all practice anyway." And get back to your work of being yourself. Read Anne Lamott's *Bird by Bird* for a scathingly honest chat about the IC (chapter entitled, "Radio Station KFKD"). Also, *Art & Fear*, by Bayles and Orland is another indispensable book about all this and the creative process.

"WHO, ME? CREATIVE?"

How many times have I heard "I don't have a creative bone in my body!" in response to decoding someone's Artist/Individualist purpose? Too many times to count and in exactly those words. If you have the Artist/Individualist purpose and that is your response, please stop and take a look at how hard you are working to fit in and conform, or how you don't recognize your own individuality and uniqueness. Does everyone around you think you're creative or individualistic or just *different*, but you just don't see it? Ask them to tell you how they see you so you can get a more accurate view of yourself ("audience" feedback). Remember that being an artist can be about creative thinking and ideas as well as about traditional forms of art or performing. It's also about being up in front of people presenting something. If you tried something creative *one time* and decided you had no talent, understand that you have to *practice* creativity, just like anything else, to find out what you've got. Also, you can try another form of creativity, and I encourage you to do so. One of my pet peeves is that, as adults, we forget that we have to learn things. The coordination of a painter's hands, eyes, and materials, or a musician's fingers, ears, and instrument, or a motivational speaker's speech delivery, or a counselor's creativity around psychological insight are all feats born out of many hours of practice, so they can express themselves through their chosen conduit. I was amazed to learn that the magician David Copperfield takes an average of *two and a half years* to develop a new act. He has a creative idea, then he has to work it out in reality by testing out pieces of it on his audiences over time to see how they react and whether he's getting the response he's after. Wow. It's when you are *engaged in* your creative pursuits that inspiration and self-discovery happens. Now there are also those who have many creative pursuits and don't know which one to pick. Ask yourself what you want to be known for and get married to it, even though it may mean leaving some of your other creative "dates" behind. I know it's hard, but how else will you become a creative master rather than a creative dabbler?

FEAR OF TOMATOES

In the old days, if you got up on the stage and the audience didn't like you, what did they do? Throw tomatoes! As an Artist, of course you are likely have a fear of criticism. Tomato Fear (as Richard Unger, the endlessly creative originator of this fingerprint analysis system, has dubbed it) comes with the territory. It is also known as "stage fright," and many talented people are renowned for being terrified of public exposure. Barbara Streisand is known for her notorious stage fright. A friend of mine said she was fortunate to see a now-famous singer-songwriter perform in a coffeehouse in her early days. The performer supposedly greeted the audience by saying something like, "Thanks for coming. I'm so happy you're here . . . so happy I could throw up!" Although these are examples of performers, Tomato Fear operates on an everyday level in terms of reining yourself in too tightly due to being afraid of being rejected by others. Some is useful so you don't walk out the door every day in your pajamas or show up at your presentation unprepared! It's a natural human thing, but if you're *overly* worried about what everyone thinks of you, it makes it very hard to be yourself.

SELF-CONSCIOUSNESS/DEFENSIVENESS/"I DON'T BELONG"

Tomato Fear can lead to an awkward, energy-depleting self-consciousness. Artists need to please themselves first. Appropriately, of course. If you are completely tuned in to defining yourself according to what others think you *should* be, then how do you find your unique self? If you are very self-conscious, you will also tend to be overly defensive. You'll be afraid of being seen or criticized by others, and you'll hide yourself. (And often, you'll find yourself criticizing others.) You may hide under a perfect not-a-hair-out-of-place façade or sometimes behind a calculated cavalier attitude and presentation of yourself (everything about you says, "I couldn't care less about what you think!"). Either way, the presentation of self is phony and superficial. We're not seeing the real you because you are afraid to expose yourself. Our reaction to you is based on the mask you show us, not on who you are. This can lead you to feel isolated and not know where you belong—the outsider always yearning to get in, but afraid to take the risk of being seen and rejected in order to find those who would applaud, appreciate, and welcome you.

As a child, I completely ruined one of my own birthday parties. For reasons I cannot fathom, I went and hid under a bush in the backyard and cried instead of attending my own party. I felt lonely and rejected and like no one loved me, even though there was my favorite cake made by my grandmother, and friends with presents, and pin-the-tail-on-the-donkey, and it was a beautiful day. Talk about a backward way to feel "special"! If you are in this boat, can you ask yourself where the real you is and gently coax yourself to come out a little bit at a time? It's likely you went through such harsh rejection that you now overprotect yourself. And who can blame you? But this level of defense keeps you from offering your true self and finding your niche in the world.

External Challenges (Doing)

When you begin to get connected to your Artist/Individualist purpose, various obstacles are likely to arise in the external world to challenge you and help you develop strength in your ability to show up. Remember, your Artist purpose doesn't guarantee creative self-expression. You have to work as skillfully as you are able with the times, the circumstances you're living in, and the people in your life, and all three are likely to confront you in many ways. Here are a few possible external challenges.

OTHERS CRITICIZE AND REJECT

Expect it. Others *will* criticize and reject and lob tomatoes at you. As if the Inner Critic and its pail of swill wasn't enough! Tomatoes are likely to fly both in your personal and your public life. As someone with the Artist purpose, who puts herself out into the public eye regularly, I understand completely that you don't want to subject yourself to it. (Can you imagine how many skeptics snort at me in outright disbelief when I present the idea that you can find your Life Purpose in your fingerprints? How many at parties have asked, in scornful disbelief, "You make a *living* doing this?") But there's no way around it. To find the applause and appreciation (and *life*) you so long for, you have to risk rejection from everyone. I had a client who is doing her creative self-expression in the spotlight through speaking (with an average audience size of three thousand—I was impressed!) and the question was how to go about offering her unique "stuff" to even *more people*. She laughed heartily, then sighed, then said, "I know I need to write a book, but I'm afraid!" She is afraid of expanding her audience, as this will mean she has little chance of controlling the response of someone reading her book when she isn't physically present to influence them. Tomato Fear in spades and, yes, more people she'll never meet *will* criticize her. Bigger audience, more tomatoes. But also, more applause and appreciation!

FINDING YOUR AUDIENCE/"WHERE DO I FIT IN?"

As you *be* yourself more and more, the beauty is that you will begin to find your "audience," the people you want in your life on all levels. The difficulty is the letting go of those already in your life who don't want you to be yourself and who pressure you to conform. "Be like us!" "What makes you think you can do something different?" "Why can't you just settle down and be normal?" "Why do you have to be so difficult/sensitive/different?" The pressure to conform can be intense. Those who are not driven to do something different may not understand that you are. Look for others who are different and living life on their own terms or moving toward it. We are out here, waiting to find you and welcome you to the Artist/Individualist tribe! Remember, you have to go through a lot of people to find the few who are meant to be part of the "audience" of your life . . . whether it's your friends, colleagues, or partner, or the public audience for your creative expression/performance. If you're not showing yourself, how do you find your "audience"? If you don't *stand out*, how do you find the place you *fit in*? Don't choose to be stuck in the "ugly duckling" role by trying to get the wrong people to applaud and appreciate you.

WORKING WITH "FEEDBACK" TO REFINE THE PRESENTATION

Now here's the tricky part. Should you reject all incoming tomatoes? No. But you must practice discernment about which tomatoes you receive and which you reject. Remember that David Copperfield, the magician, *tests* out pieces of a new act on many audiences in order to receive feedback to see if his presentations will create the effects he's after. I joke about ducking tomatoes, dodging tomatoes, but being careful not to eat them right away when they hit you in the head. When you consistently receive the same feedback about yourself or your presentation of yourself, pay attention! Are you in front of your target audience? When I speak, I pay close attention to audience feedback. Is what I'm saying making sense? Am I moving around too much and distracting them from what I'm saying? If this is the case, *I want to know*. In my personal life, if people are telling me I'm being too controlling, even though I don't want to hear it at first (*moi? control issues?*), I want to know so I can adjust accordingly. You need to be appropriately sensitive to feedback so you can discern when it's helpful to you. Unfortunately, at times people will criticize inappropriately and it will hurt. Let yourself say *"Ouch!"* Then see if there's some truth to it so you can refine your presentation. If not, then let it go the best you can. Just as you do not like everyone in the world, not everyone is going to like you. Breathe, call someone who likes you, and let it be okay. Do your best not to catch the rotten tomatoes and take them home with you.

TAKING IN THE APPLAUSE

One of the challenges of this purpose is on the other side of the fence: being open to receiving the applause, appreciation, and admiration that comes your way for being yourself, showing your paintings, singing your songs, or sharing your writing or your unique talents. Artists/Individualists don't tend to think about this challenge and many get knocked over by it. Why do you think so many celebrities drop out for a while or become alcoholics? When fame of any size comes, it can be hard to handle if you aren't prepared to take it in. In everyday life, practice saying just two words eye to eye when someone compliments you: "Thank you!" Practice taking in any and all admiration that comes your way. Notice and appreciate it, as well as those who offer it. Practice appreciating and thanking others and notice how you feel if they can't take it in. Practice *not* deflecting appreciation in any way, just take a deep breath, smile, and say, "Thank you!" If you are headed for being on a stage, imagine being in front of thousands of roaring, applauding people while they give you a standing ovation, and keeping your feet on the floor and enjoying what the audience is offering you in return for what you've just offered them!

Being It, Doing It, and Faking It (Attitude to Adopt)

Since the Artist purpose is the state of being you wish to live in, where life feels meaningful to you, you can ask yourself the following questions when you're working on adopting the attitude of your Life Purpose in order to more fully inhabit it and then *do it*.

When you feel like a *rejected, apathetic outsider*, ask:

- How do I *feel* when I am comfortable with myself? Can I stop and step into that version of me?

- Am I being *my true self* so others can actually see me?

- Am I trying to get the wrong people to appreciate me (be my audience) by doing the wrong things and compromising myself?

- When others offer me feedback, do I get defensive? Can I take a deep breath and try to be open enough to consider whether the feedback is useful or not?

- If I am already doing creative self-expression, can I expand my audience?

   "I know who I am and I show up as myself, come criticism or applause!"

Practical Everyday Expression/Steps

To build up your creative self-expression, you must *practice* the actions that create Individuality!

- *Cultivate your creativity.* It doesn't matter what you do for starters. Just take up some form of overt creativity or self-expression—writing, singing, drawing, painting, acting, or speaking in front of people (Toastmasters is great for this). Ideally, get involved with a group of people who are doing something creative, both for support and a safe, encouraging audience. Please do not take up "painting by numbers." You want to do something that gives you a chance to actually express yourself, rather than simply following along. If you *do* decide to cross-stitch, make up your own patterns, be willing to experiment, and be patient with learning how your materials work, including the "material" of your body, whether you are learning how to hold a paint brush or how to use your vocal chords. Then stick to it. Don't ditch as soon as your Inner Critic or tomatoes show up. Expect them and keep at your self-expressive pursuit. It isn't about being "perfect." It's about expressing yourself.

• *Show up!* Practice being visible, literally and figuratively. Wear something that feels a little "outrageous" or unique and attractive. Take a chance at being seen as "different." Be prepared to thank people when they compliment you (do not say, "This old rag . . . ?") and to take a deep breath if they don't like your style. Offer your opinion or thoughts about things. Notice the world around you. Compliment others for their uniqueness and willingness to show up rather than to disappear. Be mindful that you need to be the center of attention (even as you may well fear it) an appropriate amount of time . . . and then yield the "spotlight" appropriately to others. Catch yourself trying to capture attention inappropriately at times. If you were one of those who constantly raised your hand and wiggled in your chair to try and get the teacher to call on you, rein yourself in a bit. If you're one of those always trying to fade into the wallpaper, challenge yourself to step out and express yourself. Keep paying attention to how you show up or hide out everywhere you go in your life.

• *"Your opinion of me is none of my business!"* Cultivate an appropriate stance regarding others' opinions of you and who you are or what you should do. Remember that this declaration is *not* about developing a cavalier attitude ("I just ran over you with my car and your opinion of me is none of my business!") or about ignoring repeated feedback that comes your way; it's about remembering that all you have to do is be yourself and, as long as you're not being obnoxious or violating others, it's okay that not everyone is going to like you or your creative output. It's just fine. Just as you don't like everyone else in the world, not everyone is meant to be a part of the "audience" of your life (or your literal audience when you put your creative expression out in the world). When you are yourself, the audience can decide if you're what they're looking for or not . . . there's a connection or there isn't, and that's okay. "Different strokes for different folks" and "it takes all kinds to make the world go round" are both clichés because they're true.

Positive Feelings Associated with This Life Purpose

- Unique/different/special

- Seen and appreciated

- Open and unselfconscious

- Comfortable with self

"I show up!"

Questions to Ask Yourself

- What do I *show*?

- How do I *hide* and when?

- What do I *create*?

- How am I *unique*?

- What do I want to be known for?

- Who are the unsupportive tomato throwers in my life? Who are my accurate mirrors who help me refine my presentation of myself?

- Can I be myself everywhere I go?

- When am I most afraid of what others will think of me?

- When do I try to be the pleaser so others will like me, rather than just being myself?

- Do I really stop and see the world around me? The people around me?

- When someone appreciates me, can I take it in? Or do I try and deflect it?

- What can I do to *practice* being myself and letting it show?

- Am I a round peg trying to fit into a square hole?

- When do I engage in negative behaviors to get attention?

INNOVATOR

(Left Ring/Apollo Life Purpose)

Keywords: Invention/Discovery   "Maverick"
                 Fresh Perspective   Converting the Skeptics
                 Out-of-the-Box

As the Innovator, you are here to be absolutely true to yourself in the face of possible or actual fierce pressure from those close to you to shut up, sit down, and fit in—or face their harsh rejection. You have the potential to be involved with the new and the progressive, if not to be the one who actually brings outright innovation (patents or intellectual property rights pending) into the world. Innovators are here to be the boat rockers, the convention busters, the mavericks, the ones who bring or participate in positive change. They are the pace- and trendsetters, who want to be involved with things moving forward and making progress. Innovators want to improve their lives, the lives of others, and the world around them, rather than keeping their heads down and going along with the status quo, thus perpetuating customary ways of doing things.

Key to living this Life Purpose is engaging in the entire process of knowing who you really are inside, then withstanding the pressure from your *inner circle*, those closest to you (family, friends, co-workers, your boss, etc.), to not stand up and be yourself. At a basic level, when you are staunchly true to yourself, despite everyone pulling on you to do what they want that isn't aligned with yourself, you are inhabiting your Innovator purpose. To be the Innovator requires a willingness to potentially be seen as a misfit or an eccentric by your peers, until it becomes evident that what works for you is *what works for you*, even if it doesn't work for them. Innovators tend not to want to be doing what everyone else is doing, or at least not in the same way. They are attracted to the unusual and the cutting edge, and they prefer ways of doing and thinking about things that are brand spanking new in their world and not mainstream (even if it's by becoming a Buddhist—a very ancient spiritual tradition in the East, but whose practice is still relatively quite new and "marginal" in the West—after growing up in, say, the family tradition of Catholicism).

To be the Innovator, you naturally want to question the status quo, especially when it requires you to compromise yourself. This is so you can evaluate whether conforming to that compromise crosses the line over into feeling like you are prostituting yourself. Now, please understand that my use of this word is not necessarily about selling your body for money (though that is a definite possibility for some), but it's about giving up on something that is of essential importance to you in order to gain something in return (what I call an "ill-gotten" gain). It's about the idea of selling your soul, about doing something that goes against your nature in order to profit in some way that has to do with you avoiding rejection or garnering approval or making money.

In the popular movie *My Big Fat Greek Wedding*, Toula is the old-maid daughter of a Greek family. She toes the family line and is resigned to putting up with constant ridicule for not being married, showing no interest in marriage (of course, only permissible to a *Greek* man), and for being ugly. She is so prostituted out for her family's approval (and so caught up in resisting the total sellout of marrying who they might choose for her) that Toula is deflated and has no idea of who she is at the age of thirty. She is avoiding her parents' censure at a high price—by hiding inside herself and buying in to the idea that she will never be attractive or happy. No matter which way she moves, it seems the family's got her sewn up. She still lives with her parents and has no self-definition whatsoever. Like most innovators, Toula has to make a *break* with her family (literally, or in thinking and action) in order to define herself. Through a series of events, she is spurred to make that break and finally takes her life into her own hands. But to do this she first maneuvers her strict, traditional father (through her mother and aunt) and tiptoes around to take a night class and date the (ohmygosh! *non-Greek!*) man she's attracted to. Eventually, however, she's discovered and has to openly face her father's censure to marry her man and live her own life on her own terms. Toula wants to progress out of her family's traditional life model and has to risk their rejection to do so.

This is a classic story of the Innovator. Once you decide that hiding out and prostituting yourself is no longer an acceptable way to live your life, it's time to *face the critics*, and if it's possible, *convert them* to your way of thinking or doing things, which also means it's a good idea to stop and evaluate whether they are convertible. If not, then it's important to limit your exposure to the critics or to make your exit as fast and as gracefully as you can and go in search of those who are interested in your innovative self and/ or your outright innovations. Most who bring something new to the world, or who involve themselves in progress are faced with this. The world tends to keep rolling along with the idea of "if it ain't broke, don't fix it!" and you, the Innovator, come along with your gosh-darned, completely *crazy* ideas! And the rest of us are nervous about changing and losing our sense of security or whatever it is we're getting out of the status quo (sometimes money). We first put you down, doubt you, make fun of you, and threaten to reject you, or outright reject you for a while. We need some convincing until we can see how what you've got can benefit us. And it's your job, as an Innovator, to convince us. Even then we are likely to resist some more.

To be the Innovator, you must gain experience in just how far you will go in compromising yourself in order to be accepted by your personal "crowd." This is important, because those who are meant to bring an actual innovation into the world have to be able to endure the flack heaped on them from colleagues and anyone in a position to approve or disapprove of them. Innovators must be willing to drop out of the "popularity contest" of life. They have to stick to themselves when no one else will until the rest of us come around. In the movie *Billy Elliot*, Billy's father just can't accept that his son wants to take ballet classes with the girls instead of the usual society-sanctioned boxing classes with the boys. Billy persists, secretly, and when his father finds out, things explode (Dad is under a lot of heavy pressures due to the miner's strike and misses his wife who has died). Eventually, Dad comes around, sees who Billy really is, and realizes he wants Billy to have a chance to live a life outside of the dangerous coal mines where he and Billy's older brother are stuck. Dad himself faces his own moment of reckoning around whom to be true to: Does he compromise himself painfully and be shunned by his peers and his eldest miner son—by crossing the picket line and returning to the mines to make money again—in order to give Billy that chance? Or does he remain on strike? Talk about everyone catching flack on the way to possible acceptance or ultimate rejection!

People who pursue the deeply meaningful life of innovation come to a deep acceptance of themselves, which, over time, gives them a chance at commanding acceptance from others. (Unfortunately, like most things in life, there are no guarantees.) Remember that Innovators are the most likely to be "before their time" and the rest of us are playing catch-up. One of the clearest Innovator stories from start to finish is told in the ever-popular Christmas show, *Rudolph the Red-Nosed Reindeer*. When Rudolph is born, his father is mortified that his son has a bright red nose and hides Rudolph's defining characteristic as long as possible—and Rudolph hates it. He becomes very popular with his peers as he grows up . . . until his nose—his true self—is exposed. Rudolph is embarrassed, then ridiculed and shunned by almost everyone he and his family knows, even Santa Claus. As Rudolph, an outcast, wanders around he befriends another lonely misfit refusing to cave to peer pressure, the elf Hermey, who wants to be a dentist (to all the other elves' chagrin), and the two decide to leave home (they make their break) to find where they belong. On their journey they meet other "misfits" along the way, join forces with them, and discover what their personal innovations are useful for. Hermey pulls the teeth of the Abominable Snowman to save their lives, the misfit toys can be given away to adoring children by Santa, Rudolph's lightbulb nose cuts the fog that endangers the delivery of toys in time for Christmas, Hermey can attend to everyone's dental needs, and the Abominable Snowman's size is good for topping the holiday trees with decorative stars. All of these outsiders ultimately find their place by filling a niche for something others didn't realize they needed. They are all groundbreakers in their own right and finally are accepted for being so very different.

I happened to watch the movie *Dreamgirls* a couple of nights ago and found it an exquisite example of the slippery line between prostitution and breaking ground. In this story, the main character, Curtis, sees how he can reposition his stable of R&B and soul musical artists to be accepted into the larger and much more lucrative white pop market. The trouble is, it requires shady payola dealings to beat the big record labels at their own game. But the true devastation occurs as he convinces his artists to morph themselves into what will be accepted by white society, requiring them to betray their true artistic souls. Those who agree and conform to Curtis's requirements and society's preferences make a lot of money, but feel bad about themselves. Effie, the character who refuses (after already giving up her position as the talented lead singer of her group to her more conventionally "pretty" lighter-skinned, less-gospel-sounding groupmate), is shunned by the group as a troublemaker—and truly suffers the consequences. This story is an excellent study in how far people will go in bending themselves out of shape before they just can't live with themselves, and summon the courage to walk away and start over as an "outsider" on their own terms. The story presents the type of difficult decisions everyday life is littered with: do I sell out now to gain ground and can I readjust later? Curtis, the manager, *is* considered a mover and shaker by the world, but the recording artists are personally damaged by the constant compromise, and they abandon him one by one. As an Innovator, you are challenged to keep an eye on the slippery slope of compromise.

When you as the Innovator consciously begin to learn and engage in the process of self-acceptance, and staying true to self and "craft," life may not always be easy, given that you are built to be a maverick. But when you know what's true for you or invent something new and stick to it, this is the place where your life becomes meaningful and worth waking up for in the morning. Eventually others are likely to honor you and come around . . . whether it's within your lifetime or not.

If you are an Innovator, your deepest fulfillment arises from living life completely on your own terms and being deeply comfortable with it in the face of real or possible rejection. You are not willing to bend yourself too far out of shape to avoid rejection or to gain praise. You know what's best for you and stand by it—you live life in a way that is progressive for you, breaking with tradition where it makes sense and bringing a new way to approaching things into your life and into the world. You may want to invent something new and offer it to others, or you may simply be content with living your own life on the cutting edge as defined by the dictates of your own inner system.

Challenges

Just because you are an Innovator doesn't mean it's always easy to inhabit your purpose all the time and in all circumstances. You are here to grow into your being and what it requires you to do. Two types of challenges help you gain the broad experience you need in order to live this Life Purpose.

Internal Challenges (Being)

These are some of the challenges you have within yourself, the negative beliefs you may hold about yourself and about Innovation, which need to be brought to consciousness and worked with so you can do what is necessary to become absolutely true to yourself.

OVERLY CRITICAL OF SELF

Those with this purpose tend to be just the teeniest bit overly self-critical. You can give yourself a very hard time about being yourself. This is all about that Inner Critic thing again (mentioned in the Artist/Individualist section), only the Innovators can have a much more extreme case of self-rejection. We actually learn the phrase *"paralyzing* fear of rejection" in association with this purpose. That is, you feel you can't move in any direction because there's likely to be some form of rejection no matter which way you go. So you immobilize yourself, criticize yourself, and shrink down into conformity. It's like you're living your life holding your breath—afraid to make any waves at all. Ask yourself what would happen if you practiced self-acceptance instead of self-denigration? What might happen? Would the sky really fall down? Would some aspect of your life have to change that's hard to let go of?

"I JUST WANT TO FIT IN"

If you are fiercely negative with yourself, it is understandable you might feel like all you want to do is fit in. If you have been subjected to criticism from people close to you, or you're afraid of the possible rejection of those close to you, it makes sense that you might just want to keep your head down. In fact, if this is how you got through a difficult childhood, it's even worked in a positive way for you. Or, let's say you had a perfectly loving family, but now you want to go do something really different and are afraid they won't understand. Or you're afraid you'll have to leave people you really care about behind in order to be yourself or to pursue your innovation. I have a friend with this purpose who always says, "I'm just an *average* guy and I *like* being *average*." What's funny is he hardly leads an average life at all, and when I point this out he gets a funny little grin on his face and then we both bust out laughing. Remember that you may or may not need to literally leave people behind when you embark on living your true-to-you life, and you will find other people along the way who want to be supportive of you as you walk your own path. This friend of mine forced himself to live an "average" life for many years, until he felt like he just couldn't get up in the morning and do it anymore. He was so apathetic and depressed that he wasn't sure he could go on living. His true self wanted to emerge and he had to make some painful decisions, but his life went on strike until he decided to own himself.

"EVERYTHING FEELS LIKE A COMPROMISE"

For some with this purpose, it feels like everything entails too much compromise. If you constantly find yourself asking (out loud or to yourself), "You want me to do what?!" take a moment to stop and consider if there is a practical reason for the request being made of you before jumping to a critical decision about it. I knew someone with this purpose who just couldn't stand stopping at red lights. He repeatedly ran them after making a semi-stop to make sure there was no cross-traffic coming. He even did this once *right next to a police car waiting at the red light.* Despite many tickets and many trips to traffic court, he felt that having to wait at a red light when there was no cross-traffic forced him to compromise himself in an inappropriate way. It is natural with this purpose that your Compromise Geiger Counter is tuned too high or too low. If yours is too high, please consider focusing on what is practical so you don't set yourself up to be a social pariah (and therefore prove to yourself in a backward way what a maverick you are). Apply all that wonderful out-of-the box energy appropriately to doing something that is actually innovative.

"I'M DAMNED IF I DO AND DAMNED IF I DON'T"/THE DOUBLE BIND

One of the ways you can tell if you're in a compromised position is to take a look at where you feel "damned if you do and damned if you don't" in your life. Let's say (just for *fun*) that your spouse is cheating on you, you've found out, and he or she doesn't want you to leave (but doesn't want to stop having the affair either). If you leave, you lose your marriage and will become a divorced person (let's say this is totally against your plans, as you swore to yourself you'd never be a divorced person), and if you stay, you are married to a person who is dating someone else (and this in no way was part of what you wanted for yourself either). This is a stereotypical situation more people find themselves in than any of us would like to admit. Either way you go, it feels like there's serious compromise. It becomes a question of which one is really better for *you*. Which one brings you in line with what you truly want for yourself? Toula in *My Big Fat Greek Wedding* is similarly faced with this setup of compromise and rejection at every turn: if she prettifies or "improves" herself, her family will try to marry her off; if she stays frumpy, they will continue to ridicule her for being an "old maid." When you "can't win for losing," it's time to take a good look and cut your losses by discerning *where you are* in all this, then stepping up to it and facing the criticism. You need to step out and do what's best for *you*.

External Challenges (Doing)

When you begin to engage your Innovator purpose, various obstacles are likely to arise in the external world to challenge you and help you develop strength in your ability to innovate. Remember your Innovator purpose doesn't automatically guarantee your ability to be true to yourself. You have to work as skillfully as you are able with the times, the circumstances you're living in, and the people in your life, and all three are likely to confront you in many ways. Here are a few possible external challenges.

OVERLY CRITICAL OF OTHERS

You may find yourself being overly critical of the way others live in order to justify and bolster your own choices, whether you are being true to yourself or conforming to others' expectations. Watch out! Asking others to conform to *your way* is not the perfect antidote to being criticized by others. You will be doing to others what you hate having done to you. Can you go ahead and live your life in the way that best suits you and relax into a wider acceptance that allows others to live theirs?

"I GOTTA BE DIFFERENT . . . JUST TO BE DIFFERENT"

Some exhibit their Innovator purpose in an interesting way: they can't stand any restraints or limitations whatsoever and see anything and everything asked of them as a severe compromise. If you ask them to sit down with you, they will insist on standing up. If you ask them to show up on time, they will surely be late. Is this you? If so, you construe complying with *anything* expected of you as a request to sell out somehow. As an Innovator, you need to be true to yourself, but does it make sense to define yourself by being a contrarian, even when it doesn't make any sense? What's tricky about this is, rather than defining who you really are, you are mistakenly defining yourself *against* others . . . in *reaction* to them, and this will keep you from finding your true self. You are defining yourself by being automatically untrue to others' expectations, which is not the same as being true to your own. In a strange way, you're still allowing others to define you and likely "cutting off your nose to spite your face" in the process.

MAKING A BREAK

As you get clearer about what constitutes your life, you may find that you need to make a literal or figurative "break" with people who are close to you and who have played very important roles in your life (parents, siblings, your work group, friends, etc.). A figurative break could look something like breaking with a family tradition or way of thinking—choosing not to follow in a parent's footsteps into the family business, line of work, or religion, even if you don't literally leave your family behind you. Or it could mean making a mental break in your way of thinking about something expected of you, like a woman who decides she doesn't want to have children, even if her parents or in-laws want her to provide them with grandchildren. For those of you who are unable to define yourselves as long as you remain in someone's circle (perhaps because you can't hear yourself think when near this person or group, or because the person will not stop rejecting you, ridiculing you, or requiring you to prostitute yourself), a literal break may be necessary, whether it's temporary or permanent.

CONVERTING THE SKEPTICS

When you are actually engaged with your innovative self, there will be skeptics around. The skeptics are a sign that you're on track! Most innovative inventors have had to face high levels of skepticism. Timothy J. Berners-Lee developed a program to help him keep track of which researchers were using which computers in the physics lab he was working in. After connecting the computers in the lab, he was easily able to extend out to five thousand researchers' computers and beyond. The World Wide Web was born. "Until the Web made its debut in 1991, though, most people had a tough time grasping the need for such connectivity. Even Cern management was skeptical [Cern was the lab *using* Berners-Lee's innovation successfully]. 'Today,' muses Berners-Lee, 'what's hard to explain is why the concept ever seemed abstruse'" (Otis Port, "Timothy J. Berners-Lee: Spinning The World's Web," *Businessweek*, November 8, 2004).

Frederick Smith is quite famous in the business world for the original rejection of his innovative idea—an integrated overnight delivery transportation system. Smith wrote a term paper outlining the changing technological world and the need for a publicly accessible overnight delivery service. His professors passed him—with a low grade—they didn't think it was such a hot idea. After percolating on the issue during his time serving in the Vietnam War, Smith took a $4 million inheritance he'd received and raised $91 million more capital and started Federal Express (FedEx). Talk about hanging in there with being true to yourself! Though the business took time to get going (it was *not* an overnight success—pun intended—as U.S. postal regulations stood in the way), Smith persisted despite all the skeptics, and we all know how successful and well-used FedEx is today. Who's skeptical now? There are so many wonderful stories of innovative inventors. Some succeeded in their lifetimes, and others came up with inventions that were so ahead of their time that ways of thinking, cultural belief systems, and even physical technology had to catch up with them. (Leonardo DaVinci's inventions on paper—including flying machines—are an exceptional example of this.)

Being It, Doing It, and Faking It (Attitude to Adopt)

Since Innovation is the state of being you wish to live in, where life feels meaningful to you, you can ask yourself the following questions when you're working on adopting the attitude of your Life Purpose in order to more fully inhabit it and then *do it*.

When you feel like you're *compromising/prostituting* yourself, ask:

- What does it mean to be true to myself right now? Can I step into the version of myself who won't compromise inappropriately?

- Who am I trying to please? Whose disapproval am I trying to avoid? How do I feel when I approve of myself—apart from what others may think?

- Am I living my real life in secret? How can I arrange things to live my life openly? Do I need to make a "break" to do so?

- Do I try to make others *please me* inappropriately? Can I let it be okay for others to just be themselves and do what works for them?

- Can I find a way to enjoy being a "misfit" and find my own niche in life?

"I live no one's life but my own."

Practical Everyday Expression/Steps

To build up your ability to be true to yourself and your life, you must *practice* the actions that create Innovation!

- *Notice what you are attracted to.* Do you find yourself attracted to the "strange" and different? New ideas, progressive causes, pacesetters, trendsetters, and mavericks? Alternative healing, the latest technological gizmos, Montessori or homeschooling for the kids, embracing spirituality when your family is atheist? Notice what and whom you are attracted to, and find a way to engage your Innovator purpose by getting involved with that thing or person, signing up to learn how to do something cutting-edge, or setting yourself up to innovate something yourself!

- *Catch yourself selling out.* And clean up *your* act. Your mother wants to run your wedding with no regard for how you and your fiancé want to get married. Your boss asks you to cut corners on the construction job to make more money and offers you a "bonus." You get a phone call from a magazine asking you to analyze a famous rock star's thumb print (without the other nine fingerprints), and are told that all you have to do is say something positive about it and your name will go out to many thousands of people. What do you do? Catch yourself being tempted to resign yourself in the face of mom's disapproval, the boss firing you, or losing the unexpected exposure you'd like for your business, and say no if you can. (Yes, this happened to me a few years ago—I thanked the editor and suggested that he could just as easily write it himself and put his own name on it.) It's not easy, but whose life are you living anyway? At the end of the day, you have to be able to live with yourself.

- *Practice suspending knee-jerk criticism.* Internal criticism is one of the bugaboos of being human. A big part of one of the world's foremost religions (Buddhism) focuses on learning how to suspend knee-jerk human criticism so we can stop and see who *we really are inside* and who others really are around us—rather than being jammed up with assumptions based on our snap judgments and being untrue to ourselves and others. It's not about dropping all critical ability and being naïve or clueless, but about cultivating a broader accepting awareness, starting with yourself. If you practice suspending your criticism (even *after* you've caught yourself criticizing), you can start to see just who's in there begging for your own attention. You can even go so far as to practice being *appreciative* of yourself—often a radical notion for those starting out with this purpose. For example: I'm nearing six hours straight of writing this chapter today, and I'm getting just a tad stir-crazy. I've got one voice in my head saying, "What's wrong with you that it's taking so long? Hurry up already! I'm tired and want to relax! My back hurts, my neck hurts, my knees hurt, everything feels awful! If you were a better something-or-other, it wouldn't be taking this long!" Yes, this is the Inner Critic run amok. If I just listen to this, it makes it very hard to be true to writing what I have to say. Soooooo, I catch myself being harshly critical of me, and say gently to myself, "I know it's been a long day, and it won't be over until this chapter is, but I promise you we'll take a long, hot bath with nice-smelling soap and bubbles when it's all over. Of course this is hard, and we'll take a nice vacation too, after deadline. And remember, we've got the wonderful opportunity to write a book here, let's remember how fortunate we are" . . . etc., etc., etc. On the outwardly critical side—sometimes I end up embarrassed when I'm in my car and the driver in front of me stops for no apparent reason and I assume it must be an idiot trying to answer a cell phone or otherwise trying to inconsiderately *get in my way*. I'm itchy and want to honk my horn and yell, and I feel so compromised by waiting. But I manage to resist embarrassing myself out loud and then they *finally* move—and it turns out the driver was waiting for a guy in a wheelchair crossing the street.

Positive Feelings Associated with This Life Purpose

• Inventive/creative

• Okay with being different

• Unconventional

• Free to be yourself

"I'm unconventional and unwilling to give up my essential self for approval."

Questions to Ask Yourself

• Am I thinking out of the box?

• Who do I try too hard to please?

• How am I compromising myself or selling my soul in order to gain something from others? To avoid criticism?

• When am I overly critical of myself? How can I temper myself? At times am I undercritical of myself? (Do I let myself off the hook?)

• How well do I manage to compromise when appropriate, and do I know when compromise is going too far?

• Are there places in my life where I feel "damned if I do, and damned if I don't"? Can I stop and recognize the double binds in my life?

• Can I persist in spite of the skeptics?

- Am I willing to convince others regarding my innovations? Who are the skeptics to convert? Can I present my innovation to those who are most interested in adopting it, let their numbers grow, and let them exert influence on those who take much longer to change their minds?

- How can I recognize those who simply will not be converted and not waste my time and energy on them?

- Can I recognize when I am being overcritical of others and temper myself? Are there specific people I am especially critical of? Are there those I am undercritical of, who I "let off the hook" too easily?

Pinkie Finger: Communications

(MYTHICAL ARCHETYPE: MERCURY/HERMES)

Delivering a Message/"Translation"

Listening Skills

Inner Communications

Self-Awareness (Interface of Inner/Outer Communications)

Insight/Intuition/Clear Perception

Inspiration

Concept of Self

"Manipulation" (Diplomacy, Magic, Strategizing, Brainstorming, Negotiations)

Cleverness/Wit/Mental Sharpness

Language shapes consciousness, and the use of language to shape consciousness is an important branch of magic.

STARHAWK, *Dreaming the Dark*

Courage is what it takes to stand up and speak; courage is also what it takes to sit down and listen.

WINSTON CHURCHILL

If you can't explain something, you don't really understand it.

HAL HARVEY

The only real truth is the truth we discover for ourselves.

IRVIN YALOM, "Double Exposure" in *Momma and the Meaning of Life*

Don't waste your breath!

UNKNOWN

Pinkie Fingers Overview
(The <u>Communications</u> Life Purposes)

The pinkie fingers are named after Mercury, the god of communications. Mercury was the messenger who traveled freely among all the realms, those of the humans *and* the gods in the sky, the underworld, and at the bottom of the sea. Given that the other gods and goddesses and the humans couldn't travel freely among the realms, Mercury's position as the cosmic courier seemed magic and clever. Because he possessed a talent no one else had, only Mercury was aware of whether he transmitted messages true to the owner's original intent or somehow manipulated the messages—to positive or negative effect. The pinkie Life Purposes are all about communications, the accuracy of those communications, the relationships formed by communications, and the concept of ourselves and the world around us created through our ability to perceive and convey the "truth."

Those with one of the Mercury purposes are meant to span the worlds of inner communications and outer communications. Diving deep into yourself and listening to what your inner voice says, then communicating it in some way with the outer world, or listening very closely to someone or to the world around you, and then reflecting back by communicating about it so others can see some version of the truth for themselves is what those with these Life Purposes have as their highest potential. The building of relationships, both interpersonal (between people) and intrapersonal (within oneself) is what communicators do best. Take a moment to consider what it's like when you don't know what you think about something, or how you feel, or what you want, and how difficult it is then to relay to another what's going on inside of you. There are times when it is difficult to understand ourselves, and it is very frustrating when we are clueless about ourselves due to a breakdown in our internal communication system. It is equally exasperating when it is not possible to communicate with others and make ourselves understood. As I write this, I am working in Switzerland for the first time and have only my poor high-school German to try and convey myself with. I am extremely frustrated by my inability to converse at a basic level to connect with the people I meet working in cafés, at the grocery store, and on the street. I feel isolated and lonely, and misunderstood when I can't figure out when or how much to tip or how to simply wish someone a good day. I have a much better time when I have someone along who can translate between the two worlds of language so I can be connected, understand others, and be understood myself. If you have any doubts about how important verbal and nonverbal language is, try going through one entire day of your normal life without saying a word or gesturing in any way (hands, face, shrugging, etc.). People with a Mercury Life Purpose are the go-betweens of the world, the clever shapers of thought and language who make deeper connections possible.

A salesperson asks questions and listens closely to a potential client's answers to determine whether there is a match between the client's needs and the product or service being offered. The motivational speaker and author delivers a message that comes from a deep place of inspiration. Teachers translate complex material so students can understand it. Therapists and counselors listen closely to their clients so that the clients can hear and deepen their understanding of themselves. Magicians manipulate the physical world and their audience's perceptions to perform seeming feats. Diplomats listen to the perspectives of both sides of an issue and try to clarify and reduce distorted perceptions to promote understanding. Strategists understand cause and effect, and they can run through many possibilities to help plot the best course of action. Shamans act as a go-between for the physical and spiritual realms to help people heal themselves. Storytellers bend the truth to entertain, inform, and take people to visit emotional, mental, and imaginative landscapes.

Communicators have the potential to inspire, heal, and bring the truth to light, and they are required to mediate among various worlds. The two most obvious are the inner world of feelings, intuitions, ideas, and inspiration, and the outer world of other people. The Mercury purposes are very much about being in relationship (i.e., communicating with self and then relating to others—hence the word *relation-ship*) to promote closeness and the trust that emerge from true understanding.

MESSENGER

(Right Pinkie/Mercury Life Purpose)

Keywords: Mass/Public Communications   Speaking Up/Out

Speaker/Author/Teacher   Accurate Self-Concept (In Public

Delivering a Message   Relationships)

If you have the Messenger Life Purpose, you are here to figure out what you have to say and then broadcast it to as many people as you can inspire to listen. You have the potential of engaging in some form of *public communications*, in getting your message out to a public audience. As the Messenger, you reap meaning from connecting with people through speaking your truth about something deeply important to you and increasing your listeners' awareness and understanding about themselves, a particular topic, or the world around them. At your best, you can get up and pique others' curiosity and interest in questioning something so they want to know more about it. You can inspire others' interest in learning something new and then inform them about it. This is not to say that you should expect that everyone wants to hear what you have to say, however you want to say it, all the time. As a Messenger, you have to be willing to take in feedback from others, through *listening*, to gauge who's interested and whether or not you're getting your message across effectively. Communication, like everything else, requires practice. You have to grow your awareness of who the right people are for your message—those actually interested in hearing it—and not unthinkingly and obliviously impose your ideas on those who are indifferent to it.

Key to living this Life Purpose is your willingness to engage in the entire process of communications to discover what it is you have to say, then honing your message and positioning yourself to deliver it. At every stage, this requires *both halves* of communications: *listening* (receiving communications from yourself and the world) and *transmitting* (putting communications out in some form). And then it requires *listening* again to what comes back to you, then trying to *transmit* again, and so on. Transmit, receive, refine, repeat. In order to find and deliver your message, you need to engage in the entire feedback loop of communications. Writers often say that they figure out what they have to say by writing, then find out how to say it better by having others read it and point out the places where they don't understand what the writer is trying to get at. As a teacher and speaker, I often find out what I really have to say when I get up in front of my audiences and students and say something. What's on my mind tends to slip out unexpectedly, and I am often surprised at what I have to say that I was completely unaware of until it came out of my mouth—until I had to *articulate* it. This is a bit of a chicken-and-the-egg process. To find out what you have to say, you want to be willing to take on the practice of saying something in some form so you get it out in front of you, where you can see it and/or hear it and then shape it. It is necessary to consciously take part in communications so you can figure out—communications! You must have a dialogue with yourself in some form, then have a dialogue with the outer world in order to discover *and* refine your message. Of course, this is the stuff of everyday mundane life as well. At our best we are constantly trying to make ourselves understood by delivering messages ("I'd like a single, iced, decaf mocha with whipped cream, please!") and trying to make sure we are receiving/understanding properly ("Let me make sure I understand, did you say you wanted a single, iced, decaf mocha with whipped cream?"). To connect with others, we must practice both speaking up and listening.

To be the Messenger, you must practice communicating with other people. Once you are ready to embark consciously on this path, the quickest way to stepping into your purpose is to pay attention to what you are transmitting and what you are receiving every day. Practice focusing on your communications with everyone around you, both in how you speak up and how well you listen. Do you speak your truth? Can you speak up even when you are afraid of being misunderstood? Do you say what's really on your mind or do you notice yourself (or others) blathering away vacuously? Are you aware of the people you're talking to? Are they interested in hearing what you are saying? Paying attention to your communications with others is highly instructive, and it expands your consciousness quickly. It is truly eye-opening (if a bit painful), and it affords you the opportunity to improve your communications with others to create higher levels of understanding and closer connection.

I recently had a music-teacher client with this purpose who, for several years now, has been teaching the programs a colleague devises. When my client came for her session, it was, in part, because she was in the process of deciding whether or not to look for another position where she could teach her own curriculum (i.e., deliver her own message). She has a very strong sense of what she wants to convey to her students, and that message is something she already clearly expresses to their parents. She emphatically reported something along the lines of, "Look, I don't care how *well* the kids learn how to play music, since it isn't what most of them are going to do with themselves for the rest of their lives. My emphasis is on helping them discover themselves and gain confidence in expressing themselves through the playing of music. *This* is something they can take into the rest of their lives." When she told me this, I could easily hear that she has developed a strong message she's absolutely ready to deliver. And she knows how to do it since she's been teaching for many years. At our last session together, she had just interviewed for a position she'd been strongly recommended for where she would own the whole show, she would be *the* music teacher for the school, and she was weighing whether the position would give her the freedom to deliver *her* message.

When I get clients with this purpose, they often are already involved in some type of communications as part of their work. I've had quite a few life coaches who are doing corporate training, and at first they liked it, but now the meaning is draining out a little bit at a time every day. It is so easy to see that they are getting to the point where they've practiced communications and developed their own voice, and now it's time to find their own message, take what they've learned, and write their own materials, or a book, or create their own speaking programs or trainings and do them. It's time to deliver *their own* message instead of spreading someone else's.

People who deliver a message have to go through the process of finding their own message, developing their own voice, and deciding what form the message wants to take, and then delivering it. There are various ways you can look around for what your message might be about, and they all have to do with engaging in some form of communications with yourself. One of the exercises I find most useful is to ask my clients to take a look at what they are preoccupied with, especially, "What books do you read?" "If you could keep only five to ten books, which ones would they be?" "What are those books about, and is there a theme they have in common?" (Often my clients say, "Oh! Duh!") Another way to find your message is to do some journal writing so you can see, over time, what's on your mind. You can also go ahead and do something that gives you the opportunity to speak in front of other people so you can start practicing. Can you volunteer to run the staff meeting at work, be the one to give a toast, get involved with a speaker's group? How can you take on the challenge of speaking up more so you can keep refining your communications skills? If you stop and think about it for a moment, any time you are delivering a message you are "selling" something—trying to get others to understand what you have to say, to persuade others to accept your ideas. In a way, outer communication is constantly about persuading people to see things the way you see them, to understand the "truth" as you see it.

But, as with all the purposes, there is a fine line to walk with this. One of the errors Messengers make is to think they are the only ones who know the capital-T Truth, then go about *telling* others that this is the *only* Truth and ignoring the fact that humans don't like to be *told* what to do or how to do it. ("Let me tell you what you should . . .") As a Messenger, you can feel like no one wants to hear what you have to say. In short, many Messengers have not learned the fine art of persuasion, and they don't understand when people are unable or unwilling to see their point of view. These Messengers are missing out on *listening*, so they don't take in feedback from others and the world in order to learn how to deliver their message. They don't realize that their way of seeing things is *not* the only way and that we all need to be *persuaded* to see another view of things. And we will not be swayed if we do not feel heard, understood, and have our perspective considered. It's just human nature. People don't want to be told what to do. We want to think for ourselves (which is why most of us will reject perfectly good advice if we didn't ask for it). Good "sales" people, and trained counselors, know this very well and are taught to listen to and validate others' perspectives before presenting their view of the truth. If you are a Messenger and find that other people in your life don't seem to want to hear what you have to say, stop and notice whether or not *you* are open to what others are saying . . . even when you don't like it and especially when you're getting the same feedback from multiple people (don't stubbornly persist that *everyone else is wrong but me*). Good Messengers open a dialogue that has room for many perspectives and openly welcome them in the service of expanded awareness.

When you as the Messenger consciously begin to learn and engage in the full process of outer communications, you find your voice and message by practicing speaking up, and you learn how to deliver what you have to say by listening to the world and the people in it. This broadens your understanding of "life, the universe, and everything" and how to communicate with it all. Your awareness expands, and your view of yourself and how the world works becomes more accurate (more truthful) due to paying attention to others' reactions to you and yours to them. As you grow, the number of people you regularly communicate with, and the horizon of your awareness, widen exponentially and you open up to the world we all live in.

If you are a Messenger, your deepest fulfillment ultimately arises from connecting to and inspiring many people at one time. If you are a teacher or trainer, you have groups of students; if you are a motivational speaker or singer, you have audiences; if you are a writer, you've got readers. You thrive on speaking your truth in order to inform and persuade others. You contribute to enlarging others' understanding by helping to expand your listeners' awareness of themselves and offering your view on one of the many inner and outer worlds we inhabit.

Challenges

Just because you are a Messenger doesn't mean it's always easy to inhabit your purpose all the time and in all circumstances. You are here to grow into your being and what it requires you to do. Two types of challenges help you gain the broad experience you need in order to live the Messenger Life Purpose.

Internal Challenges (Being)

These are some of the challenges you have within yourself, the negative beliefs you may hold about yourself and about public communications, which need to be brought to consciousness and worked with so you can do what is necessary to become an excellent Messenger.

"NO ONE WANTS TO HEAR WHAT I HAVE TO SAY"

Many with this purpose felt like they weren't heard or listened to as children (and they often weren't), so they gave up. "Children are to be seen and not heard." Once you're grown up, it's time to try again. How do you know if anyone wants to hear you if you don't speak up? If it turns out that people in your life truly don't listen to you, it may be important for you to point this out to them. If they still don't hear you, then you need to go find those who will listen. On your end, make sure you're saying things worth listening to and not just chattering away emptily. Make sure you also *listen* to others so they will want to listen to you.

INACCURATE CONCEPT OF SELF

Most with this purpose go through the painful process of gaining an accurate concept of themselves, which means having a grossly inaccurate one to begin with (we use the more pointed word *clueless* to describe this condition). There is the funniest version of this told in Elizabeth Gilbert's book, *Eat, Pray, Love*. While living in an Ashram, Gilbert decides that she is always talking too much and that she needs to try being totally silent for a while to work with this. She has a fantasy of being called "That Quiet Girl," and being admired for being mysterious and pious by everyone in the Ashram. As soon as our extroverted narrator decides this, she gets called to the office where Ashram visitors receive their service assignments and is taken off floor-scrubbing in order to become the *social greeter* for several upcoming retreats where the visiting meditators will be in total silence for a week. She will be the welcome wagon, the one to help them when they need help, and she will be the only person the participants can talk to if they are having a problem. She is informed that this position is called "Little Suzy Cream Cheese" due to the necessity of its holder to be "all bubbly and smiling all the time." Gilbert laughs at the irony of this and surrenders to the fact that she is outgoing and that this is not a bad thing (while vowing to do better at not interrupting others when they are speaking . . . something she *does* need to work on). The inaccurate concept of self comes from being cut off in your communications . . . both on the transmitting and receiving ends. Notice that Gilbert's greeter position requires that she be communicative on both ends of the equation. And that she surrender to the truth of who she is as others see her—an extrovert—instead of hoping to get others to see her as quiet and reserved. The inaccurate concept of self can cut in many directions at once: you may think you're fat when you're thin, good at math when you aren't, poor when you're well-off, dumb when you're smart, telling the truth when you're actually lying, etc.

"I DON'T KNOW WHAT I HAVE TO SAY"

Well, if this is you, it's time to pay attention to what you are already saying, all the time, to everybody. I had a client recently who said this to me verbatim and, after our session, he sent me a *three-page single-spaced* e-mail delineating everything he has learned about himself over the years. He took the time to transmit to me actual practical strategies he's developed around communicating with very difficult people in his life. I chuckled when I received his long communiqué and mused back to him whether he might know what he has to say after all and whether there might be people in the world who might be interested in his hard-won wisdom and the communication techniques he's discovered and practiced in his own life. If you don't know what you have to say, then take some time to journal—it's an excellent way to see what you are thinking about. If you got (and took) the chance to say something to a room of a thousand people about something, what would it be? Ask friends to tell you what *they* think you have to say. Then listen.

"MY TRUTH IS THE ONLY TRUTH"

So many of us can see the various difficult states the world is in because of diverse groups of people thinking they have the only version of the Truth. You have your version of the truth, and it's important and true for you, but please be open to how other people see the truth and what others have to say about the truth as they see it. Try practicing being open enough to respond to others' views with, "You're absolutely right!" (out loud or in your own head) before presenting your view. Otherwise you will find yourself *telling* others what to do or how to think and they will not listen to you and then you will think that no one wants to hear what you have to say (a vicious cycle). In this case, what's more accurate is that no one wants to hear you *telling* them what to think or do. Try listening to others and finding a way to agree with them (or at least understand where they are coming from and *respectfully* disagree) while presenting the way you see things. Be open to coming to a mutual understanding, even if you don't come to a mutual way of seeing things. The Sufis have a wonderful story of many blind men each grasping a different part of an elephant and stubbornly proclaiming that they each know the true God. As you can imagine, they argue, none of them listens to the others, and they are all right and all wrong and all feel misunderstood. As a Messenger, you want to expand your awareness about the many perspectives there are on any given thing and then be able to acknowledge the validity of those perspectives while adding your own.

External Challenges (Doing)

When you begin to get connected to yourself and others, various obstacles are likely to arise in the external world to challenge you and help you develop strength in your ability to communicate. Remember that your Messenger purpose does not guarantee that you will deliver a message to many. You have to work as skillfully as you are able with the times, the circumstances you're living in, and the people in your life, and all three are likely to confront you in many ways. Here are a few possible external challenges.

INDISCRETION

This refers to not knowing *whom* to tell what to and telling the wrong people what you have to say. Gossip is one good example of this. With this purpose, you want to have something to say and to say it, but what about when you find yourself divulging personal information entrusted to you by someone else? I once heard gossip defined as "anything you wouldn't say in front of the person being talked about" and have found it a handy guide ever since. Indiscretion in this context is about discerning *who* you relay your message to. Who is the proper target for your message? If you are upset with your spouse, but find yourself telling your best friend all about it (but not your spouse), then you are talking to the wrong person. You can also be indiscreet in the way you deliver your message—as in tactless. "I'm telling you what I think of you for your own good." Or perhaps you tell other people how they should do their job. Watch out as this is terribly insulting, especially when you don't really know anything about where others are coming from or what things look like from where they are sitting (lack of awareness on your part). Divulging personal details of your own life to the wrong people could also be a form of indiscretion.

"I'M SPEAKING UP BUT NOT BEING UNDERSTOOD/HEARD"

Are you *listening* so you can appropriately "manipulate," or shape, your communications? Are you taking the target of your communications into account? Consider this common scenario: If you speak English and you're trying to talk to someone who doesn't, raising your voice isn't going to help. Translation is needed, not volume. Think about a time when you're having a misunderstanding with someone and you keep restating what you're thinking and feeling over and over again verbatim and it isn't getting through. Oops. You probably need to say it a different way. You need "translation." Or you need to take time out if neither of you is able to listen (you're both *unreceptive*) and try again later once everyone's frustration level goes down or emotions cool off. (And then, there *are* the people who cannot and/or will not listen, and you're wasting your breath.) When I speak and teach, I find that when everyone comes in and is chattering away, there is no way I can get people to quiet down if I just try and use my voice. I end up screaming to try and be heard and sound like a shrew (and feel like one). I finally realized that I can use other things to get everyone's attention. I've used gongs, music, tapping a glass, and also standing silent at the front of the room until my audience or class becomes aware that they are missing what they came for!

WHEN TO SPEAK UP, WHEN TO SHUT UP

There is also the timing of your communications. *When* is the right time to speak up and the right time to keep your lips zipped? Do you take up too much of the conversations you have with others? Not enough? Can you "get a word in edgewise"? Can the people you talk to get heard by you? When are you "wasting your breath" on someone who just won't listen? When is the best time to bring up what you have to say? During class time or at the staff meeting? Or later on, in private? Do you interrupt others regularly? Do you allow others to finish what they have to say before responding? Do you make sure others allow you to finish what you are saying?

INAPPROPRIATE MANIPULATION

Make no mistake. Every time you communicate with others you are "manipulating" the truth. You are *arranging* what you have to say and the way you say it and deciding what to say and what not to say. This can add up to diplomacy, good negotiation skills, good "bedside manner," and the creation of illusion that is the magician's special thrilling skill. Or it can add down to lying to get what you want, whether you are concealing what you have to say or what you know (the truth) or bending it completely out of shape for your own gain. It can be difficult at times to discern when "manipulation" is helpful and when it isn't. When is it appropriate to tell your truth, or keep it to yourself, or arrange it very carefully to avoid misunderstanding? My teacher, Alana Unger, had a client with considerable manipulative possibilities and in response to Alana pointing this out, the very old German woman said proudly, "That's right! I lied to save many Jews from the Nazis during the War!" But when do you lie (outright or by omission) to people "for their own good" or because they "can't handle the truth," or to get what you want at another's expense?

Being It, Doing It, and Faking It (Attitude to Adopt)

Since the Messenger purpose is the state of being you wish to live in, where life feels meaningful to you, you can ask yourself the following questions when you're working on adopting the attitude of your Life Purpose in order to more fully inhabit it and then *do it*.

When you feel *misunderstood/unheard*, ask:

- Am I speaking up (and to the appropriate person)? What does it feel like to be understood? When do I communicate well? Can I step into this version of me and say my piece?

- Am I *listening* to others so I can understand them and so I can say things in a way that gets me understood?

- Do I listen to others so they feel understood and are then willing to listen to me? Can I practice listening without interrupting others so *I can understand them?*

- Can I practice speaking my truth appropriately?

- When do I feel like I have something to say and how does it feel to say it?

"I know what I have to say and when to speak up and when to shut up."

Practical Everyday Expression/Steps

To build up your ability to use your power in the world, you must *practice* the actions that create connected communications!

- *Mind your mouth.* Pay attention to what you are saying and how you are saying it. Listen to yourself. Practice the *who, what, where, why, when,* and *how* of communications. To whom do you communicate? What are you trying to convey? Where should you convey it? When is the best time? And how do you want to say what you have to say? (E-mail or phone or letter? Bluntly or softly? Public speaking or writing or teaching? In what words and/or gestures?) Practice not giving up (and shutting up) on communicating with others when misunderstanding happens. When someone isn't understanding what you're trying to say, take a deep breath, and try different ways of saying it.

- *Look in the "mirror" of others.* Pay attention to how all the people in your world respond to you everywhere you go, from your family members, your spouse, kids, friends, and co-workers, to the strangers you interact with on the street and in stores and cafés (or do you not interact with people you don't know?). Practice really listening to and watching how people react to you or don't. You can learn so much about yourself in such a short time from doing this, especially about how connective *you are.* You'll also start to see a consistent picture of yourself . . . both positive and not so positive (which then gives you opportunities to improve your communications). There is nothing like increasing your awareness of yourself and how you interact with the world so you can improve your interactions and your sense of connectedness on a life scale.

- *Get involved with group communications.* Put yourself in a place where you can immediately practice your one-to-many communication skills. If you choose writing as your mirror, you can join a writer's group for feedback; if you think you'd like to teach or speak, consider joining a speakers group like Toastmasters or Speaking Circles. Set yourself up to teach a small group of people how to do something you already know how to do. Studying sales communications in a group setting is also an excellent choice (as it emphasizes attentive listening, something most of us are not so good at without some conscious work). If you are a Messenger who is already involved in speaking, writing, or teaching/training, you will want to consider a couple of things: Are you delivering your own message yet? Are you delivering someone else's message or materials verbatim? It tickles me when I get a client with this purpose who is already employed in such a way, but who is beginning to feel frustrated with delivering someone else's message because it's time to find his or her own. Is it time to write a book? Or speak? Or teach what you know so others can deliver your message and spread it?

Positive Feelings Associated with This Life Purpose

- Heard and understood

- Connected—(to others or the world)

- Inspired and inspiring

- Intelligent/sharp/quick

"I speak up!"

Questions to Ask Yourself

- What do I have to say?

- How well do I speak up for myself?

- Can I negotiate for myself?

- When do I go mute?

- When do I talk too much?

- When do I have a hard time *listening*? Can I practice listening closely to others?

- What can I choose to do to find my message? About everyday things? About what I have to say to a wider audience?

- What form do my communications want to take (speaking, teaching, writing, painting, etc.)?

- Where are my blind spots about myself? In what ways am I naïve about myself and/or the world around me? Am I willing to perceive the truth about myself and others rather than ignore incoming feedback that I don't like?

- Do I sometimes think I am the only one who knows what's best for others and try to *impose* my ideas on them?

- Can I see others' perspectives as well as my own? Can I stop and try to understand others' points of view? Can I formulate my own point of view as well and not just unquestioningly take what others say as the truth?

- Can I stop and make sure to be aware of the people I am speaking to and not just "run off at the mouth" as if the person in front of me doesn't matter as long as I have someone to talk to?

- When do I feel heard?

HEALER

(Left Pinkie/Mercury and Double Pinkie/Mercury Life Purpose)

Keywords: Inner Communications

"Intimate" One-to-One
Communications

Personal Growth/Awareness

Self-Acceptance

Accurate Self-Concept (In Personal
Relationships)

If you have the Healer Life Purpose, you are here to inspire and empower other people to grow through surrendering to their own process of inner communications. As a Healer, you find fulfillment by guiding people in listening to themselves and gaining insight into what their inner voice is trying to tell them. Healing is about helping others trust and accept themselves, as they are, right now in the present moment, so they can take a look at who they are. You want to be in a position to guide others through a process of self-inquiry—to foster their curiosity about who they are inside. You have gained deep psychological insight—you have earned it through your own challenging self-discovery process, which was spurred on by working with your emotional and psychological "woundings," so you can guide others in healing their own pain. This is not to say you are meant to heal others' wounds for them, but your work is to facilitate personal growth by helping others figure out who they are, why they are having a hard time, how they've gotten to where they are, and then assist them in discovering the ways they can *help themselves.*

Key to living this Life Purpose is developing your own trusting relationship with yourself—your psychological insight into you. This happens by engaging in your own personal growth, unearthing the truth about yourself, and listening very closely to your inner voice, even when you don't like what it is trying to say. As a Healer, you must first be open and curious about your own innermost processes, especially those having to do with the ways in which you were hurt and the ways you have chosen to protect yourself, but which later block your ability to relate to yourself and others. You must practice self-acceptance and get comfortable with being who you are. This includes increasing your self-awareness by looking at how you relate to your "intimates," the people you are closest to. These people are like mirrors for you because they reflect you back to yourself by providing feedback about what you are transmitting. This is why people work with healers when their lives are not functioning well, because many of our difficulties as human beings boil down to our (in)ability to connect with ourselves and with other people on a personal level. Healers of all sorts are, ideally, proficient in both the inner process of self-reflection and the skills required for good external personal communications (mirroring). Which means they have been engaged in their own growth process and have learned some form of healing to facilitate others through the personal growth process.

As you gain self-trust and compassion (and, hopefully, a sense of humor about your own foibles) from doing your own personal growth work, you become someone to whom others feel they can entrust themselves. As you progress on the Healer's path, you want to open up to the inner worlds of others and develop your ability to empathize—to see what the world looks like from someone else's shoes—and help others find the truth of themselves and their interactions with the world. As a Healer, it is not your job to try and change people or to control them by telling them what to do (this is counterproductive as it *dis*empowers them), but to help them trust their own sense of being. As most professional healers know all too well, "You can lead a horse to water, but you can't make it drink!" Healers provide an open, accepting, close relationship for others to discover and learn about themselves and then do their best to inspire and help them find their own power to take a drink and see what happens next.

One of my favorite Healer stories is that of the originator of this system of fingerprint analysis, Richard Unger. A long time ago, Richard worked in insurance. His sales communication skills were exceptional, and he was on the way up. As he talked with prospects, he naturally found himself taking a lot of extra time learning about their dreams, aspirations, and the various life conundrums they were wrapped up in. This was the part of his work he enjoyed the most. He found people's life stories fascinating and liked helping them find solutions to their problems. He had a high closing ratio (that's the number of sales completed compared to contacts made), but one day his supervisor sat him down and said something along the lines of, "Unger! You aren't your clients' rabbi! Sell them the insurance they need, if they need it, then move on to the next prospect. You've got great potential as a salesman, but you can't afford to spend this much time with each prospect." His boss was right. Richard, like many clients who come to see me, was successful because of his ability to inspire people to grow, but it wasn't what he was actually getting paid for. Happily, he figured this out and eventually dedicated himself to full-time Healership. Thirty years later he is still inspiring and empowering people to live their Life Purposes, and getting paid to do it.

The most common error I find Healers making has to do with counseling everyone around them (often starting with their own family members), but not from a place of overt permission. There is nothing wrong with lending an ear or offering advice to friends or co-workers, as long as they lend an ear and offer advice back to you when you ask for it. But Healers urgently want to help others and usually jump in to try and help anywhere and everywhere they see it's needed and then get a mixed response. Some people want your help and seek it out, and others may dislike your advising them without their permission. I had one client, who was in an administrative position, and everyone in the company stopped by her desk at some time during the day to bend her ear. It got so bad she had her boss request that people stop parading by her desk, as it was preventing her from doing the work she was getting paid to do. It was very clear what was going on when we found she has the Healer purpose and needed to move into a position where people could officially bring their problems to her. Healers often find people want to talk to them, even when those people are complete strangers. One of the challenges when you are a Healer is figuring out how to offer your insight skills so they are what you're getting paid for. This entails more than a change of career or position, it requires that you consciously put yourself in the seat of vulnerability where you are responsible for holding the accepting space needed for others' growth and well-being.

As you advance in your psychological insight through your work with yourself, your Healer purpose wants to be engaged with your own and others' personal growth in a professional (i.e., paid) capacity. This is not exactly the same as offering people your everyday advice or opinion. It is about choosing a form of psychological insight work and learning about appropriate advisement (i.e., first asking people if they want your advice), asking reflective questions, and employing active listening. There are many ways a Healer can help others with self-discovery, and most Healers develop an area of "expertise" springing from the wisdom gained from the work they have done around their own area of wounding or from their own deeper questions about what it means to be human. How can you be the best Healer you can be if it's something you do "on the side" rather than committing to it full-time?

When you consciously begin to learn and engage in the process of inspiring and empowering others to grow, it is clear that you are constantly studying people, starting with yourself, and what makes us all "tick." You intentionally observe and take on the study of some form of psychological insight work so you can hone your inner and one-to-one communication skills. You choose to become a professional healer who has permission to guide others in self-exploration. You make yourself a good mirror for others by asking the questions that steer someone into a deeper curiosity and awareness of how they think and feel. You help others question what is motivating their actions and help them see the relationship between cause and effect in their own lives. What results are they creating through their actions so they can consciously behave in ways that help them live life in deep consonance with themselves?

If you are a Healer, your deepest fulfillment arises from guiding others to blossom in their ability to relate to themselves and others so they are well connected and have closeness and understanding in their lives, as well as offering open acceptance and understanding to others. You feel best when encouraging others to be themselves, rather than wasting precious energy trying to be someone they are not.

Challenges

Just because you are a Healer doesn't mean it's always easy to inhabit your purpose all the time and in all circumstances. You are here to grow into your being and what it requires you to do. Two types of challenges help you gain the broad experience you need in order to live this Life Purpose.

Internal Challenges (Being)

These are some of the challenges you have within yourself, the negative beliefs you may hold about yourself and about Healership, which need to be brought to consciousness and worked with so you can do what is necessary to create deeply trusting relationships.

"I DON'T KNOW WHO I CAN TRUST"

Many Healers have been through difficult close relationships of one sort or another and wrestle with figuring out who they can entrust themselves to. Some have a hard time entrusting anyone with any information about themselves and feel isolated and misunderstood. They control by not telling us much, so we have a hard, if not impossible, time relating back to them since there is very little to respond to and we aren't mind readers. This under-trusting Healer tends to be overly suspicious of others and doesn't trust that others might respond to him or her openly and with acceptance. The over-trusting

Healer is not suspicious enough of others' motivations. These Healers entrust too much of themselves too fast without developing relationships gradually over time, and they can find themselves regular victims of deception in close relationships ("I didn't see it coming!"). These folks need to practice slowing down the process of building relationships rather than diving right in, surrendering themselves, then finding out who they're dealing with after the fact.

VULNERABILITY ISSUES

Certain personalities with the Healer purpose believe that they are supposed to go through life as tough stoics. I find this especially true for men with the Healer purpose (men aren't supposed to show "weakness"), but it is also true for women. These are the people who survived their "woundings" by unplugging from themselves and maintaining as much control of themselves, and the people and world around them, as possible. Right away I want to acknowledge the usefulness of this approach at times, especially when it got you through harsh times . . . whether you've survived emotional or physical abuse, a life-threatening illness or accident, poverty or war as a child, or being tough was valued within your family, or you had to survive being beaten-up by peers, or you had a very unpredictable parent, etc. "When the going gets tough, the tough get going!" and "Pull yourself up by your bootstraps!" can be very useful in some life situations. But later on, the question becomes, can you figure out when it is okay to open up truthfully so you can allow others to get close to you? Can you be vulnerable to yourself and know how you feel and take your directions for yourself from the inside (instead of defining yourself and life by what might go wrong "out there")? If you are one of the "tough ones," can you allow others to be "soft" and express the emotions you consider "weak" (sadness, tenderness, fear, love, worry, etc.) so they can be real and truthful in their relationship to you? Can you go through the vulnerable moment of asking for help and support from others even though they may turn you down?

FEAR OF ABANDONMENT

Some Healers had abandonment experiences when young. Whether there was a literal abandonment by a parent who went out of your life (through death, divorce, giving you up for adoption), a figurative abandonment involving the loss of closeness with a parent (who couldn't express feelings and be close, or who had to work three jobs and couldn't be home much), or you gave yourself up—abandoned yourself—in order to be loved by a parent, any form of abandonment tends to make it a dicey proposition to risk allowing someone to get very close to you again. If you are working with a fear of abandonment—fear that the people close to you in your life will leave you or stop communicating with you if you reveal your true self—it is important to do some work with a counselor or some other type of healer to cultivate your relationship with yourself so you know that there is one person in your life who will never abandon you—*you*. Healers practice the opposite of abandonment—they stay present and aware and help others learn to stay present to self regardless of whether other people stick around or not. As a Healer, you want to help others learn to express themselves in the face of the fear of abandonment, and you must be able to be present to yourself in order to be present for others.

INNER COMMUNICATIONS/SELF-AWARENESS

Healers are challenged to become highly aware of their feelings, thoughts, and motivations through getting in touch with themselves. It is no wonder, then, that Healers are people whose potential lies in their willingness to visit the shipwrecks of their life in order to learn about what happened, how they felt about it, how they relate to those wounding experiences, and how these experiences are driving them unconsciously to do what they are doing now—both usefully and to their detriment. Healers are those built to visit their own unconscious places so they can bring themselves to consciousness, up into the light of day, a little piece at a time. Their job is to take light down into the dark places so the truth can be known and wholeness regained over time. It all sounds very nice and poetic until you are in the middle of actually doing it and are face-to-face with the skeletons in your closet, the truths you hid from yourself because they hurt too much, your now questionable judgment of years past—or a current betrayal rips open another layer of rage about being abandoned. The task of gaining self-awareness is often painful and loaded with anxious feelings you'd just rather not have, not right now anyway, thanks a lot. But there it is: you are here to get really good at communing with yourself and accepting yourself, so you can tolerate being with others as they examine their lives and express their uncomfortable feelings. It takes a very self-aware and psychologically savvy person to be able to hold an open space for others. It takes the kind of compassion that allows you to be a witness to others' suffering, without drowning in it yourself, because you trust the process of consciousness enough to let things unfold, to surrender to the process of another as you have practiced surrendering to your own dialogue with yourself.

External Challenges (Doing)

When you begin to listen deeply to yourself and others, various obstacles are likely to arise in the external world to challenge you and help you develop strength in your ability to inspire and empower others to heal and grow. Remember, your Healer purpose doesn't guarantee that you will inspire and empower others to grow in an appropriate context. You have to work as skillfully as you are able with the times, the circumstances you're living in, and the people in your life, and all three are likely to confront you in many ways. Here are a few possible external challenges.

FALLING IN LOVE WITH "FIXER-UPPERS"

Let's face it: on some level we are *all* "fixer-uppers." None of us is perfect and most of us are riddled with emotional scars and bewildered by the complexities of human life. But, as a Healer, you want to beware of surrounding yourself, in your personal life, with very wounded people in order to have people to counsel, and also to feel in control of, just because you might be in slightly better shape than they are and can take the superior role (and thus avoid vulnerability by being the person who is constantly dispensing advice and coming to others' rescue). A place where this becomes very pointed is in your intimate relationship life. It is common for those on the Healer's path to fall in love with someone's potential rather than with the person he or she already is. The Healers are often grossly disappointed when their intimate partners don't change, seem to have no interest in doing so, and actually resist the Healers' exhortations to "Grow, darn it!" This is one of the most challenging places to learn that healing is not about making anyone do anything, but about accepting people as themselves, and relating to them as they are here and now.

TRYING TO "FIX IT" FOR OTHERS

As a Healer, you want to help others, but remember that helping others is not about "fixing it" for them, it's about facilitating someone's healing process so that individual takes as much responsibility for it as possible. Years ago I was bitten by a dog and landed in the hospital with a life-threatening infection that spread from the bite on my right hand up my arm. Once the infection was routed out, my right pointer finger was curled in from the thick scar tissue at the site of the worst puncture wound. I was sent to an orthopedist who set me up for physical therapy, but didn't let me out of his office until he showed me *what I could do* to work on it myself. For the week until the physical therapy appointment, I did exactly what he told me to do every day and returned my hand to full functionality myself. I didn't end up needing the physical therapy, and I was grateful to the doctor who empowered me to do what I could to heal myself. As a Healer, it is so important to understand that you mostly cannot "fix it" for others, no matter what part you are playing in someone's healing process. You can't make others grow or give them the desire to participate in their own healing or even their own lives. The best you can do with those who are interested and willing is "teach them how to fish," and encourage them to take as much responsibility for themselves as they are capable of. Beyond that, all you can do is surrender to the truth of the unfolding process of growth, whether it moves quickly or creeps along.

THE WATER COOLER COUNSELOR

Are you one of these? I met a "water cooler counselor" at my writing café today, a friendly retired man who accosted me by booming, "So, are *you* retired?" I was momentarily puzzled since I'm obviously nowhere near retirement age and everyone in the café, like me, was working hard on a laptop computer. "I'm working on a book," I told him, cautious of what might come next, given the judgment implied in his aggressive question. All of a sudden he started giving me advice about how I am too smart to be hanging around this place. (This café? Oakland, California? The West Coast?) "What are you doing here?" he bellowed, and he asked why I wasn't living in New York with all the other smart respectable writerly people, or at least in San Francisco where the beatniks used to hang out, or down around Stanford (I surmised he or his children went to Stanford). He thought he was being sage, but he just wanted to counsel someone about something and I happened to be at the wrong place at the wrong time. Poor confused soul, he *was* quite jovial along with being a tad bit pushy and unaware. He looked like a retired successful CEO who might consider volunteering as a counselor at the Small Business Administration instead of advising anyone he can find. As you can surmise, we humorously use this name for those who hang around the "water cooler" at their place of work, dispensing advice to the hapless visitors who come by for a drink of water (or coffee!) and receive the water cooler counselor's two cents as an added "bonus."

If this is you, please consider training in some official form of advising people. Go study it, then set yourself up to encourage those who come to you for it.

WALKING YOUR TALK/"BACKSEAT HEALER"

Of course, an ongoing challenge for you as a Healer is to keep expanding your personal awareness so you can "walk your talk." How can you counsel others to take risky steps that you yourself are not willing to take in your own life? Healers find that although it isn't possible to have every life experience under the sun to counsel from, it is vital to keep taking your own corollary, empowered growth steps so you can honestly inspire others to take theirs. It is unavoidable that where you have blind spots you are likely to collude in some way with others' blind spots when they match up—you may "hire" or urge others to do the growth work for both of you, or not see where someone is stuck because it's where you're stuck and don't want to see it, or you may project your judgment of yourself around your stuck spot onto others (there's something wrong with *them*, not me!). You may find that when something about a client really bugs you, it's because they are exhibiting something *you do* that you don't like and are trying to stay in denial about. It isn't possible to go over all the ins and outs of this. The psychotherapy profession has well-developed training and many good books on transference and countertransference. But whatever type of healing you engage in, your own self-discovery process is wonderfully spurred on by working with people whose predicaments bring to light the places where you are not walking your talk, and this gives you many opportunities to take your next step.

Being It, Doing It, and Faking It (Attitude to Adopt)

Since Healership is the state of being you wish to live in, where life feels meaningful to you, you can ask yourself the following questions when you're working on adopting the attitude of your Life Purpose in order to more fully inhabit it and then *do it*.

When you feel *isolated* and *mistrustful*, ask:

• How do I feel when I most *trust myself*? Can I step into this version of myself?

• What do I need to do to *not* abandon myself?

• How can I stop and pay attention to what I know about myself and surrender to it?

- How do I communicate myself in my personal relationships? Can I be appropriately vulnerable?

- How can I cultivate a good relationship with myself?

> "I strive to understand myself and to communicate
> effectively in my personal relationships with others."

Practical Everyday Expression/Steps

To build up your ability to be a Healer, you must *practice* the actions that create acceptance of self and others!

- *Healer heal thyself.* This seems obvious, but when you have the Healer Life Purpose, your own healing process needs to come first in your life. You are constantly learning the reality of the *process* of personal growth, of the gradual deepening of your relationship with yourself, and of the futility of believing that a day will come when you are completely "fixed." Healers need to be consistently vulnerable to themselves. You are required to keep looking into your internal truth mirrors and the reflection of your close relationships to continually discover the truth about yourself. You will develop compassion and patience through the humbling process of seeing who you are, even the parts you don't like. This allows others to entrust themselves to you as your judgment is tempered regularly by your own healing process. Make time for your own personal growth work, whether or not you are already in a professional position as a healer. Remember, your ability to inspire and empower others to grow and heal rests entirely on your ability to do the same with yourself.

- *Focus on communicating with your intimate partner.* Because Healers are growing and changing rapidly on this life path, and healing and intimate relationship both require appropriate trust and surrender in communicating with another, honing your one-to-one communication skills at home is important. A healthy, living, intimate relationship requires you to keep revealing your changing feelings, shifting views on things, and evolving thinking about your life with your partner. This can feel, and is, mighty risky. ("What if my partner doesn't like the latest 'version' of me and therefore 'abandons' me?") If you stop communicating with your partner about your self-discovery process (and/or stop being curious about his or hers), your relationship will come to a point where you can't keep the evolved version of yourself stuffed inside anymore. And when that newer version of you comes out, your partner may wake up wondering, *Who are you? This isn't the person I thought I committed to!* Remember that your intimate partnership and your Healer purpose require the same thing—trusting, close communication—so your intimate partnership is an integral part of your training ground for your Healer purpose. Whether you are currently in or out of an intimate relationship, you can choose to investigate, in all your close relationships, the ways in which you "keep things under control" by withholding parts of yourself. For instance, exclaiming, "I don't like the way you're looking at me!" is quite different from stating, "I'm afraid of what you might be thinking about me right now," which is quite different from asking, "I'm scared—what are you thinking about me right now?" Each of these expressions is a vulnerable communication, but each one is successively more vulnerable and requires a more risky level of openness and a deeper level of communication. There's what passes for vulnerability (first statement), but true vulnerability is about putting yourself into a position to actually receive feedback and then be open to it (third question).

- *Associate with other healers.* The early stages of your Healer purpose involve a significant amount of self-healing, so "associating with other healers" at this stage implies working with someone who is a professional healer of some sort or taking healing, self-discovery-oriented workshops/classes (in which case you also have others engaged in healing as your cohorts). If and when you go professional, you still need to connect with other healers so you have peer relationships where you can talk shop. In my work with many healers (and many types of healers), I commonly find that they go through a period where they shed people from their pre-healer lives (their unofficial "clients") and then feel isolated and wonder just where everyone went. Healers develop a very different way of seeing people and the world around them, and this unique view can create a sense of estrangement. It is of paramount importance to you as a Healer to make the effort to find other healers to relate to and be supported by. (Irvin Yalom advocates eloquently for this in his book, *The Gift of Therapy.*) It is also vital to be willing to re-enter the healing relationship as a client when you get hung up on another round of your own healing process. Remember that you are on a personal growth path that doesn't quit!

Positive Feelings Associated with This Life Purpose

- Aware/awake

- Perceptive/insightful (seeing inner truth)

- Connected (to self/spirit/other people on a personal level)

- Receptive

"I trust myself."

Questions to Ask Yourself

- How well do I *listen* to myself?

- Am I willing to practice my inner communications? How can I improve my self-awareness through growing my trust in myself?

- What kind of relationship do I have with myself?

- Do I find myself "counseling" everyone I know everywhere I go? With (or without) their permission?

- How can I cultivate my psychological insight skills? What form do they want to take? In what capacity would I like to inspire and empower others to grow/be the best they can be?

- What are the wounds I am healing for myself?

- Do I give myself enough "cave" time . . . time spent on my own personal growth?

- Who in my life do I try to "fix it" for? Can I stop trying to rescue others?

- Can I surrender and trust the ongoing *process* of growth and healing?

- Can I resist giving others advice unless they ask for it directly? Can I ask others for permission before offering my advice to them?

- How can I keep sharing and communicating my own growth process with my intimate partner?

- How comfortable am I with my all of my own feelings? How comfortable am I with others' feelings?

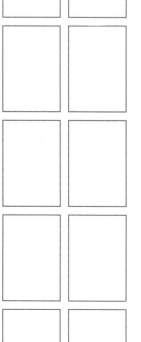

5 The Four Group (Aggregate) Life Purposes

. . . and the truth is that as a man's real power grows and his knowledge widens, ever the way he can follow grows narrower. Until at last he chooses nothing, but does only and wholly what he must do . . .

URSULA K. LE GUIN, *A Wizard of Earthsea*

When you have *six or more* high-ranking fingerprints, the focus of your Life Purpose is heavily colored by the essential nature of the *type* of the predominant fingerprint (arches, tented arches, loops, or whorls).

For those who have *six to ten* of the same high-ranking fingerprint type, the Group Life Purpose is your Life Purpose.

Depending on the arrangement of the *six or more* high-ranking fingerprints, it is often possible to decode your Life Purpose according to finger placement and the ten Individual Life Purposes, particularly by looking at the doubles. In addition, you will want to read the overlay of your Group Life Purpose. For those with ten of the same fingerprint, your purpose is the Group Life Purpose.

The four potential Group Life Purposes are:

Master of Peace: ten arches required.

Master of Wisdom: six or more tented arches required, with the remaining fingerprints arches.

Master of Love: six or more loops required, with the remaining fingerprints arches and/or tented arches.

Master of Service: six or more whorls required, with the remaining fingerprints any of the other three types.

Ten Arches: Master of Peace

Life in Balance

Inner Peace

Calm/Serene/Ease

Grounded/Anchored/Centered

Present/Awake/Aware/Focused

Safe/Secure/Solid

Comfortable with the Physical Body

Time Is on Your Side

Existential (Life and Death) Issues

Purity/Simplicity

I don't want to not live because of my fear of what could happen.

> LAIRD HAMILTON, big-wave surfer, in *Riding Giants*

Many refuse the loan of life to avoid the debt of death.

> OTTO RANK

There is nothing to fear but fear itself.

> FRANKLIN D. ROOSEVELT

Courage is rightly esteemed the first of human qualities . . . because it is the quality which guarantees all others.

> WINSTON CHURCHILL

Danger—if you meet it promptly and without flinching—will reduce the danger by half. Never run away from anything. Never!

> WINSTON CHURCHILL

I don't want to end up simply having visited this world.

> MARY OLIVER, "When Death Comes"

When the going gets tough, the tough get going.

> JOSEPH KENNEDY

Presence is the most valuable gift we can give another human being.

> RAM DASS

If you have the Master of Peace Life Purpose, you are here to find a sense of inner peace that comes through living a fully present life. You have an extra sensitivity to the questions of embodied existence and want to be engaged, literally or figuratively, with life-and-death issues and what it means to live life to its fullest. As a Master of Peace, you reap meaning when you face the reality of impermanence, the harsh fact that nothing in life is really secure or certain (except death). When the reality of death is faced, you find the peace of mind that comes from being present for every minute of your precious life while it lasts. Being peaceful is not about enduring life by being a heroic stoic, instead it's about cultivating full awareness of what's happening around you and remaining focused enough to experience it. This purpose is about finding your core sense of *being* that exists no matter what you do, or what happens to you, or around you. Like the focused, calm eye of the storm surrounded by chaos, being a Master of Peace is about allowing yourself to be affected by life, even when it feels dangerous, rather than playing it so safe that you don't live it at all or sleepwalk through life.

Key to living this Life Purpose is engaging in the process of cultivating grounded, focused presence so you can choose to live life to its fullest while you have your physical body to live it. This requires you *be here now*, to be embodied fully, so you can best assess what is going on around you and act accordingly. With this purpose you are seeking to inhabit *balanced vigilance*. The *Encarta Dictionary* defines *vigilance* as "the condition of being watchful and alert, especially to danger." On the upside, you are meant to be alert and aware of the world around you. On the downside, you can be fixated on the possibility of danger—and be panicky about it—even when it isn't present, or you can numb out so as to avoid your fear of mortality as much as possible. As the Master of Peace, you need to admit your feelings of fear so that you can evaluate whether or not they're warning you of something you need to protect yourself from. A retired police officer I met in passing told me a striking story in which he demonstrated focused vigilance while a bystander to the crime displayed life-threatening levels of stubborn obliviousness. From his motorcycle, parked at the curb in a crosswalk, the officer trained his gun at an armed robber exiting a jewelry store. As the getaway car, piloted by an armed driver, rounded the corner to pick up the robber, a pedestrian strolled up, glanced at the guns the officer and the robber had aimed at each other, and obstinately planted himself in the line of fire between them. He demanded that the officer move out of his way so he could cross the street in the crosswalk. Despite the officer's admonishments, and being wedged between two pulled guns, the guy wouldn't budge. The officer stayed calm, quickly considered his options, and decided to use foul language to wake the pedestrian up and to get him to move out of harm's way. After the incident was over, the bystander was still insensitive to the fact that his life had been in real danger, and he filed a report against the police officer for obscenity! How well do you stay calm and present in order to react appropriately to your circumstances? To find presence and become awake, aware, and alert to the world around you, you have to be willing to feel your fear when it's appropriate without being carried away by it, so you can most accurately assess what to do. In the robbery scenario, the police officer was acutely aware of the dangers around him, and he remained grounded and present to the situation so he could take proper action, but the bystander had his fear completely turned off and therefore could not protect himself. His lack of vigilance also further endangered the police officer.

As the Master of Peace, you desire intense, attention-focusing experiences, which bring you in direct contact with the here-and-now, the present. But there is no way to live in the intense, focused awareness of the here-and-now without eventually becoming aware of the reality of death. Seeking balanced vigilance is vital so you can begin to live a life that harmonizes your desire for intense attention-focusing experiences *with* the prospect of facing your fears regarding the limits of your existence. The challenge lies in becoming aware of *how* you get your need for intense experiences met. When you space out to avoid your fear of mortality yet long for intense experience, you are likely to err in one of two directions, both related to being spaced out. We call the overly busy version of a spaced-out person with arch fingerprints "Mr. Sticks and Plates," after the vaudeville act where a performer exhausts himself by spinning as many plates on sticks as possible. Mr./Ms. Sticks and Plates starts with one spinning plate and adds more until all he or she can do is switch from one stick to another to keep the plates aloft until they all come tumbling down in a chaotic, crashing heap. Do you go into overdrive mode and *do* too much until you're in a daze, pushing yourself mercilessly to keep going at the expense of everything else in your life? (Cram too much into too short a time frame and keep forcing in more to the detriment of your health, relationships, and ability to love life as you're living it?) Overwork until you drop? (Working so hard you have to get sick or injure yourself to "take time off"?) Do you lose your ability to enjoy your life because all you do is work or overdo? ("All work and no play" makes you very dull and humorless indeed, and too exhausted to smell the flowers or savor your vacation.) Do you tend to make scenes by blowing small everyday events out of proportion and make "mountains out of molehills" so there's a an intense crisis to be met? Do you turn every little mishap into an "end of the world" disaster? ("Eek! Ants in the kitchen! Oh! What are we going to do? What if they take over the house and crawl on us when we're asleep?")

At the other space-out extreme is Mr./Ms. Mellow, who sleepwalks through life, at best getting by on automatic pilot with a secure but meaningless job, or, at worst, paying so little attention to taking care of basic security needs that things tend to slide into crisis mode. ("Well, I didn't work enough this month, so now I can't pay my rent, I'm getting evicted, and I will have to live in my car." Or, "I never bothered to lock my car and now it got stolen." Or, "Your house burned down? Did you hear if the Dodgers won yesterday?") It's also common to combine Mr. Sticks and Plates *and* Mr. Mellow: "I was too busy to pay my electricity bill and now my utilities have been turned off for two weeks, and my father is coming to visit tomorrow!" (Mr. S&P). "But, oh well, these things happen" (Mr. Mellow).

If you are living in the extremes of the Master of Peace purpose, how can you funnel your need for intensity into appropriate channels? What can you do to get present enough to discern how much work you need to do (to create security) versus how much play? Can you be present enough to know when to fight and when to flee? When to act and when to wait? How do you harmonize *doing* and *being* rather than living a state of continual numbness or a state of panic, or even swinging regularly between the two?

Every aspect of the captivating and intense big-wave surfing documentary *Riding Giants* exemplifies the issues of this purpose. The early pioneers of this dangerous sport lived on the beach in Hawaii, entirely focused on surfing, barely making ends meet by living off the land. In numerous interviews, the surfers echo each other with the idea, "Surfing wasn't something you *did*, it was something you *became*," something that allowed them to discover a deep-rooted sense of *being* through the marriage of intense experience and a clear awareness of physical danger. Surfing was their complete life, five to ten hours a day, with "no dates, no money, no car, nothing." They had no discernable material security, and surfing big waves is life-threatening, but they all had a sense of inner peace and stability stemming from engaging in an activity where they were choosing constantly to face death and choosing to live life in a meaningful way. This confrontation made them want to spend their time fully enjoying life. Life was simple in its scope and they were all engaged in an intense practice, commanding one-pointed, alert focus to survive. Surfer Ricky Grigg says, "When you come down the face of a mountain [of water], you're on fire, your heart is exploding, the endorphins are just busting out in your brain and you want to, not just prove that you can do it, but discover what you're made out of."

The surfers' needs for intense, meaningful experience are met positively through surfing big waves and engaging the borders of life and death. They know their lives can be easily lost, or limited by injury, and challenging this fosters alert, awake living. Behind all the interviews you can plainly hear the theme: *Life is precious! Live it now despite your fears!* And these guys do not hesitate admitting they have to work with fear. They are not operating from a numbed-out state. Jerry Lopez, known as "Mr. Pipeline," relates the story of his first time out to one of the largest breaks in the world: "The first time I surfed Peahi, I remember getting so uptight on the way out, just going, 'Oh man, so much anxiety!' that I was thinking, 'I'm just . . . I'm not going to be able to surf!' And I remember finally having to go, 'Okay . . . I guess this is a good day to die.'" Some of the others interviewed point out the sanctuary provided by such focus. Jeff Clark, who surfed the cold, shark-infested coastline dubbed "Mavericks" in Northern California alone for fifteen years says, "It was my sanctuary, I could leave the shore and go out there and be so focused and so in-tune and feel the ocean with every fiber in my body, and I was a part of it." In other words, he can be nowhere but merged with the here-and-now when surfing, and this provides him a sense of peace. Dave Kalama says, "There's something about riding a sixty-, an eighty-foot face wave that draws something out of you. The wave commands so much focus and so much attention that it is the only thing that matters for a few seconds. It's very purifying." What is important is brought into focus by surfing, and it's being in the *present tense*, here and now. The challenge inherent in identifying who you are so strongly with what you do, is also brought to light by Laird Hamilton, who openly admits to depression and a loss of identity when there are no waves to surf. "I question that [who he is, his identity] all year long, except when it's thirty feet and I'm out surfing."

You reap the satisfaction of your Master of Peace Life Purpose by working with your fear of being alive in a transitory physical body. You rise to the challenge of "feeling the fear and doing it anyway," whether you work on an ambulance or lead others through meditation. You remember that there is no courage without fear. You find that facing your fears creates a deep sense of inner peace. You learn that your fear is an important part of your system, and therefore important to be in touch with, as it serves the function of warning you when something might not be safe. Over time, you cultivate enough presence so you can tell the difference between your fear of what might happen and your instincts, which are trying to tell you something really is wrong so you can protect yourself. You re-decide every day to get up and live your precious life to the fullest and encourage the rest of us to look at the reality of life and death so we can realize how lucky we are to be alive, despite life's trials and tribulations, or perhaps because of them.

When you consciously begin to learn and engage in the process of being present, you choose to work, literally or figuratively, with life-and-death issues. You may pilot airplanes and keep everyone safe for the trip, be a safety inspector, work in an emergency room saving lives, sit with people who are dying, teach others self-defense, or surf big waves. Some help others in their search for a deeply meaningful life through some form of counseling, or help others get present through some mode of working with or nurturing the body. Still others involve themselves in attention-focusing practices such as meditation, yoga, tai chi, or martial arts.

If you are an actualized Master of Peace, your deepest fulfillment arises from being acutely awake and aware and present to life. You are able to be tolerant of life's uncertainties and desire to look closely into what it means to be alive, with all its highs and lows and its inevitable end, without being entirely carried away or over-identifying with the passing show of temporary circumstances. You are aware that things change, that everything is impermanent, and that you are continuously cultivating a deep acceptance of the terms of existence and mortality. This motivates you to appreciate the gift that life is for all of us, and to stay focused on the importance of *how* you pass the time of your life (including the time of your death). Because of this larger view, you are able to keep things in perspective and truly enjoy life by living in the moment. You choose to savor every day of your life so much that, on some level, every day is a good day to die because it's also a good day to live. You can see death as just another stage to go through when the time comes. You want to aspire to loving and living life to its fullest, as Mary Oliver does in her life-and-death embracing poem, "When Death Comes," which proclaims, "I don't want to end up simply having visited this world."

Challenges

Just because you are a Master of Peace doesn't mean it's always easy to inhabit your purpose all the time and in all circumstances. You are here to grow into your being and what it requires you to do. Two types of challenges help you gain the broad experience you need in order to live the Peace Life Purpose.

Internal Challenges (Being)

These are some of the challenges you have within yourself, the negative beliefs you may hold about yourself and about Peace, which need to be brought to consciousness and worked with so you can do what is necessary to find true inner tranquility.

"LIFE IS HARD"

You may feel like life is hard because your life truly has been difficult, and you are absolutely right that living life in a human body on planet Earth ain't no piece of cake. By the same token, if you focus on everything being hard, or only on what's difficult, then it will be, and you'll miss out on the parts that are wonderful. Without denying your life situation or your feelings about it in any way, whether it was hard or still is, can you look up, right now, from this book and find something that is delightful to your eye? Can you remember a kind word or deed from someone? Can you make a list of things you can be grateful for? Can you name one thing that is precious to you? Can you take a moment and remember or notice any of these things and enjoy it? Can you taste the bite of food you are eating and savor it? Can you pay attention to the seemingly small things in life that can be an anchor for you and keep you going?

"LET ME OUTTA HERE!"/LIFE ON THE RUN

Those with the Master of Peace purpose have an extra sensitivity to the reality that life ends in death ("None of us gets outta here alive!") and that the world is a dangerous place. The awareness of death is something most of us do our best to keep in the periphery of consciousness because it is so terrifying. Those with this purpose tend to struggle with these issues on a life scale, compared to the rest of us who may or may not go through a major confrontation with death. Depending on how high this realization rises in your consciousness, some part of you is likely to ask, "What's the point of it all if I'm just going to die anyway? Let me outta here!" Now, "Let me outta here!" ends up translating into all kinds of things. There are many ways to "escape," space out, or bypass the extreme anxiety produced in most people when they confront death and realize it applies to them. You can get extremely driven and busy to defend yourself against this awareness, you can numb out by watching television all the time, or tune out by taking drugs or drinking. Or are you someone who chooses to flirt with death through life-threatening pursuits that focus your attention so strongly that you feel completely alive in the moment? (Positive: race car driving, mountaineering. Negative: reckless driving, heroin.) If you have this purpose, how do you "run"?

"I AM MY WORK"

I had a lovely client with the Peace purpose who told me all about the work she used to do and how she had finally downshifted (and took a lower salary) because she didn't know who she was anymore. She had become her work and felt like a human *doing*. She had an extremely successful career in international sales and traveled incessantly for it. She was super busy. She was living her life on the run and enjoyed it at first, but over time she was exhausted and had no sense of home or of who she was apart from her work. Her life was secure in terms of dollars in the bank, but there was nothing settled or calm or peaceful or balanced about it. She was like a nonstop whirlwind with no time to enjoy her life or the money she was making. If you are like my client, it is too easy to be overdriven and "escape" through working constantly, until all the rush and pressure and stress and ungroundedness catches up with you.

LIVING WITH YOUR BODY

Because Peace is about the challenge of being present and focused and in your body, it is very much about how you treat your body. Do you see it as something to be driven or ignored or resented because it can get sick and is mortal? This purpose has an overlap with the body issues of the "Family" purpose, but the motivation has a different flavor. With the Peace purpose, you are challenged to accept that you are living your life in a physical body and feel grateful for your body as the vehicle of your existence. You cannot exist without being embodied. Taking care of your body, rather than treating your body as if it's unimportant or an enemy, is an important focus of your life. Paradoxically, if you ignore your body and treat it poorly, it will have trouble, and that trouble is there to pull you back into focused presence with yourself. Your body is the foundation for your life, and you just can't get along very well without it. "Your health is everything," is true. It is not easy, and it can be close to impossible to enjoy life, if you are in regular pain or fatigued or fighting cancer. If you are someone with this purpose and have health challenges, you know all too well that life is precious and the body much more fragile than most of us want to acknowledge.

External Challenges (Doing)

When you begin to get present to yourself and the world around you, various obstacles are likely to arise in the external world to challenge you and help you develop strength in your ability to find balance. Remember your Peace purpose doesn't guarantee feeling calm and secure. You have to work as skillfully as you are able with the times, the circumstances you're living in, and the people in your life, and all three are likely to confront you in many ways. Here are a few possible external challenges.

WHEN IS ENOUGH *ENOUGH?*

As you get present to yourself and feel your anxiety, can you consciously practice relaxing over time into the fact that there is always something to do regarding reaffirming your security? Can you be aware that you can have an internal sense of safety and security whether you have one dollar in your pocket or one million? Of course, you would think you'd feel more secure with a million, but you'd be surprised. Plenty of people are anxious, regardless of what they actually have. Since this is the purpose, ultimately, of *inner peace*, you are here to learn that peace is about your state of consciousness, regardless of your outer circumstances. Remember the big-wave surfers who owned almost nothing and lived on the beach? Their sense of serenity came from passing the minutes of their precious lives in a meaningful way, and as long as they had something to eat and a safe place to sleep, they had enough. Because their lives were focused and meaningful, they had a deep sense of security and serenity. If you have enough in the bank, and you are still anxious (which is not unlikely), can you stop to look for the actual source of your anxiety so your fears about material security (including the fact that your body is not materially permanent) don't drive you into not being able to enjoy your life? Remembering that "you can't take it with you" (your material possessions) can help in appreciating what is truly precious about life—*how* you live it.

KEEPING THE BALANCE

With the Peace purpose, you are here to learn that living a balanced life is an ongoing dynamic process, like walking a tightrope or learning to balance on a ball. How do things balance out? Your life tends to be a study of extremes—too much "work," too much "play," or too much "slouching on the couch." If you exert yourself too strenuously (mentally, emotionally, or physically), then, to recover, you will need a commensurate amount of time to do nothing at all. If you slouch around too much, then life tends to lose its meaning. As a Master of Peace, you are challenged to balance your own life out. How much doing? How much being?

IDENTITY ISSUES

As a Master of Peace, you tend to identify strongly with work or with what you are *doing*, so it can be uncomfortable to slow down, take time off, and relax into a calm sense of just being. It can be very hard to sit still. You can find yourself confronted with the anxiety of wondering who you are when you aren't working or doing. People with this purpose often report having a very difficult time putting enough R and R time into their schedules because of the identity crisis that surfaces when they stop moving. The first few days of a vacation can be positively itchy and miserable if you've been on overdrive for a long time. It can feel like everything inside you is still rushing ahead even though you're lying on the beach. It's difficult to decelerate. You can also worry because once you do slow down, you feel you won't necessarily want to accelerate again (fear of losing your drive). Can you recognize that you tend to identify with your circumstances and lose track of who you *are*? How do you find the steady core of your being that goes beyond anything you actually *do*?

"CRISIS AND PANIC SURROUND ME"

It is not uncommon, as you find your center and get your own life calmed down and more secure, for others in your life to be panicky or for crises to show up. You may find that somehow you've been surrounded by people in perpetual crisis for most of your life. Remember, as the Master of Peace, you have to learn not to over-identify yourself with your circumstances, but instead find the core of your being that is the touchstone of your existence beyond any particular situation or transient state of affairs. It is about doing what you need to do to find and maintain your own equilibrium and your own basic security and sense of safety. So it is no surprise when clients report that, just as soon as they get their own footing, higher levels of crisis and panic challenge their balancing skills. This isn't to say that there is anything wrong with those around you undergoing a difficult time (unless they are generating false crises to suck you back in so they have some company—remember misery does love company). Life throws a lot of curve balls; the question is, how do you maintain your equilibrium in the face of crisis without shutting yourself down to get through it? If you've chosen a career that is about working with people in crisis of some sort (which would be very appropriate to this purpose), how do you enjoy life and take care of yourself enough to avoid being depleted by it?

Being It, Doing It, and Faking It (Attitude to Adopt)

Since Peace is the state of being you wish to live in, where life feels meaningful to you, you can ask yourself the following questions when you're working on adopting the attitude of your Life Purpose in order to more fully inhabit it and then *do it*.

When you feel *spaced out or panicked*, ask:

- How do I feel when I am calm and peaceful and centered? Can I take a deep breath and center myself right now so I can be aware of myself and my surroundings *in this moment*?

- What is causing me to be spaced out? Do I need to get myself moving or slow myself down?

- How do I feel when my life is balanced? What things can I do to find my balance point? Do I need more self-care time? Or more work to get myself focused?

- What things do I have or do in my life that make me feel happy to be alive? How can I get more of these things into my life? Can I remember them when I'm feeling "What's the point?"

- How do I lose my perspective? What can I do to regain it?

"I am awake and aware and live life to the fullest."

Practical Everyday Expression/Steps

To build up your ability to stay grounded and present in the world, you must *practice* the actions that create peace!

- *Notice when you space out.* When do you space out? What causes it? What triggers your fears or anxiety? What feelings are you avoiding? See if you can notice your numbness and what feelings you might be avoiding by numbing out. Be gentle with yourself. If you have this purpose and tend to say, "I'm not afraid of anything!" can you notice the absence of your other emotions? Where did they go? Can you create a safe space to experience them? Stoicism is very useful at times, but when does being armored block your connection to yourself, other people, and the world around you? When does being tough *not* serve you? Can you figure out when to put your armor on and push through on and when it's safe to take it off?

- *Cultivate grounding and presence.* What brings you back into the moment where you can take a look at what is making you uneasy? During an anxious moment, can you stop and take a deep breath and notice the feel of your feet on the floor? Over time, do you engage in activities that allow, encourage, and require focus? Physical activities such as walking, running, bicycling, yoga, dance, etc., work well for many. Gardening or being close to nature regularly is great for others. Reading in the bathtub and other forms of relaxation are excellent as well. What can you take time to do regularly that puts you in touch with your body and the physical aspects of existence? Some find housecleaning or cooking or washing the car fits the bill nicely. Anything focusing you into the here-and-now is excellent.

- *Practice balance.* Are there ways in which your life is out of balance? All work and no play? All play and no work? Too busy all the time with no time to spare? Or are you perpetually slouched on the couch? The arch fingerprint is about extremes and the challenge of finding the steady middle ground of equanimity. This includes the possibility of emotional extremes. Some with this purpose are stoic, and others seem to always be in crisis and constantly creating panic for themselves and others. (Swinging back and forth between these extremes is a possibility as well.) Can you take a look at the ways your life is out of balance, then see what you can do to redress the imbalance?

Positive Feelings Associated with This Life Purpose

- Grounded and calm

- Awake/aware

- Focused

- Balanced

"I'm happy to be alive!"

Questions to Ask Yourself

- When do I panic? How do I create crisis and chaos in my life? How can I step back and see how it might be easier?

- When am I stoic and tough? Is it appropriate to the situation I am in? Can I be tough when necessary and vulnerable when appropriate?

- How do I manage my time? Do I misjudge and cram more in than is humanly possible and stress myself out? Or is it hard for me to be on any kind of structured schedule because I can't focus?

- When do I feel like I'd rather not be living my life? Can I keep re-deciding to see my life as precious and to live my life to the fullest?

- How do I care for my body? How aware am I of its needs? Can I see it as a friend and not an enemy? Can I take proper care of my precious body and see it as the miraculous vehicle for my existence that it is?

- Do I push myself to extremes by doing too much, then end up with unenjoyable time off because I'm sick or injured from driving myself too hard?

- How much do I enjoy life? Smell the flowers? Taste the food I eat? Hear the birds singing? Notice the color of things? How can I stop and enjoy life wherever I am and find the pleasure in it?

- Do I take care of my security needs? Can I do what I need to do to make my life feel as safe as possible, whatever my circumstances?

- What can I do to cultivate being present to myself and the world around me?

- In what way do I want to engage with existential issues?

- Are there ways my life is out of balance?

- What does it mean to love my life and live it to its fullest?

Six or More Tented Arches:
Master of Wisdom

Experience Gained

Appropriate Risk

Participation

Good Judgment

Compassion

Insight

Thinker

Teacher/Instructor

To dare is to lose one's footing temporarily; to not dare is to lose one's life.

SØREN KIERKEGAARD

He who would be everything cannot be anything.

ARTHUR SCHOPENHAUER

Jack of all trades, master of none.

PROVERB IN USE SINCE 1600S

Courage . . . it's when you know you're licked before you begin but you begin anyway and you see it through no matter what.

ATTICUS FINCH in Harper Lee's *To Kill a Mockingbird*

Unfortunately expectations based on illusion lead almost always to disillusionment.

DAVID BAYLES AND TED ORLAND, *Art & Fear*

Good judgment comes from experience, and often experience comes from bad judgment.

RITA MAE BROWN

Not answers, but questions; not dogmas, but doubts.

DAVID INGLEBY

You don't know until you go.

UNKNOWN

If you have the Master of Wisdom Life Purpose, you are here to teach or instruct others from the accumulated wisdom gained from your practical experience. At your best, you learn and theorize about a focused field of endeavor and then choose to apply what you've learned by testing out your theories in practical reality. With this Life Purpose, you are here to be the Man or Woman of Wisdom who teaches, informs, or advises others so we can better navigate whatever endeavor of life in which we are striving to gain experience and understanding. Your challenge is to avoid being the "know-it-all" who collects a lot of knowledge but does nothing with it. As the Master of Wisdom, you reap satisfaction from teaching others about something, and encouraging them to gain their own real-life experience of it, and therefore become wise themselves.

Key to living this Life Purpose is engaging in the entire process of learning *about* something then learning *from* doing it. Wisdom = knowledge + experience. As a Master of Wisdom, you naturally want to collect as much information as possible. You are a data-collecting being who likes to know a little of this and a little of that and who likes to *think* about it all. Those with this purpose are likely to hold multiple educational credentials or *almost* be the holder of multiple degrees. You may be very well educated indeed. But at some point the challenge is: Can you take some piece of what you have learned and apply it, use it, and take action on it? Can you travel the path from being someone who knows a lot, to being someone who can honestly say you've "been there and done that"? To be wise requires more than just having read a book or an article or hearing a report on the radio about something—it requires participation, action, and practice. It demands acquiring a body of experience from which you draw the insights you pass on to others. You can read many books on figure skating and learn the names of the jumps and spins and moves in the field. You can watch the competitions on television and study the best skaters. But can you really teach someone to skate if you have never even strapped on a pair of those stiff boots with their eighth-inch blades, and balanced, and learned how to propel yourself, and fallen down, and gotten up?

Can you be wise about skating and competing if you haven't put in the countless hours of practice and had people watching and judging you as you do it? Upon what would your instructions and opinions be based if you can't describe to your student what to focus on and what it should feel like in his or her body? If you sit on the sidelines telling someone how to skate when you've never done it, all you can succeed at doing is exposing your lack of experience with it—your ignorance.

To be the Master of Wisdom, you must get off the sidelines and commit to participating in something. To begin, you want to be willing to get an education and follow all the way through on gaining whatever credential you might need. And as soon as possible, you want to start applying what you are learning by doing it in whatever way is suitable. There are some things you can only learn by practicing them, and practicing them with some instruction *is* the education. Skating is a great example of this. You can learn only by putting on the skates and getting on the ice. There is very little a book can tell you about it. With other subjects, you need some book-learning and then hands-on instruction. Learning to fly an airplane is like this. You go through "ground school" first, because you must learn many things about the plane, the physics of how it works, and how the instruments work before you get in the cockpit at all. To become experienced enough to fly solo, there are a certain number of hours to be logged with an instructor, and so on. Other endeavors require much more book study before you can even begin to put what you've learned into practice. Becoming a doctor is a good example of this, as is becoming a pharmacist. So, first you get your education and complete the basic levels necessitated by the particular field. Then it's time to apply what you've learned and actually *do it*. I love the quote by Thomas Kempis that I came across: "The object of education isn't knowledge, it's action." You are on track with your Master of Wisdom purpose when you learn about something, then act on it so you can learn from it, which, in turn, makes you wise.

The movie *Good Will Hunting* is a great example of this purpose. The main character, Will, is a mathematical prodigy working as a janitor at MIT. He spies on the classes and leaves solutions to complex problems scrawled where they can be found, but he is living his entire life on the sidelines and thinks he knows far more than he does just because he is smart and observant. He may be brilliant at math but it doesn't mean he knows much about living life, especially when it comes to relating to other people. This is obvious to others, but not to him. Will gets hooked up with a therapist and spouts off cleverly about anything and everything, and he generally makes an ass of himself with the psychologist, who has been through some pretty tough life experiences. Will's brilliance has not been tempered by experience, and he sits in a seat of compassionless judgment, which hurts others. The movie is about his timid steps to engage in life (by getting a girlfriend and by letting himself relate to his therapist) and open up to experience instead of holding himself apart where he is stuck in know-it-all-ism. He has to put himself in a position of not knowing everything, of learning from making mistakes, and of being wrong to eventually become the compassionate, wise man we see he could be.

People who gain wisdom open themselves to experience rather than taking a defensive skeptical position behind what they know and having to "know more than you do." At their best they are mentally curious and eager to see how their theories play out in reality. They are happy to share what they have learned, and they can be honest about the difference between something they know a little about and those experiences they have actually been through. Wisdom Masters do not try and impose what they know on others or pose as "experts," but ask permission to share what they know, and they are willing to expose themselves from an appropriate position where people can seek them out for their advisement. Wisdom Masters choose to be teachers and writers, speakers and consultants, and are happy to exhibit their credentials—both those gained through formal education and those earned through the hard knocks of the school of life. They are committed to a field of endeavor and finding out everything they can about it through direct practice. When you inhabit your Wisdom purpose, you have the deep compassion that comes from being tumbled and humbled by reality knocking away your sharp judgmental corners. You thought you knew, but real life was something else again, for better or worse or somewhere in between. Wisdom Masters are humbly in awe of it all and know they don't know everything.

The biggest banana peel to slip on with this purpose is to hesitate and procrastinate and avoid gaining experience. You don't commit solidly to anything. You do too many things and can't move forward with any of them or you do nothing at all. You've got too many ideas. Many with this purpose put things off, then put them off a little more, as life passes by and the clock keeps ticking, until there's no more time left. You tell yourself, "I'll do it when x, y, and z are just right." "I'll do it tomorrow, or next week, or next year, or when the kids are grown." You stand at the crossroads of decisions, small and large, wringing your hands and worrying about all the pros and cons of something for so long that you never leap. You can't stop asking, "What if it doesn't turn out the way I want?" You look back, lamenting, "If only I'd done such-and-such,

I would be where I wanted to be now." You make excuses for why you didn't and, even worse, why you don't. All of this instead of seizing the day and doing it *now*. All this thinking about the past and thinking about the future and missing out on this very moment, which is the only time you can ever actually *act* and participate in life.

When you consciously begin to participate in life and learn from that involvement, you begin immediately to accumulate wisdom. You stop making the mistake of trying to become wise by *knowing it all*. Instead, you engage in taking action now, which allows you to *know it deeply* by entering the realm of the body of experience encompassed by your pursuit. For instance, knowing all the rules of grammar and spelling won't make you a good writer—actually sitting down and writing (and then applying grammar as you need it) will, with practice, make you a better writer. And learning *from* writing itself is what you will find to be the most rewarding thing after all.

If you are a Master of Wisdom, your deepest fulfillment arises from taking your ideas of the way things could be and engaging in the actions required over time to bring them into being. You delight in sharing your experience with others so they can find their own truth and gain insight into their own life experience. You see life as a great experiment and take joy in giving life to the world of ideas and how they can be applied to everyday life. Because you have gained your own hands-on, real experience, you become someone who has your head in the clouds with your feet firmly planted on the ground, a bridge between the world of dreams and their realization.

Challenges

Just because you are a Wisdom Master doesn't mean it's always easy to inhabit your purpose all the time and in all circumstances. You are here to grow into your being and what it requires you to do. Two types of challenges help you gain the broad experience you need in order to live the Wisdom Life Purpose.

Internal Challenges (Being)

These are some of the challenges you have within yourself, the negative beliefs you may hold about yourself and about Wisdom, which need to be brought to consciousness and worked with so you can do what is necessary to become truly wise.

SKEPTICISM/CYNICISM

As the Master of Wisdom, you may find that you doubt and question everything or, just the opposite, that you are too credulous and naïve and believe anything presented to you without question. Neither of these extremes is ideal. If you are overly skeptical, you will tend to make snap judgments based on what you think, rather than on actual experience. You can be so invested in what you think that you blind yourself to any contradictory truth that is right in front of you. If you are on this side of the fence, I encourage you to not believe what anyone tells you, but make sure to *gain your own experience* before passing judgment and *be willing to find out you're wrong*. You pride yourself on your rationality, but how rational is it to make a decision based on no experimentation? What if you took a risk? To think well for yourself means you must be open to experience before making up your mind about something. If you are the gullible type, you also need to gain your own experience instead of just believing anything anyone presents to you. Can you stop and think for yourself, instead of having to learn by leaping without looking? Can you stop and learn from being taken advantage of so you will consider a little more carefully next time? Each of these types tends to be afraid of becoming the other one—the cynic doesn't want to be unsuspecting and taken advantage of, and the innocent doesn't want to become jaded and closed off. Both need to borrow a little from the other so they can each get into the middle territory of gaining and learning from experience.

JUDGMENT/DOGMATISM

Wisdom Masters tend to be just a tad bit judgmental. Because you want to be the wise one who knows it all, it is too easy to think you know the right way of doing things (dogmatism—*my* way is the *right* way) and to be willing to sit in judgment of others. The challenge here is to cultivate good judgment without being inhumanly critical of yourself and/or others. Your job is not to *impose* what you think is right onto others, but to be secure enough in your own way of thinking to have compassion for all us humans traveling the bumpy road of life and learning from it (as you are). What is right for you is great, but it doesn't mean it's right for everyone else. Everyone has a right to think for themselves rather than being told what to think. And your strongly held beliefs and opinions ideally stem from your own experiences and thinking, rather than being adopted wholesale from a rigid system of ideals.

PROCRASTINATION

Masters of Wisdom tend to have lives riddled with procrastination. We call this "Mr. Next Year." There is a tendency to put things off and to constantly have "reasons" for doing so. Conditions are never sufficient right now. Things are delayed until some future date when everything is "perfect." "I've always wanted to take piano lessons, but I have to wait until my kids grow up and go to college first." "I've got three degrees related to child development, but I think I need another before I become a teacher; I don't know enough yet." "I want to do some public speaking, but I should read some books before thinking of joining Toastmasters."

When you are the Master of Wisdom, there is always a reason to put off doing what it is you think you'd like to do until life has passed you by. Why is this? Wisdom Masters have very strong mental images about the way things *could be* if everything was perfect. This enables you to envision things, which is fantastic. But when you go to make a move toward it by taking action, you can find yourself thinking of all the ways *it might not work out*. And you're right. It might not work out in the way you envision it. You don't know exactly how things will turn out. So it's just much easier to *think* about what you *might* do than to actually face your fears about what *might* happen.

"IF I CAN'T WIN, I WON'T PLAY"

So if there's just the *possibility* of reaching my vision, and there's work and disappointment involved, why should I bother committing myself to something? "If there is no guarantee I'm going to become an exceptional pianist, then I don't want to bother." There is a tendency to want to know the end of the story before it even begins. You have to remember that this is *impossible*. There are no guarantees. All you can do is decide to engage in something, to play the game of life and see what happens. I'd suggest you try looking at it all another way . . . things will *never* be the way they could be if all you do is think about it. *You can't win if you don't play.* There is no time like the present, so you might as well take the first step toward your vision, so it can begin to exist *now*. There will likely be disappointments along the way. There will be effort involved. You will not become a proficient piano player overnight. Who knows if you will become great at it? But if you get started, there is the *possibility* of being a good piano player someday. And as soon as you start playing the piano, you will actually *be* a pianist because you are playing the piano. You're *doing it*. Besides, as a Wisdom Master you like to learn things. Much of your satisfaction comes from the learning experience itself. So what are you waiting for? Take the *first step* on something you'd like to do *today*, and remember that Rome wasn't built in a day.

External Challenges (Doing)

When you begin to become aware of your urge to transmit wisdom to others, various obstacles are likely to arise in the external world to challenge you and help you develop strength in your ability to become a Master of Wisdom. Remember that with the Wisdom Life Purpose, getting yourself into a position to instruct others isn't automatically guaranteed. You have to work as skillfully as you are able with the times, the circumstances you're living in, and the people in your life, and all three are likely to confront you in many ways. Here are a few possible external challenges.

GIVING UNSOLICITED ADVICE AND OPINIONS/THE "KNOW-IT-ALL"

This is the purpose most likely to give unsolicited advice and opinions (topping even the Healer's propensity for this). With the Master of Wisdom purpose, you have a tough-to-resist urge to share (read between the lines here: *impose*) what you know, what you think, or what you *think* you *know* with others. You want to be seen by others as someone who *knows*—the expert. Of course you want things to be the way they *could be* at their best for everyone, but aren't you really just succumbing to the urge to be right and to know better than others so that you feel wise? With this purpose, you need to get yourself into a position where people seek you out for your wisdom. And when you see that something you know or have experienced may provide good guidance for someone, can you *seek their permission* before advising or instructing them? And then be clear that *your* experience was *x*, but *their* experience may well differ since they are not you? Offer your experience up in the spirit of shedding some light on theirs, but understand that they've got to acquire their own experience so they may gain their own wisdom.

THE ARMCHAIR CRITIC

Do you sit safely on the sidelines, attempting to direct the show of life, without actually participating in it? Armchair critics are those who think they are wise because they watch—even if they do not act. And of course, your capacity to observe is very important. But remember, true scientists set up experiments so they can take a theory and then apply it and see how it stands up to reality. This is what makes things juicy and exciting for Masters of Wisdom. They willingly and openly engage in finding out the truth for themselves by applying it or observing it, in action, in practical terms. Isn't it a good thing that pharmaceuticals are tested before being made available for us to take? Is someone's *idea* about what a drug *may* do sufficient to dispense it?

Years ago, we had a classic example of the armchair critic at the skating rink. Inevitably, while I was practicing jumps (and, of course, falling on my butt), he would sidle up and start instructing me on how I could improve my jump. First of all, I didn't appreciate being judged when I hadn't asked for it, and secondly, he couldn't jump at all, didn't want to learn to jump (due to the falling down and looking foolish part of the process), had no teaching experience, and had no idea of what he was talking about. His directives were ridiculous and only served to make *him* look foolish (exactly what he was trying to avoid!) rather than wise. See if you can catch yourself being the armchair critic and try and laugh at yourself when you do.

THE EXPERT

So where are you on the scale of owning the Master of Wisdom's desire to be seen as an expert? There is nothing wrong with wanting to be an expert; the question is, *what* are you expert at? Do you pose as an expert at things you have no earned experience with? Or hide from being an expert because you don't recognize or value your hard-won experience? Are you afraid to expose yourself to others' questions or doubts, or experience that is different from yours? Do you need to find a conduit through which to channel the experiences you've had and knowledge you've collected? Journalists are a great example of this—they take everything they know and everything they've done and pour it into their writing. Teachers have learned how to teach and can relate well to their students because they are perpetual students themselves. Teachers ideally know a lot about many things and can point students in the right direction to find the knowledge they may need. Can you engage your expert nature appropriately?

APPROPRIATE RISK TAKING

One of the big challenges with this purpose centers on discerning what risks to take. How much time do you spend evaluating before taking action or abstaining from it? What do you commit yourself to doing? What's too risky? When do you know enough to go ahead and jump off the diving board? ("There's water in the pool, I know how to swim, let's go!") When do you decide *not* to jump off the diving board? ("I don't know how to swim," or perhaps the pool is empty.) Do you tend to risk too much (stake all your money on the lottery, get married when you've only known someone for two days, try a double jump on ice skates when you've only skated twice)? Or do you risk too little? ("We've been together ten years but I don't know if I can commit to him . . . what if he leaves me?" "I've always wanted to try ice skating, but what if it turns out I'm terrible at it?" "I've saved lots of money . . . but I bury it in my backyard because what if the banks fail like they did in 1929?") With this purpose you are challenged to balance evaluation with action.

Being It, Doing It, and Faking It (Attitude to Adopt)

Since Wisdom is the state of being you wish to live in, where life feels meaningful to you, you can ask yourself the following questions when you're working on adopting the attitude of your Life Purpose in order to more fully inhabit it and then *do it*.

When you feel *skeptical and hesitant*, ask:

- How do I feel when I *do* what I'm thinking of doing? Do I want to sit on the fence all my life and regret what I didn't do? Do I want to say, "Well, I *thought* about it"?

- What do I need to do to gain experience and, therefore, wisdom?

- When do I know enough to go ahead and do something? When can I apply what I know?

- Can I submit to the learning and practice of something in order to gain experience? Can I let it be okay to be a student when I am one and not pose as an expert? Can I then own what I've learned and put it into practice?

- Can I balance taking things seriously (in order to commit to them) and not take myself too seriously?

" I put my ideas into action so I can become wise!"

Practical Everyday Expression/Steps

To build up your ability to be an expert, you must *practice* the actions that create Wisdom!

- *Make decisions.* When you hesitate, procrastinate, and think things over until the "twelfth of never," you are avoiding making decisions. Once decisions are made, they require action and applied effort. And what if it turns out that your ideas don't work out in practical reality? Well, how do you know what will happen if you don't give it a shot? Your idea or vision may be strong in your head, but how can reality ever match it if you don't do what it takes to make it work out in practice? Theories are important—most things start off as an idea—but then there's what happens once you decide to put the pedal to the metal. If you are indecisive, you get completely hung up, and your ideas about the way things could be never have a chance to come true. It's true that you have to let go of options. When you *decide*, you *are* slaying or killing other options. But you are eliminating them so you can move forward and actually bring one of them to life. Do not be like the hen who lays eggs all over the place, who cannot sit on any one of them long enough for any of them to hatch! Practice catching yourself mired down in indecision, and do whatever it takes to *decide*.

- *Take committed action.* Once you have decided, then you can take action! This turns out to be the most exciting part, after all. Who would've thought it would be so satisfying . . . to give life to your idea? Ahhh, to finally be able to commit enough to something to act on it, gain experience, and move closer to the way it could be! It turns out this is what you really wanted and what satisfies you. It may feel, at times, like you've *lost* the freedom to choose from amongst many ideas and opportunities, but you've actually *gained* the freedom to move forward and become experienced. After all, things could turn out better than you expect or take a different turn. The anesthetic Novocaine was developed by German chemist Alfred Einhorn. Einhorn created something that had a much wider practical use than he could have ever envisioned—things turned out *better* than he could've ever imagined! (Ironically, his *idea* was that it was for medical doctors, and he was very disappointed when it turned out to be better for dentists—an interesting twist on being disappointed with reality.) I had a friend whose son was on the first-string hockey team *and* the first-string soccer team, and he began to have to travel for both. He was equally talented in both sports, but his wise coaches finally asked him to choose between the sports so that he could focus on one and move toward the potential of becoming truly great. How can you choose one thing to take committed action on so you can move toward the possibility of being the best you can be at it and eventually becoming wise about it?

- *Develop your sense of humor.* With the Master of Wisdom purpose, the tendency is to be overly serious and dogmatic because you have to be *right* about what you know. Can you catch yourself being judgmental, critical, or know-it-all-ish, and stop and laugh at your all-too-human attempt to trump up your self-importance? When someone else shows you up because they actually have experience at something you've been "talking out of your hat" about, can you accept that you're wrong and lighten up? Even though you want to know it all with this purpose, one of the biggest signs of wisdom is knowing how much you do not know and acceding to the wisdom of others. You learn so much more when you are curious and questioning about the experiences of others, rather than trying to prove you know more than they do. Those who are wise can take things lightly because they understand that no one knows everything, least of all themselves!

Positive Feelings Associated with This Life Purpose

- Free

- Curious

- Open-minded

- Experienced

"I learn from taking action."

Questions to Ask Yourself

- When am I overly judgmental and critical of myself and/or others?

- How do I set myself up for disappointment because my ideas about the way things *could be* and the *reality* of where things are don't match? How can I *do* something about it? Get my hands dirty? Take the risk of acting to bring my ideas and reality closer together?

- When am I most indecisive? What am I really hesitating and procrastinating about? Can I "get off the fence" and get moving?

- Can I catch myself thinking some version of *If I can't win, I won't play* because things might not turn out the way I want them to? When am I a "poor sport"? Do I feel I have to know how things will turn out before I can commit to them?

- How good am I at assessing the risks I take? Do I tend to leap before I look? Look but not leap? Can I put myself at stake? Or choose not to?

- In what capacity do I want to convey wisdom? What experience do I have that I would want to teach or share with others?

- When do I take myself too seriously?

- When do I believe that I'm the only one who knows the "right" way to live or think?

- Do I feel trapped once I commit to something or someone? Can I remind myself that this is something I want to do?

- How do I scatter my focus? Am I a "Jack/Jane of all trades" but "master of none"?

- Can I catch myself making up a long list of reasons for not doing or committing to something or someone?

- Am I overly skeptical, cynical, or jaded because I committed to someone or something and it didn't work out? Can I try again?

Six or More Loops:
Master of Love

Emotional Authenticity

Feelings

Relationships

Closeness

Understanding

Openness

Connectedness

Unconditional Love

Empathy/Sympathy

Self-Acceptance

Let's not forget that the little emotions are the great captains of our lives and we obey them without realizing it.

VINCENT VAN GOGH

The distinction between children and adults, while probably useful for some purposes, is at bottom a specious one, I feel. There are only individual egos, crazy for love.

NICCOLO MACHIAVELLI

To give vent now and then to his feelings, whether of pleasure or discontent, is a great ease to a man's heart.

FRANCESCO GUICCIARDINI

Emotion turning back on itself, and not leading on to thought or action, is the element of madness.

JOHN STERLING

The walls we build around us to keep sadness out also keep out the joy.

JIM ROHN

When dealing with people, remember you are not dealing with creatures of logic, but creatures of emotion.

DALE CARNEGIE

The world needs anger. The world often continues to allow evil because it isn't angry enough.

BEDE JARRETT

If you have the Master of Love Life Purpose, you are here to enjoy close, understanding relationships with everyone you come into contact with, like the butterfly, who visits many flowers in one day and has an intimate reciprocal connection with each one. The butterfly drinks nectar from a flower, pollinates it in return, then carries pollen to the next flower. Thus, the Master of Love is someone who connects with people through relationships, while also connecting people together, just as a butterfly connects with each flower *and* connects disparate flowers through pollination. The Master of Love purpose is not focused on running around trying to love everyone—it is about having a good relationship with yourself through feeling all of your feelings, loving yourself enough to open up to the whole delicious human emotional experience, and connecting with others through the appropriate expression of your feelings so you can have what you yearn for most: a sense of closeness and connectedness, of being accepting of others and accepted by them.

Key to living this Life Purpose is first engaging in the process of relating to yourself, discerning your own feelings, and cultivating a close loving relationship with yourself. As a Master of Love, you want to love yourself enough to surrender, appreciate, and value *all* of your emotions. After all, your feelings are your first and foremost internal guidance system. It's your feelings that tell you what you like and don't like, what you want and don't want, who you like and who you're uncomfortable with, whether you're safe or there's danger nearby. Your feelings are your chief source of information about you and your environment; they drive how you interact with and relate to the world. Being in touch with your feelings is of paramount importance and it's your chief challenge. When you are a Master of Love, there is a tendency to judge a subset of your emotions as *un*acceptable and to deem yourself as unacceptable for having them, so you stuff them down in an attempt to avoid them. Some with this purpose stuff the supposed "negative" feelings, such as anger, fear, sadness, jealousy, or shame, and others avoid the "positive" emotions such as happiness, joy, pride in self, or tenderness. Either way, the issue is, how can you get in touch with your feelings? For example, if you think it isn't okay to be angry and you stuff it, can you ponder why anger is a necessary part of your system and why it might be important to feel it when it arises? I ask my clients, "What would happen if you were to put your hand on a lit stove burner if you didn't feel pain? You would still get severely burned, right?" Physical pain isn't pleasant, but it warns you that something is wrong so further damage can be avoided. Anger is the alarm system for your emotional body, it lets you know when there is the potential for violation or that violation has occurred—whether someone is treating you badly, you are disrespecting yourself, or you are in danger of harming someone else. Others with this purpose stuff their "positive" feelings for various reasons. If you have the Love Life Purpose, you are here to welcome the full range of human emotional experience so you can first have a connected compassionate relationship with yourself.

As you cultivate emotional presence with yourself, a simultaneous layer of challenge is in how you relate to others. How do you build close understanding relationships with other people? Who do you talk to about your feelings and how? How vulnerable do you make yourself by letting others know how you feel? How vulnerable do you allow others to be with you? Do you "spill your guts" to everyone in hopes that they'll understand? Hide your feelings from everyone because you don't want to burden them or find out they don't like how you feel? Expect others to *guess* how you're feeling without your having to voice your emotions? How much do you open your heart to others, not in a fuzzy nonspecific way, but by being emotionally in the moment with them and expressing yourself appropriately? Figuring out *whom* to tell your feelings to, *when* to do it, *where* to express yourself, and the *intensity* of your emotional expression can get pretty complicated. This is what you are meant to *master*, your understanding of feelings and how their expression creates relationships.

To have relationships, we have to *relate* to one another. Sometimes it may be appropriate to yell and scream (you're being attacked and you holler to try and warn off your attacker, or you raise your voice with your partner who repeatedly does something that hurts your feelings despite your requests to desist). At other times it may be best to put a lid on it, sort your feelings out or cool off, then express yourself later or not at all (there is an earthquake and you need to stay calm and get out of the building and emote later, or your baby is driving you crazy waking you up at night). The extremes can be obvious, but it's everything in between that can be so difficult. Do you yell at the person who cuts you off in line at the grocery store? Do you say nothing and just let it slide? What constitutes overexpression and what constitutes underexpression? When do you decide something isn't worth getting worked up over, and when are you just upset and simply need to feel it so you can move through it? All of this takes repeated experience to build your emotional communication skills.

Although I do not know her fingerprints, one of my favorite examples to use for the Master of Love is the Indian "hugging saint" known as Amma. Amma inspires millions of people by simply connecting with them through giving them a loving, affectionate hug. She doesn't tell people how they should feel; rather, she accepts them as they are with the compassionate recognition that, as human beings, we all suffer in various ways and have more in common to empathize with than we have differences. She also emphasizes that it is not enough to *feel* love, it also needs to be *expressed*. From her website, www.amma.org: "Love is the foundation of a happy life. Knowingly or unknowingly we are forgetting this truth." She promotes no particular religion—in fact, people of all religions come together and connect through her all-accepting nonsectarian work, and she encourages everyone to get to know themselves through whatever means suit them. Amma's whole life is about connecting with many people and encouraging them to connect to themselves and others. She is like a butterfly making a connection with many flowers, or like a flower visited by many bees who, because of their congregating around her, get an opportunity to meet up with all the other bees. Ama's followers discover that there is no reason for them to live lives of disconnection and loneliness. There are innumerable people to connect with if you connect with your own tender, vulnerable heart and open yourself to connecting with others.

A more mundane story for the Master of Love is of the character Evelyn from Fannie Flagg's novel, *Fried Green Tomatoes at the Whistle Stop Cafe*. Evelyn is a woman of a certain age who wakes up to her feelings after a lifetime of trying to be loving and understanding to everyone *but* herself. As you can imagine, she's pissed at not heeding her own feelings for so long and finds it's gotten her nowhere but stuck. Her marriage and her stale life have been running along by rote and she feels completely isolated and lonely. Because she hasn't known her feelings, she hasn't known herself. For a while, Evelyn has an extremely short fuse and constantly fantasizes about taking revenge on all the various bad people in the world. Her husband catches a lot of flack, and it jars him awake to his own disconnection. But, as her story progresses, and she lets off her steam over time, she starts to know herself through discerning her feelings and what she wants. She begins to be able to express it and reaches out to others in a genuine way. She develops friendships, starts her own business, and she and her husband get to know each other all over again.

When you are having a hard time with your Master of Love purpose, everything will boil down to some sort of difficulty with making a connection with yourself or to others. You may be out of touch with your own true feelings or stuck on a particular emotional state. (Sad all the time? Flat? All "love and light and everything's perfect," even in the presence of intense suffering?) You may be withholding your feelings ("shutting up and putting up") so others don't know what you're feeling. I've had many clients with this purpose report that they've just cut people off with no explanation because they didn't want to tell them how they felt or didn't want to deal with a friend's feelings, or because they expected someone to just *know* how they felt. I always remind these people that it would be great if we could guess what they're feeling all the time, but since it isn't possible they might want to consider giving us the chance to understand them by communicating their feelings. It's also possible to over-emote as a way to keep people at a distance. Gushing your emotions all the time, at high intensity, without consideration for others' feelings, will surely push people away. Telling other people what they are feeling or what they *should* feel, or ignoring their feelings, are other sure-fire ways to block relating and understanding.

As the Master of Love, your purpose is not about keeping emotions and relationships *under control*. Instead, you want to become *masterful at understanding feelings and the authentic appropriate emotional expression* that allows you to connect to other people with warmth and empathy. You understand how to create and foster understanding relationships through the glue of emotional expression. You allow yourself and others to be okay as the messy, contradictory human beings we all are. You understand that everyone feels the way they do for some reason, whether or not it seems rational and whether or not you feel the same way.

If you are a Master of Love, your deepest fulfillment arises from your willingness to feel the full range of your feelings with acceptance. You love yourself enough to sympathize with yourself and have patient understanding of yourself. Because of your compassionate, loving acceptance of yourself, a space of open acceptance is created around you, which gives others permission to simply be themselves no matter how they feel in this moment. Your appropriate expression of your own feelings allows others to relate to you and to become more deeply connected to themselves.

Challenges

Just because you are a Master of Love doesn't mean it's easy to inhabit your purpose all the time and in all circumstances. You are here to grow into your being and what it requires you to do. Two types of challenges help you gain the broad experience you need in order to live the Love Life Purpose.

Internal Challenges (Being)

These are some of the challenges you have within yourself, the negative beliefs you may hold about yourself and about *authentic emotional expression*, which need to be brought to consciousness and worked with so you can do what is necessary to become truly *connected to self and others*.

"I HAVE 'BAD' FEELINGS"

For those with the Love purpose, there is a tendency to deem a subset of your emotions unacceptable or "bad." For many it's the so-called negative emotions getting stuffed down. Anger, jealousy, fear, sadness, frustration, desperation. For others it's the so-called positive emotions that are to be avoided. Happiness, delight, joy, love, caring. At first glance it seems to make more sense that someone would want to avoid the emotions on the "negative" list, but consider someone with this purpose who grew up with an alcoholic, suicidal parent who was (for obvious reasons) emotionally unavailable. Doesn't it make sense that it might be difficult for this person to delight in life, both because of being accustomed to the emotional climate they grew up in and also because they might feel guilty for surviving when the parent didn't? Feeling happy can feel like a betrayal. "Survivor guilt" is no joke. Or what if your parents always struggled with money, and now you find yourself having a very difficult time enjoying your own success, which has outstripped theirs? What if, on top of it, those parents are jealous of your success, and you suppress your own pride in yourself and your achievements in order not to lose your connection to those parents? For those who prefer to ignore the "positive" feelings, anger feels powerful rather than weak, wallowing in perpetual sadness can be a way to solicit sympathy, and repeatedly flying into jealous rages certainly is one way to get your partner to reassure you of your centrality in his or her life. Remember, none of the emotions are "bad." If this is your purpose, you are here to expand your capacity to experience the *full array* of human emotions. There is no particular way you "should" feel.

No matter what your particular life experience to date has been, you are challenged to develop your emotional range and understand that there is a time and place for all of the feelings. You are here to figure out what they are trying to tell you.

EMOTIONAL "PERFECTION"

Many with the Love purpose have a very particular picture of how they are *supposed* to feel—about themselves, other people, and the world around them. It's okay to be stoic, but better not show fear ("big boys don't cry"). Suspicious and doubtful, but never trusting ("you can't trust anyone but yourself"). Sad, but not angry ("women are more emotional and always turn on the waterworks"). In love, but never saying "I love you." Distressed, but not self-sufficient or strong ("damsels in distress"). And then there's the old adage "children should be seen but not heard." When you are dealing with a strong internal sense of having to be "perfect" emotionally, it requires you to shut down vast parts of yourself, to lie to yourself about how you feel, to disown and reject yourself; basically, to treat yourself and others in a very *un*-loving, uptight manner. If you don't allow yourself to feel anger, how do you know when someone is violating you so you can protect yourself? If you avoid your sadness, how comfortable can you feel in lending a shoulder to someone who is grieving? If it isn't okay to be happy, how can you enjoy life? When you stuff any of your feelings down, you deplete the energy you have for living life and end up out of touch with yourself.

"WHAT AM I FEELING?"

When you are a Master of Love, you are here to connect deeply with yourself through feeling the full range of human emotion. How do you become proficient at this? You start out by having a hard time recognizing or being able to identify what you're feeling, whether it's one particular emotion or all of them. How do you possibly begin to identify what you don't even recognize? This is where your relationships with others and their objective observations can really come in handy. You're driving down the road and your companion notes, "You seem really tense. Are you okay?" And you bark back, "Tense? I'm not tense!" And your companion replies, "Oh. Well, you're gripping the wheel so tight your knuckles are white, your teeth are clenched, and you're frowning." This might be a good moment to pause and check yourself out. *White knuckles, yep. Clenched jaw, yep. Frowning, yep. Hmmm. Is this what it means to be tense? Okay, then I guess I'm tense.*

Paying attention to the *consistent* feedback you get from the people around you is one of the best ways to learn what you're feeling when you don't know yourself. I've known several angry people who think they aren't angry, but everyone in their lives knows they are and avoids them. The angry individuals don't understand why no one sticks around and refuse to acknowledge their seething and lashing out at anyone who gets at all close to them. They are unable to recognize that they are angry and don't see that everyone is responding to it. For some reason they are keeping everyone at a distance because they're afraid to get close. Can you stop and notice how other people respond to you and be curious about what it says about how you are feeling and expressing yourself?

STUFFED FEELINGS

So you've got some feelings you'd rather not have and you're stuffing them, avoiding them, denying them airplay. This is par for the course with this purpose. No need to beat yourself up about it, as this just leads to more self-rejection and more self-hatred rather than building an accepting relationship with yourself. Who can blame you for not wanting to feel those intense stuffed feelings? Your job is to: (1) begin to unstuff your baggage, and (2) become conscious of how you stuff your feelings so you can begin to change your emotional process. First off, I want to point out that these things are both parts of a *process*. Building a loving relationship with yourself is something that happens over a lifetime, not overnight. Your purpose is to build your emotional awareness and acceptance.

External Challenges (Doing)

When you begin to get connected to yourself and others, various obstacles are likely to arise in the external world to challenge you and help you develop strength in your ability to appropriately express your feelings. Remember, your Master of Love Life Purpose does not guarantee emotional authenticity or good relationships. You have to work as skillfully as you are able with the times, the circumstances you're living in, and the people in your life, and all three are likely to confront you in many ways. Here are a few possible external challenges.

"WHAT WILL OTHERS THINK OR FEEL (ABOUT WHAT I FEEL)?"

When you are a Master of Love and you begin to discern what you *really* feel, the next step is to figure out *how* to express it. But your concern about what others might think or feel about what you're feeling can cause you to go right back to stuffing or withholding your feelings and keeping others at arm's length. You want closeness and connection, but what if you tell others how you feel and they react with strong rejection? What if they don't want to be close to you anymore? What if they tell you the way you feel is *wrong*? It's true, this can happen. But if your concern for what others think outweighs your expression of your feelings, how will you ever get the connection you long for? How will we ever get the chance to understand you if you don't tell us how you feel? Could it possibly be okay to feel the way you feel and express it, *and* okay if someone else doesn't feel exactly the same way you do? Can you ask that someone listen to how you feel and try to "hear where you're coming from," without having to agree with your feelings or change them? Having *some* concern for others' feelings is very appropriate. After all, you don't just want to blast someone with all your baggage, but how much concern is just the right amount? You have to practice to find out.

FAIR-WEATHER FRIENDS

Once you start to let others in on how you are feeling, it's likely that some of them aren't going to like it. To your chagrin, you may find that some people in your life are happy to be your friend when you "put on a happy face," but flee when the going gets rough and real in any way. On the dark side of this equation, if you have been in a relationship based on habitual grousing about how rotten things are, you could lose that relationship when you get happy, get a better job, stop playing the victim, or succeed. This is painful stuff. When you find out that someone isn't really there for you (when the emotional truth comes out or your emotional climate broadens), you can really feel the loss. But consider this: If someone is not interested in knowing you, both when the chips are up *and* when the chips are down, were they really well connected to you in the first place? How good a friend were they if you had a semi-accepting relationship with them? It can help to realize that there are some people you can depend on for some things, but not others. You can have different relationships to fulfill different areas of your life. But in the big picture, is it a bad thing to clear your decks of relationships with those who don't really want to know and empathize with all parts of you, so you can make space to find those who want to get to know all about you?

APPROPRIATE EMOTIONAL EXPRESSION

As you express your feelings more fully, you want to pay attention not only to communicating authentically, but also *appropriately*. When you share your feelings, you need to be aware of appropriate *time, person, place,* and *intensity*. When you are unhappy with your spouse, do you complain to your friends but not share your discontent with your spouse? If your mother is jealous of your success, do you call her up first to share your elation when you advance in your career if you know she's just going to try and deflate you? If someone disrespects you in a staff meeting at work, do you in turn make a cutting comment about them in front of all your co-workers or take it up later in private? If the smoke alarm goes off, do you freak out and freeze or do you get yourself out of the building, find out if there's a fire, then emote? This is where it all gets as complex as your feelings can be. Being *authentic* is one thing, but being *appropriate* along with it is another. You are not required to make yourself emotionally vulnerable to those who are unsafe or in an unsafe environment, nor are you supposed to spew your feelings all over someone else in the name of being emotionally truthful. The way you tell your best friend you're hurt or angry will probably be different from the way you express this to a boss or co-worker or someone who cuts in front of you in line at the grocery store. Can you allow yourself to practice appropriateness in the expression of your feelings, given that sometimes you will overdo it and others will underdo it? Can you keep figuring out the best way to get your feelings understood?

EMOTIONAL REMOTE CONTROL

One of the great temptations with the Master of Love purpose is to try and control others' feelings so you don't have to feel the emotions that are uncomfortable for you. If you don't like being angry, you will tell other people why they shouldn't be angry. ("I didn't mean to hurt your feelings, don't be mad at me!" Or, "I think anger is bad and people should rise above it." Or, "She didn't mean to kill your houseplants by not watering them like she promised to. Why can't you just let it go?") You may also tiptoe around and not express yourself so you don't elicit anyone else's ire. Another form of this is an emotional game called "hot potato," which is about eliciting your stuffed feelings from other people so they express your feelings for you (and you can say, "See, I'm not angry/sad/jealous, it's you! You're the one with the problem, not me!"). Or you might withhold your feelings to try and ensure that someone will love you. Or try to get people to agree with the way you feel in an attempt to validate how you feel. ("If others feel the same way I do, then my feelings must be okay.") For the Master of Love, this is not the type of mastery we're talking about. As the Master of Love, you keep growing awareness of your feelings, how they operate, how they are necessary and important, and how working with them requires feeling and expressing them in order to be close to yourself and close to others. The only way beyond any of your feelings is to experience them, understand what they are trying to tell you about yourself, and go through them by giving them an appropriate outlet. When you notice that you're trying to control others' feelings, stop to see how and why you are trying to avoid or validate your own.

Being It, Doing It, and Faking It (Attitude to Adopt)

Since emotional authenticity is the state of being you wish to live in, where life feels meaningful to you, you can ask yourself the following questions when you're working on adopting the attitude of your Life Purpose in order to more fully inhabit it and then *do it*.

When you feel *disconnected* from yourself or others, ask:

- How do I feel when I know my own feelings? When I accept others' feelings? When my feelings are understood and accepted? Can I allow myself to feel whatever I feel in this moment?

- What can I do to accept my own or others' feelings? Can I accept the way others feel even when I don't feel the same way? Can I accept my own feelings, even if they are uncomfortable for me? Take a deep breath and stay emotionally present?

- How do I feel when I am close to others? What do I need to do to let someone else know about how I feel? What feelings do I tend to withhold from others?

- Can I *practice* expressing my feelings? Allow myself to express more, or try to express less, so I can figure out what's just right and gets me understood?

- How would I express my feelings, right now, if I was already skilled at emotional self-expression?

"I accept all of my feelings and express them appropriately to others."

Practical Everyday Expression/Steps

To build up your ability to connect with yourself and others, you must *practice* the actions that create good relationships!

- *Stop and notice what you're feeling.* As you go through your day, can you regularly pause and pay attention to what you are feeling? Are you tired? Relaxed? Hungry? Sad? Frustrated? Tense? Content? Happy? Psychology uses an easy-to-remember palette: Are you feeling bad, mad, sad, or glad? More than one emotion at once? Can you first take a moment to allow yourself to feel whatever emotion is there, without worrying about why you're feeling it, and without judging it—or yourself—for feeling this way? Try taking a few deep breaths and just be with yourself and these emotions. Notice how your body feels while you feel this way. Then be curious about why you feel the way you do rather than discounting your feelings or rationalizing them away. Can you notice if you would rather avoid these feelings? Do you feel the exact same thing, all the time, every time you check in with yourself? Are there numb spots? Try making a practice out of noticing your feelings in an uncensored manner, and being curious about them and where they come from, with as little judgment as possible. Is some particular feeling noticeably absent? Stop and take a deep breath. Think of it as the very interesting experiment it actually is and have mercy on yourself for being perfectly human.

- *Catch yourself withholding your true feelings.* Whether you tend to overexpress or regularly underexpress yourself, the real questions are: Are you expressing your true emotions or withholding them from yourself and others? Which feelings do you stuff the most? For some it's anger, for others it's fear, and some with this purpose are afraid to express their "positive" emotions to others because it feels too vulnerable to do so. It's common for men with this purpose to have a harder time showing their "softer" emotions because they've been taught that love and tenderness equal weakness. For many women, it's okay to cry, but absolutely forbidden to express their anger openly. Can you catch yourself in the act of withholding your feelings and simply note it? How often do you withhold how you feel? From whom? What are the results of withholding your feelings?

- *Practice <u>understanding</u> without <u>agreement</u>.* Being close and connected to other people is not necessarily about feeling the same way they feel or trying to get them to feel the same way you feel. It's about making an effort to understand why others feel the way they do and asking them to make an effort to understand the way you feel. "I feel what I feel, you feel what you feel, and it's okay." Everyone's feelings are valid, especially since feelings aren't "right" or "wrong." This is what empathy and sympathy are all about. There are times when you may not even be able to understand why others feel the way they do, and your inability to understand your differing feelings makes it impossible to relate to each other, but you can still be respectful. It's always possible to work toward an understanding of each other's emotional positions without agreeing or feeling the same way. Striving for *understanding* instead of agreement is what ultimately fosters a good connection.

Positive Feelings Associated with This Life Purpose

- Warm

- Sympathetic/Empathetic

- Connected to self and others

- Loving

"I love and understand myself."

Questions to Ask Yourself

- Which of my feelings do I tend to judge and deny and stuff?

- What feelings am I uncomfortable with when others express them?

- Do I have close, connected relationships with others?

- Can I allow myself to have all of my feelings and recognize they are all important and necessary? Be curious about why I feel the way I do?

- When am I uncomfortable with other people's feelings? Which ones are hardest for me to witness and be present for?

- Do I believe I am supposed to feel a certain way about myself, other people, or the world?

- Do I tend to be stuck on one particular emotion? Try to be happy all the time? Feel sad about everything? Get angry or frustrated in response to everything?

- Do I try to get other people to feel my feelings for me so I don't have to? Poke at others to make them angry, or hurt their feelings to make them cry (while I stay calm and collected and in control)?

- Does it seem like I am surrounded by people who all feel a particular way? Is it possible that they are expressing what I am stuffing down? Mirroring my own unacknowledged feelings?

- Do I have too many "fair-weather friends"? Can I take the risk of letting some of them know more about how I really feel so I can find out if they are truly understanding and supportive of me?

- Can I give others the opportunity to understand and get closer to me by letting them know what I feel?

- Do I expect others to *know* how I feel without telling them?

Six or More Whorls:
Master of Service

Help

Assistance

Giving

Sharing

Choice/Liberty

Awareness of Desires/Appetites

Appropriate Indulgence

Individuation

The first duty of a human being is to assume the right functional relationship to society—more briefly, to find your real job, and do it.

CHARLOTTE PERKINS GILMAN

Personal transformation can and does have global effects. As we go, so goes the world, for the world is us. The revolution that will save the world is ultimately a personal one.

MARIANNE WILLIAMSON

I don't know what your destiny will be, but one thing I know: the only ones among you who will be really happy are those who have sought and found how to serve.

ALBERT SCHWEITZER

Give a man a fish and you feed him for a day. Teach him how to fish and you feed him for a lifetime.

LAO TZU

How can I be useful, of what service can I be? There is something inside me, what can it be?

VINCENT VAN GOGH

Consciously or unconsciously, every one of us does render some service or other. If we cultivate the habit of doing this service *deliberately*, our desire for service will steadily grow stronger, and will make, not only for our own happiness, but that of the world at large.

MAHATMA GANDHI

The greatest good you can do for another is not just to share your riches but to reveal to him his own.

BENJAMIN DISRAELI

If you have the Master of Service Life Purpose, you are here to reap the joys of sharing inherent in acts of selfless service. You have the potential to give to others and the world, springing from a deep desire to offer valuable needed help and assistance. As the Master of Service, you reap meaning from knowing you have something to offer, something someone else needs, and then giving it generously with "no strings attached," without expecting anything in return. This is not to say that you are meant to serve indiscriminately, to give everything you have away, to try and help anyone and everyone who needs help, or to give with no regard to the outcome of your service. Rather, you are meant to learn how to make sure that your giving is to the benefit of *everyone* involved. With this purpose, you are here to serve yourself, serve others, *and* serve the world, and be enriched by it.

Key to living this Life Purpose is engaging in the entire process of learning what true service is—and what it is not. You are here to discover the difference between *service and sacrifice.* The traditional notions of service most of us hold involve giving everything you have away, considering everyone else before yourself, saying yes to any request made of you, living in some form of impoverishment (particularly material), and being appreciated by others for giving up everything of value to you for some greater good. In the French movie *Amélie*, the title character fantasizes that she has lived a life of service/sacrifice by working for the poor and downtrodden of the world, and that she has died from exhaustion. This is all enacted visually as she and we watch a television tribute to her life with an audience of people cheering and thousands of people thronging to her funeral to shed debilitating tears of devotion. She gave it all up and won the hearts of the world in return. But this is not what true service is actually about. It is not about impoverishment or servitude or giving everything you have in order to be admired by others. If you serve/sacrifice until you drop, then you can no longer be of service to anyone. True service is about asking the following *Service Test Questions:* (1) Is it good for me? (2) Is it good for them? (3) Do I want to do it? Then it is about pausing to make a *deliberate* decision about the best action for everyone in-volved—starting with yourself. At first this can sound terribly "selfish" to you if you have this purpose. "Doesn't being a 'Master of Service' mean that I should be okay with doing anything for anyone at any time they need me?" The answer is *no!* When you do this you are *not* engaged in service, you are *sacrificing*, which, ultimately, isn't good for anyone since someone in the equation is being depleted, undervalued, disempowered, or impoverished for another's gain.

As the Master of Service, you get to work with a paradox: you must be "self-ish" (appropriately self-oriented) in order to become selfless. I use the following story to il-lustrate this is: Imagine that Albert Einstein (who, with seven whorls, was a Master of Service) was good at fixing plumbing, and that everyone in his neighborhood knew it and called him up with their plumbing crises, and he always jumped to help them out. What if word spread and all his time was taken up with other people's plumbing problems? If this were the case, would Einstein have had enough time and energy and resources to work on his physics and make his great discoveries? I think you can see where this is leading. It's clear that it's a good thing Einstein was self-oriented enough to stay focused on the work that was *his* work. The best way Einstein could serve the world was through his discoveries in theoretical physics, discoveries that continue to serve us today, long after his death. Einstein devoted himself to fulfilling his individual potential, and the fulfillment of his potential served the world in a much greater way than helping others with their individual crises ever could. He passed the Service Test Questions: what he did was good for him, good for them, and he wanted to do what he did. In fact, he was acknowledged with the Nobel Prize in 1921 for his "*services* to theo-retical physics."

Many students and clients who are counselors with the Master of Service purpose have similar stories of struggling mightily with it. They are all people doing service in accordance with their special gifts and talents, but were very burned out because of seeing too many clients one-on-one. All are successful in terms of being overbooked and in high demand. Some also had additional commitments to train other students or peers in their respective fields. They all wanted to help as many people as possible and didn't know how to draw the line and say no in order to take care of themselves. Most were sick with fatigue and on the verge of emotional, physical, and energetic break-down, which would force them to stop sacrificing themselves for others and serve *only* themselves in order to recover and restore their lost energy. All were faced with figuring out how to serve more people with considerably less energy output since they were already running below empty. This feat would require them not only to stop taking on more, but to *scale back* their schedules in order to recharge themselves so they could have enough energy to devise some way to work with more people at once, to focus "self-ishly" on developing another way of delivering their services. One realized that she needed to write a book, another saw that she wanted to create and run workshops, and yet another saw that he could simply refer new business to colleagues (and be of service to them) instead of believing he should extend himself into an even longer day to help "just one more person." These Masters of Service all had to understand that if they weren't serving themselves properly they couldn't sustain their service to others. And that if they were living burned-out, overextended lives, they were hardly good models for their clients. When each of them asked themselves the Service Test Questions, they found one or more of the answers clearly came back *no*, particularly for the question "Is it good for me?" but also in response to "Is it good for them?"

People who serve make sure that it is good for everyone involved. They realize everyone must be well served for anyone to be well served. Service is about an exchange; it is a form of giving and receiving that empowers both the giver and the receiver. To have something to give, you must be able to receive. That interaction is not always directly between the giver and the receiver, but the giver must receive (be served by self and others) in order to have something to give. If you make your first dollar and then give it all away to your neighbor who needs to buy food, then you put yourself in a position of needing help from someone else to get by. You have *sacrificed* yourself, and now perhaps *both* you and your neighbor are starving. You need to fill yourself up to a sufficient level so you can sustain yourself before you can give substantially to others. Think of some of the large philanthropic foundations that provide money to help many different causes. When John D. MacArthur started making money, he didn't immediately give it all away to serve others. He built up a lot of money and then started the charitable foundation. There were so many resources accumulated ($1 billion) that just the interest generated off the principal of the money is a phenomenal amount of service to many causes in need of help. And this money perpetuates itself and will continue to serve the needs of many people over an indefinite period of time.

I am not suggesting that you shouldn't help anyone out with anything along the way, just that you need to mind your own resources so you have enough for yourself and don't put yourself in such a position of need that you are literally unable to help others.

Friends of mine belong to a Muslim community with strong service values. They donate 5 percent of their modest income to their community to help others in need and to fund educational services for the community. They may or may not be in need of some of those services themselves someday, but they feel good about giving and their own living is not in jeopardy. Their giving meets the Service Test Questions.

It is also important to check to see if what you do for others is actually *good for them*. Because you want to be needed and want to help and want to serve, you can make the mistake of doing things for others that they should do for themselves. When I see men with the Master of Service purpose I hear a common story: He's working very hard to provide for his family, but all they want is *more*, and they take what they have for granted. They have no idea what it takes to make the money and just *expect* husband/Dad to do whatever it takes to give them what they want. He's the man, he's supposed to make the sacrifices to provide for his family, right? Isn't that what men are for? When I get such a client, I try to help him see how he has tripped on his Master of Service purpose by giving his family everything they want (and more), expecting very little in return, and basically training them to be selfish. How empowered will the kids be, once they grow up, when they find out they will have to *work* for money and they've learned to be lazy? How good can the marital relationship be if the client is too tired to enjoy life and he feels resentful about working too hard and being taken for granted? Could it possibly be true service to make the kids earn some things for themselves rather than thinking money grows on trees? When you find yourself thinking, "this is what I get after all I've done for you!" then you know that it's time to ask the Service Test Questions. Maybe you are doing things for others that they didn't even ask for and would rather do for themselves? Maybe they should do these things for themselves in order to become competent and capable and strong? Maybe it's better to "teach them how to fish"? When you find that there is resentment anywhere in your transactions with others, it is a red flag indicating sacrifice is happening, not service.

When the Master of Service consciously begins to learn and engage in *choosing* to serve, rather than sacrificing, or being coerced into servitude, you become truly helpful to others. You are able to balance your service to yourself with your service to others and everyone wins. It becomes easier to discern what is best for everyone, and you develop your ability to focus your service so it can have a real impact, rather than mistakenly scattering and wasting your energy. You get more comfortable with letting other people know what you expect in return for what you give so you can serve each other, and you are able to see when you are "giving to get" and manipulating others, rather than giving with no strings attached. You are willing to keep practicing *appropriate* self-ishness in order to become truly selfless. You keep enough of your time, energy, and resources for yourself so you can cultivate your potential and then allow that to serve the world in a larger way.

If you are a Master of Service, your deepest fulfillment arises from clearly saying yes to service and no to sacrifice, of being more and more savvy about the difference between the two of them and negotiating the fine line between them. You are able to stop and make a conscious decision about what you do for others instead of acting under a sense of duty and burdensome obligation. Life doesn't always make it easy to tell the difference between service and sacrifice, but you keep learning that it's the *spirit* with which you give and receive, rather than the action itself, which constitutes true masterful service.

Challenges

Just because you are a Master of Service doesn't mean it's always easy to inhabit your purpose all the time and in all circumstances. You are here to grow into your being and what it requires you to do. Two types of challenges help you gain the broad experience you need in order to live the Service Life Purpose.

Internal Challenges (Being)

These are some of the challenges you have within yourself, the negative beliefs you may hold about yourself and about Service, which need to be brought to consciousness and worked with so you can do what is necessary to become truly helpful.

KNEE-JERK SERVICE (SACRIFICE)

When you have the Service purpose, you feel like you *have* to help others and jump to do it, without considering whether it's the best thing for everyone involved or not. You see someone having trouble and spring to the rescue, whether or not they have asked for your help, regardless of the bigger picture or the consequences. You don't stop and make a conscious choice, and because of this you get to learn the bitter truth of the saying "the road to hell is paved with good intentions," as your well-meaning actions can miss the mark and someone ends up getting sacrificed. You're depleting yourself, depriving someone else of learning what they need to learn, disempowering them by doing it for them, or just plain getting in the way because you've just *got* to feel like you're doing something for someone, you're looking for something in return (even if it's a simple thanks), and you're not happy if no appreciation is forthcoming. If you can anticipate someone reacting by saying, "I didn't ask you for your help!" you are most likely in trouble. How can you learn the difference between sacrifice and service so you know when to help and when to refrain from helping?

"I DON'T KNOW THE DIFFERENCE BETWEEN SERVICE AND SACRIFICE"

To tell if your intended actions will fall in the realm of true service or dastardly sacrifice for yourself or others, stop and practice asking yourself these Service Test Questions: (1) Is is good for me? (2) Is it good for them? (3) Do I want to do it? At first this may be difficult to do. You're used to jumping to "help" and have to learn to catch yourself. You might feel guilty and selfish for asking, you may not want to think beyond yourself to your impact on others, or you may find it very difficult to get answers to one or more of these questions. But this is the place to start once you realize you are engaged in self-sacrifice—or expect others to sacrifice or live in servitude for you.

FACING THE "BIG I DON'T KNOW"

Once you start to ask the Service Test Questions, it can be painful to discover you don't know the answers. It can be frustrating to face the "Big I Don't Know," that black hole in yourself. You've been so disconnected from yourself or from others that you don't even know what's good for you or good for them or good for the bigger picture. It's enough to make you squirm and run back to your old ways of riding the coattails of others' needs or "doing nothing for no one but me." It's hard to engage true service when you don't know what's best for you or others. The worst can be seeing how you don't even know what you want. You've been sacrificing for others for so long that you've been absent from yourself. (Or you've been so self-serving that you haven't noticed the rest of the world.) Can you sit in the "Big I don't know" when you find it? There is a place inside where you *do know*, but it's as if you haven't listened to it for so long that it thumbs its nose at you and replies, "*Now* you're asking? Why should I tell you anything! We never do what I want anyway!" (Or, when you finally ask others what works for them, they can be reluctant to trust you enough to tell you because you've shown no concern for them until now.) It is of paramount importance that you keep asking yourself the Service Test Questions so you can reconnect with the part of you who knows exactly what it wants, and then serve yourself. It is equally important to ask others what they want so you know how to serve them properly, if you choose to do so.

"I *EXPECT OTHERS* TO SERVE ME"

One of the internal obstacles you may have to work with is the *unconscious expectation* that others should serve you. After all, you're giving to them, shouldn't they give back to you? The answer is *not necessarily*. In fact, if you find yourself *expecting* something from someone (without a spoken or written agreement involved), as if it is their duty or obligation, or it's in return for what you've done for them, then you need a red flag to go up. Sacrifice is going on, not service. When you find yourself thinking or saying, "After all I did for you, this is what I get!" note that you were expecting something in return and you weren't engaged in true service. You were trying to bargain for something through manipulation. Another version of this centers on expecting others to read your mind and serve you. ("I know what others need, isn't what I need as obvious to them?") And yet another is about believing that you deserve to receive from others constantly, without giving anything in return. ("Others serve me, I don't have to serve them.") This is what perpetuates slavery, which is still practiced all over the world to the tune of 27 million people being held and forced to work through the threat of violence. See www.iabolish.org.

External Challenges (Doing)

When you begin to balance Service to yourself with Service to others, various obstacles are likely to arise in the external world to challenge you and help you develop strength in your ability to serve. Remember, your Master of Service purpose doesn't guarantee *balanced service*. You have to work as skillfully as you are able with the times, the circumstances you're living in, and the people in your life, and all three are likely to confront you in many ways. Here are a few possible external challenges.

"IT'S HARD TO SAY NO"

You're stopping to ask yourself the Service Test Questions, and some of them are coming up *no*. It's one thing to know within yourself that something isn't good for you, good for them, or you don't want to do it—congratulations for practicing asking yourself! Now it's quite another matter to open your mouth and tell someone "No" when they are asking for or expecting your help. And life situations don't always make it easy to turn others down, but just see if you can take a deep breath and practice saying no when you know you'll be sacrificing yourself if you say yes. Make it your grand experiment. And be prepared for others to dislike it.

"THEY DON'T LIKE IT WHEN I SAY NO"

Others are used to getting their needs and wants met through you. You've been a "yes" man or "yes" woman for so long that they are shocked when you finally say no. Your challenge is to withstand anyone who pulls out the stops to manipulate you to continue sacrificing yourself for them. I've heard many versions of this from clients, including the following: *Flattery.* ("You're so much better at this than I am!" "It takes you so much less time to do it than me.") Being *thanked* for sacrificing. (I had a client whose husband cleverly pre-empted her considering serving her own career desires by thanking her lavishly and regularly for giving up her own career in order to travel with him for his.) *Feigned helplessness.* ("I'm not strong enough to do it." "I just can't deal with it!") And flat-out *emotional blackmail.* ("You don't love me anymore!" "You used to be so nice." "Why don't you want to help me?" "You're so selfish! You think of no one but yourself!")

If this is your purpose, I'm sure you can come up with more examples of how others try to keep getting themselves "served" by you, even when it isn't good for you, good for them, or you don't want to do it. The good news is that when you choose service and say no to sacrifice, you stop allowing people to take you for granted, and they may eventually learn to respect you for serving yourself and appreciate you when you choose to do something for them.

INTERFERENCE/MEDDLING IN OTHERS' BUSINESS

One of the challenges with the Service purpose is to catch yourself jumping in to help without an invitation to do so. It's one thing to to use the Heimlich maneuver on someone who is choking, it's quite another to tie your children's shoelaces for them forever just because they aren't good at doing it, or take over the computer when someone asks you a question about how to do something. But you want to feel needed. I was at a conference last year and had such a long line of people waiting to see me that the form my clients fill out to sign up for an appointment got passed down the line. This was no problem. But then the sheets got shuffled, and when the clipboard got back to me, I paused a moment to straighten things out. A waiting client noticed I was overwhelmed, grabbed the sheets from me, and started arranging them—when she had no idea how they went together. In fact, she made an even bigger mess out of them and thought she was being helpful. She just couldn't resist her compulsion to "serve" and mistakenly interfered in my business to my detriment and to time lost for those waiting. And, yep, once I looked at her fingerprints, there she was with the Service Life Purpose. I had another client who had just signed up for a session; we'd looked at her fingerprints, and scheduled her appointment. When I talked to her a bit about service, sacrifice, and the possibility of meddling with others' business she was a little befuddled and said, "I used to do that, but not anymore." Then I mentioned that I was finishing up a book and she *immediately* volunteered to give up her appointment time (sacrifice it) and schedule it for after my deadline (months later) and, and, and . . . and I looked at her and grinned, and she did too as she realized that she'd just jumped to sacrifice what she wanted and was trying to manage my time for me in order to make the sacrifice. It was all done in the spirit of considering my needs, but it was meddling just the same, in the name of trying to be helpful. Oops!

IT'S HARD TO RECEIVE FROM OTHERS . . . OR HARD TO GIVE

If you are someone who constantly gives to others in the name of service, you may find it difficult to allow others to serve you. How can you feel that you might be serving others by allowing them to serve you? Just as you wish to help others, there are people who would like to help you. Can you let others accumulate some service brownie points, or do you always have to hog them all for yourself? Can you let them feel that they are full enough to have something to offer? The truth is, when you don't allow others to do things for you, you are cutting off the deep sense of sharing that makes life feel good to you. Service is a two-way street requiring both giving and receiving. True service empowers both the receiver and the giver. How does it feel when someone refuses your help? Can you be vulnerable enough to receive? If you are on the other side of the fence with this, expecting to be served without ever giving in return, the same thing applies. Balanced service is about being able to both give and receive so that everyone is well served. If giving or receiving are blocked, true service is thwarted and what you are really doing is maintaining control.

Being It, Doing It, and Faking It (Attitude to Adopt)

Since Service is the state of being you wish to live in, where life feels meaningful to you, you can ask yourself the following questions when you're working on adopting the attitude of your Life Purpose in order to more fully inhabit it and then *do it*.

When you feel like you're *sacrificing*, ask:

- How do I feel when I *consciously decide* to serve?

- Am I capable of turning down requests for help? How does it feel to do so?

- Do I find my agenda by hitching onto others' needs and desires? Do I know what I want so I can serve myself instead of *expecting* to be served by others?

- Can I see myself as the first and foremost person who needs to serve me?

- What would I do right now if I were already balancing service to myself with service to others?

"I engage in deliberate Service and can choose to serve or not."

Practical Everyday Expression/Steps

To build up your ability to be of true Service, you must balance what you do for yourself with what you do for others.

- *Practice <u>choosing</u> what you do for others.* Ultimately, Service is a consciousness more than what you do or don't do for others It's about being *at choice* about what you do for yourself, for others, and for the world. Before jumping to "help out" or sign up for something you feel you "have to" or "should" do, practice restraining yourself and asking the Service Test Questions. When you think you've got the answers, stop and ponder your options. Making this moment conscious, the moment of choice, is what begins to make all the difference in the world for you. Given that you're free, you *always* have choices, even if the circumstances look like you don't, and you're having to choose between the lesser of two evils, or you're dealing with an obligation you've already made and now you're not too happy about it. Let's say you've got the Master of Service purpose and you've had a baby, and it turns out your baby is colicky and up all night screaming for days on end. Tough situation. Who wouldn't start to feel trapped and resentful and helpless and frustrated and like there is no choice in the matter? Or that the choices are very limited: abandon your child or continue being a slave to this little being you cannot reason with. Now, for many, abandonment wouldn't even come up as an option. But what if you *considered* it (as well as stopping to see if there is anyone you can ask for help)? And then what if you made your decision again, every day, anew, to be of help to your baby? What if you realized that *you are making a choice* and you *could* make other choices, but you are making a willing choice to help and comfort this little being? Wouldn't your mental state be different than that of feeling resentful and of *having to*? Can you keep reminding yourself that you *chose* to have a child in the first place? I'm using this as an example because most people reading this book would balk completely at abandonment as an option, but it is, and it happens all the time, even if it's not the choice you would make. There *is* a choice being made. No one is forcing you to stay with your child. Can you do your best to *own your choice* and transform your sense of sacrifice into the consciousness of service when it is appropriate to do so?

- *Balance giving and receiving.* If you are someone who gives and gives and gives some more, and you're energetically, emotionally, financially, or physically exhausted, you are learning that you cannot serve others without being served yourself or you just end up a sacrificed-out martyr. To have something to give, you must be able to receive, both from yourself and from others. If you burn out you will no longer be able to help anyone but yourself. You'll be broke, or sick, or perpetually tired, or resentful of how much is expected of you, and disillusioned about receiving nothing in return. You'll get yourself into a position where you must put yourself first and allow yourself to be helped because you've done such a poor job of serving yourself. It's as if you've fed everyone else all your food and starved yourself down to nothing, and you don't understand why you can't keep rolling along like this. With the Service purpose, this is a perfectly normal extreme to go to, if necessary, so you can learn the art of being served, albeit the hard way. If you have not yet gone to such extremes, can you start paying attention to what you need and want and take care of it for yourself? Can you start asking for help from others? If you have hoarded everything selfishly for yourself, like Scrooge in Dickens' *A Christmas Carol*, can you make a choice to start sharing yourself and your resources (of all kinds—your piano playing, your time, your money, etc.) with others so you can begin to enjoy your fullness?

- *Notice when you're engaged in "silent bargaining."* Pay attention to when you are *giving to get*, that is, you are doing something for others (whether they asked for it or not) and you are expecting something in return, but *this has not been openly expressed, so a negotiation didn't happen.* When you do this, you are sacrificing yourself and expecting others to sacrifice themselves in return. One version of this has to do with your *not knowing* what you want, so you give others what you think they want and hope that they will guess your needs or desires and fulfill them in return. Yikes! This is a recipe for disaster. No one can know what you want but you, and it is unfair to manipulate others to get something from them that they may not want to give. There is nothing wrong with wanting to give and get something in return, but it must be an above-board negotiated deal so both parties have a chance to *choose* what they give and receive (true service), rather than get all tangled up a sacrificial bargain with no one getting what they desire.

Positive Feelings Associated with This Life Purpose

- Choice

- "Giving is its own reward"

- Energetic/full

- Helpful

"I enjoy serving others and enjoy being served!"

Questions to Ask Yourself

- Do I know what I want to do? What do I do that isn't good for me? What do I do that I really don't want to do?

- Can I see what is in the best interest of others? What do I do that is disempowering for others?

- Do I never serve anyone but myself? In what ways am I selfish?

- What do I do for others that leaves me feeling drained?

- Can I see how and when I give to get, rather than consciously giving for its own sake?

- Do I know what I want and need to serve myself? Do I know what my own agenda for myself is?

- Can I catch myself jumping in to be "helpful" when I'm actually getting in the way or interfering with someone else's business?

- Does my life feel like it's loaded with duty and burdensome obligation? Can I stop and see how I am *choosing* or *not choosing* to do the things I do for others?

- What do I believe I *have* to do for others?

- Can I ask and allow others to serve me?

- Do I allow others to take me for granted?

- Can I let it be okay to ask, "What's in it for me?" as well as consider, "What's in it for them?"

- When do I feel burned out from doing too much for others?

APPENDIX

Practice Charts

practice chart #1

	Thumb	Pointer	Middle	Ring	Pinkie
Right	♌	◉	♌	♌	♌
Left	♌	♌	♌	♌	♌

#1. Life Purpose is _____

practice chart #2

	Thumb	Pointer	Middle	Ring	Pinkie
Right	♌	◉	♌	♌	♌
Left	♌	◉	♌	♌	♌

#2. Life Purpose is _____

practice chart #3

	Thumb	Pointer	Middle	Ring	Pinkie
Right	—	♌	◉	♌	—
Left	◉	♌	◉	♌	—

#3. Life Purpose is _____

practice chart #4

	Thumb	Pointer	Middle	Ring	Pinkie
Right	—	—	—	—	—
Left	—	—	—	—	—

#4. Life Purpose is _____

practice chart #5

	Thumb	Pointer	Middle	Ring	Pinkie
Right	♌	—	♌	♌	—
Left	♌	—	⊥	⊥	⊥

#5. Life Purpose is _____

practice chart #6

	Thumb	Pointer	Middle	Ring	Pinkie
Right	♌	▬	▬	♌	♌
Left	♌	▬	▬	♌	♌

#6. Life Purpose is _____

practice chart #7

	Thumb	Pointer	Middle	Ring	Pinkie
Right	◎	♌	◎	♌	◎
Left	♌	♌	▬	♌	♌

#7. Life Purpose is _____

practice chart #8

	Thumb	Pointer	Middle	Ring	Pinkie
Right	♌	◎	◎	♌	◎
Left	♌	◎	◎	♌	◎

#8. Life Purpose is _____

practice chart #9

	Thumb	Pointer	Middle	Ring	Pinkie
Right	▬	⊥	⊥	⊥	⊥
Left	▬	⊥	⊥	▬	▬

#9. Life Purpose is _____

practice chart #10

	Thumb	Pointer	Middle	Ring	Pinkie
Right	♌	⊥	♌	♌	♌
Left	♌	⊙	♌	⊙	♌

#10. Life Purpose is _____

practice chart #11

	Thumb	Pointer	Middle	Ring	Pinkie
Right	⊙	⊙	⊙	⊙	⊙
Left	⊙	⊙	⊙	⊙	⊙

#11. Life Purpose is _____

practice chart #12

	Thumb	Pointer	Middle	Ring	Pinkie
Right	♌	♌	♌	♌	♌
Left	♌	R ♌	♌	♌	♌

#12. Life Purpose is _____

practice chart #13

	Thumb	Pointer	Middle	Ring	Pinkie
Right	♌	♌	♌	♊	♌
Left	♌	♌	♌	♊	♌

#13. Life Purpose is _____

practice chart #14

	Thumb	Pointer	Middle	Ring	Pinkie
Right	◉	◉	◉	◉	◉
Left	Ⓢ	◉	Ⓢ	◉	Ⓢ

#14. Life Purpose is _____

#1. Leader. #2. Leader. #3. Family Mentor. #4. Master of Peace. #5. Successful Artist in Business. #6. Master of Love *or* Successful Healing Artist. #7. Successful Messenger in Business. #8. Master of Service *or* Leading Healing Mentor. #9. Master of Wisdom *or* Leading Mentoring Creative Communications. #10. Passionate Innovator. #11. Master of Service. #12. Master of Love *or* Live My Passions. #13. Artist. #14. Master of Service *or* Successful Leading Creative Communications in Business.

Summary Sheet for Identifying Life Purpose

(Make copies so you can use more than once, or visit www.DestinyAtYourFingertips.com to download this page.)

Step #1—Four Basic Fingerprint Types *(see book for subtypes, if necessary)*

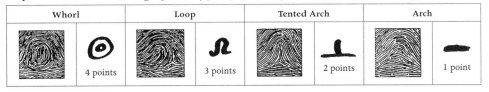

Whorl	Loop	Tented Arch	Arch
4 points	3 points	2 points	1 point

Step #2—Identify Fingerprint Type(s)

Step #3—Fill in Fingerprint Chart with Symbols

	Thumb	Pointer	Middle	Ring	Pinkie
Right Hand					
Left Hand					

Step #4—Add Ranking Points in Corner for Each Fingerprint

Step #5—Decode: Circle Your High-Ranking Fingers and Read On!

	Thumb *Results*	Pointer (Jupiter) *Power*	Middle (Saturn) *Responsibility*	Ring (Apollo) *Creativity*	Pinkie (Mercury) *Communications*
Right Hand Outer or "Public"	Public + Results SUCCESS	Public + Power LEADER	Public + Responsibility "BUSINESS"	Public + Creativity ARTIST/INDIVIDUALIST	Public + Communications MESSENGER
Left Hand Inner or "Personal"	Personal + Results "FAMILY"	Personal + Power PASSIONS	Personal + Responsibility MENTOR	Personal + Creativity INNOVATOR	Personal + Communications HEALER

#5a: If you have **fewer than six** fingerprints tying for high rank, decode according to the chart above denoting **Each Individual Finger's Life Purpose**. Check for doubles, then string all the words for your Life Purpose together and write below.

#5b: If you have **doubles** tying for high rank (for example: *both* thumbs or *both* pointer fingers have high-ranking fingerprints), use the purposes below.

Double Thumb = Success   Double Ring = Artist

Double Pointer = Leader   Double Pinkie = Healer

Double Middle = Mentor

#5c: If you have **six or more fingerprints** tying for high rank, use the **Group Life Purpose** associated with the fingerprint type itself and write in below.

Ten arches = Master of Peace   Six or more tented arches = Master of Wisdom

Six or more loops = Master of Love   Six or more whorls = Master of Service

My Life Purpose Is: _____

See Life Purpose chapters for full explanations.

271

BIBLIOGRAPHY/RESOURCES

Books, Essays, and Articles

Bayles, David, and Ted Orland. *Art & Fear*. Eugene, OR: Image Continuum Press, 2001.

Flagg, Fannie. *Fried Green Tomatoes at the Whistle Stop Cafe*. New York, NY: McGraw Hill, 1987.

———. *Welcome to the World, Baby Girl*. New York, NY: Ballantine Books, 1998.

Gilbert, Elizabeth. *Eat, Pray, Love*. New York, NY: Penguin Books, 2006.

Glickstein, Lee. *Be Heard Now!* New York, NY: Broadway Books, 1998.

Hill, Napoleon. *Think and Grow Rich*. Meriden, CT: The Ralston Society, 1937.

Ingleby, David. "The Importance of Being Peter Lomas: Social Change and the Ethics of Psychotherapy." In *Committed Uncertainty in Psychotherapy: Essays in Honour of Peter Lomas*, edited by Lucy King, 139–150. London, UK: Whurr Publishers, Ltd., 1999.

Lamott, Anne. *Bird by Bird: Some Instructions on Writing and Life*. New York, NY: First Anchor Books, 1995.

Lee, Harper. *To Kill a Mockingbird*. New York, NY: Popular Library, 1960.

Le Guin, Ursula K. *The Farthest Shore*. New York, NY: Bantam Books, 1972.

McLaughlin, Emma, and Nicola Kraus. *The Nanny Diaries*. New York, NY: St. Martin's Press, 2002.

Oliver, Mary. "When Death Comes." *New and Selected Poems*. Boston, MA: Beacon Press, 2005.

Port, Otis. "Timothy J. Berners-Lee: Spinning The World's Web." *Businessweek*, November 8, 2004, http://www.businessweek.com/magazine/content/04_45/b3907023_mz072.htm.

Shinoda Bolen, Jean. *Gods in Everyman*. San Francisco, CA: Harper & Row, 1989.

———. *Goddessess in Everywoman*. New York, NY: Harper & Row, 1984.

Starhawk. *Dreaming the Dark*. Boston, MA: Beacon Press, 1997.

Unger, Richard. *LifePrints*. Berkeley, CA: Ten Speed Press, 2007.

Wilson, Frank. *The Hand*. New York, NY: Vintage Books, 1998.

Winterson, Jeanette. *The PowerBook*. New York, NY: Vintage Books, 2000.

Yalom, Irvin. *Momma and the Meaning of Life*. New York, NY: HarperCollins, 1999.

———. *The Gift of Therapy*. New York, NY: HarperCollins, 2002.

Zander, Rosamund Stone and Benjamin Zander. *The Art of Possibility*. Boston, MA: Harvard Business School Press, 2000.

Movies

Amélie (2001)

Billy Elliot (2000)

Dreamgirls (2006)

Good Will Hunting (1997)

The Karate Kid (1984)

Miracle (2004)

Miss Potter (2006)

Mumford (1999)

My Big Fat Greek Wedding (2002)

Riding Giants (2004)

Rudolph the Red-Nosed Reindeer (1964)

Schultze Gets the Blues (2003)

Sicko (2007)

Websites

Creative Juices Arts (Chris Zydel): www.creativejuicesarts.com

iAbolish: The American Anti-Slavery Group: www.iabolish.org

www.amma.org

Music

Barenaked Ladies, "Box Set" (song from their album, *Gordon*)

Free Catalog

Get the latest information on our body, mind, and spirit products! To receive a **free** copy of Llewellyn's consumer catalog, *New Worlds of Mind & Spirit,* simply call 1-877-NEW-WRLD or visit our website at www.llewellyn.com and click on *New Worlds.*

LLEWELLYN ORDERING INFORMATION

Order Online:
Visit our website at www.llewellyn.com, select your books, and order them on our secure server.

Order by Phone:
- Call toll-free within the U.S. at 1-877-NEW-WRLD (1-877-639-9753). Call toll-free within Canada at 1-866-NEW-WRLD (1-866-639-9753)
- We accept VISA, MasterCard, and American Express

Order by Mail:
Send the full price of your order (MN residents add 6.5% sales tax) in U.S. funds, plus postage & handling to:

Llewellyn Worldwide
2143 Wooddale Drive, Dept. 978-0-7387-1324-3
Woodbury, MN 55125-2989

Postage & Handling:

Standard (U.S., Mexico, & Canada). If your order is:
$24.99 and under, add $3.00
$25.00 and over, FREE STANDARD SHIPPING

AK, HI, PR: $15.00 for one book plus $1.00 for each additional book.

International Orders (airmail only):
$16.00 for one book plus $3.00 for each additional book

Orders are processed within 2 business days.
Please allow for normal shipping time. Postage and handling rates subject to change.

Sail into Your Dreams

8 Steps to Living a More Purposeful Life

KAREN MEHRINGER

Sail into Your Dreams is the perfect book for anyone who's ever asked, "Is this all there is to life?"

Unsatisfied with her busy life in Seattle, Karen Mehringer embarked on a six-month, life-changing ocean odyssey to Australia, Indonesia, Fiji, and, most importantly, toward the joyful, fulfilling life she had always wanted.

You don't have to leave land to make your dreams come true. Karen shares the wisdom and practical tools she learned on her ocean odyssey, showing us how to focus on what truly matters. Journal entries and inspiring stories from Karen and others highlight how to slow down, nurture yourself, connect with others, and tap into your life force energy—the source of infinite possibilities.

This eight-step program will help you assess your life and eliminate toxic relationships, emotional trauma, physical clutter, and debt—making space for new experiences that awaken your passion and spirit.

978-0-7387-1053-2
240 pp., 5 x 7 $13.95

To order, call 1-877-NEW-WRLD

Prices subject to change without notice